HOME OFFICE

SENTENCES OF IMPRISONMENT

A Review of Maximum Penalties

Report of the Advisory Council
on the Penal System

LONDON: HER MAJESTY'S STATIONERY OFFICE

ISBN 0 11 340145 0

ADVISORY COUNCIL ON THE PENAL SYSTEM

Members who took part in the review:

*The Right Honourable Sir Kenneth Younger, KBE (Chairman until May 1976)
The Baroness Serota of Hampstead (Chairman from May 1976)[1]
Professor Sir Arthur Armitage
*Mr. Alan Bainton, CBE
† Mr. Louis Blom-Cooper, QC
*The Honourable Mr. Justice Stephen Brown[2]
Mr. Derek Gladwin, OBE
Mr. Alan Goodson, OBE, QPM
Mr. Milton Hargreaves, OBE
*His Honour Judge Hines, QC
The Right Honourable the Earl Jellicoe, DSO, MC[3]
*His Honour Judge Richard Lowry, QC
The Lady Rothschild, MBE
*Mr. Hugh Sanders, OBE
*Dr. Peter Scott, CBE[4]
Mr. W. R. Stirling
*Professor Nigel Walker
*The Right Honourable Lord Justice Waller, OBE
*The Baroness Wootton of Abinger, CH

Secretaries

Mr. N. R. Varney (until September 1976)
Mr. C. L. Scoble (from September 1976)

---

* Member of the sub-group on maximum penalties.
† Chairman of the sub-group on maximum penalties.
[1] Baroness Serota was appointed Chairman in May 1976 following the death of Sir Kenneth Younger.
[2] Mr. Justice Stephen Brown joined the Council in May 1977.
[3] Lord Jellicoe was a member of the Council until March 1977.
[4] Dr. Scott was a member of the Council until his death in August 1977.

Home Office
Queen Anne's Gate
London SW1H 9AT

28 February 1978

Dear Home Secretary,

In July 1975 your predecessor, Roy Jenkins, asked the Advisory Council on the Penal System to carry out a review of the present system of maximum penalties of imprisonment, and to assess how far they represent a valid guide to sentencing practice. In May last year, we submitted to you an interim report on *The Length of Prison Sentences* to deal with the pressing question of the reduction of sentence lengths for the ordinary offender. At that time we indicated that our deliberations were drawing to a conclusion and that we hoped shortly to present our final recommendations. Accordingly, I now have the honour, on behalf of the Council, to submit for your consideration our final report of the review.

The review has presented us with many complex and difficult problems. We would wish to stress that the new system of penalties recommended in Part B of the report, although creating a novel structure, is not in any way a revolutionary proposal. Based as it is upon the current sentencing practice of the courts, it represents rather a formalisation of the existing situation. As we indicate in our final chapter, we hope that you will be able shortly to undertake a general consultation on our proposals with all the interested parties and, assuming a favourable reception for our scheme, to test out during an experimental period those features of it which do not require legislation.

In our view questions of sentencing practice are of prime importance to the working of the criminal justice system and the penal system, and have suffered in the past from a woeful lack of public consideration and discussion. The fact that ours is the first comprehensive review of the system since the 1840s speaks for itself. We hope that our report will make up for the lost opportunities of the past and will now open up a new area of debate on the sentencing structure of the future.

Yours sincerely,

BEE SEROTA.

The Rt. Hon. MERLYN REES, MP,
Her Majesty's Principal Secretary of State
    for the Home Department.

CONTENTS

INTRODUCTION

"Has not the time come for new maxima?"

Winston Churchill, in a minute
on a Home Office file (1910)

CHAPTER 1

THE REFERENCE AND THE REVIEW

Introduction

1. We were given the following terms of reference[1]:

> "to consider the general structure and level of maximum sentences of imprisonment available to the courts; to assess how far they represent a valid guide to sentencing practice; and whether further provision needs to be made regarding the suspension of periods of imprisonment and the combination of existing forms of non-custodial penalty and disability with sentences of imprisonment; and to make recommendations."

Membership

2. The period of the review was sadly marked by the death of two of our members, Sir Kenneth Younger (our first Chairman) in May 1976 and Dr. Peter Scott in August 1977. Both were founder members of the Council in 1966 and have over the years made an important contribution to its work. They will be greatly missed. Baroness Serota of Hampstead, already a member of the Council, was appointed Chairman on Sir Kenneth's death. In March 1977 Lord Jellicoe left the Council because of the pressure of his many other commitments. In May 1977 we welcomed Mr. Justice Stephen Brown as a new member.

Procedure

3. The review was undertaken by the Council as a whole, although much of the detailed work was carried out by a sub-group of 11 members, chaired by Mr. Blom-Cooper. In all, the sub-group has devoted 31 meetings and the Council parts of 12 meetings (including a residential week-end conference at Wye College in Kent) to completing the review. The sub-group also established a small working group which was charged with calculating the new maxima we have set out in Appendix A. The working group met four times in accomplishing this task. We decided early on that we would not issue a general invitation for evidence since we felt that the subject matter of the review was not entirely appropriate to such a proceeding. Rather, we invited a selection of individuals to come and talk to us informally; their names are recorded in Appendix U. We are most grateful for the help and opinions which they freely gave, many of which have had a strong influence upon the recommendations in this report. Halfway through the review we debated whether, in line with contemporary practice, we should issue a consultative paper, at least to those involved in the administration of the criminal justice and penal systems. We concluded, however, that a consultative process of this kind would delay for a further year the publication of our report, and since our final recommendations would, in any

---

[1] The original reference in July 1975 was limited to a consideration of maximum penalties; the questions of suspended sentences and combined penalties were added later.

3

event, be the subject of widespread consultation and consideration, we were keen that the public debate should start as soon as possible. This report, therefore, records our views on maximum penalties and related matters, but may serve also as a part of the wider debate on what kind of penal system we should have in the future.

4. Throughout the review we have kept in touch informally with those bodies whose current work has overlapped our own—the two standing official law reform bodies, the Criminal Law Revision Committee and the Law Commission; the Committee on The Dangerous Offender, set up by the Howard League for Penal Reform and chaired by Mrs. Jean Floud, Principal of Newnham College, Cambridge; and the Insolvency Law Review Committee, set up by the Department of Trade, whose remit includes the question of criminal bankruptcy with which we deal in Chapter 15. This process was made easier in some cases by an overlap of membership; during our review Lord Justice Waller was appointed a member of the Criminal Law Revision Committee,[1] and Professor Walker and Mr. Blom-Cooper are both members of the Committee on The Dangerous Offender.

5. In June 1977 we issued an interim report on *The Length of Prison Sentences* to deal with a pressing, but not a central, theme of our review: our strongly held opinion that the length of sentences passed upon ordinary offenders could be reduced without any effect on the level of serious crime. When we issued our interim report, we had already reached an advanced stage in the formulation of our proposals, and the views we expressed in that report have inevitably informed much of our thinking in this one.

Origins of the review
6. This is the first official review of the whole system of maximum penalties of imprisonment which has taken place since the work of the Commissioners on the Criminal Law in the 1830s and 1840s. True, there have been attempts to construct a complete penal code, such as that by James Fitzjames Stephen in 1878,[2] but these have generally been the result of individual initiative and have petered out in failure. The idea for this review originated at the time of the passage through Parliament of the Criminal Damage Bill of 1971. At the Committee and Report Stages in the House of Lords,[3] it was suggested that, in view of the significant changes in the penalty structure contained in the Bill, the Council should be given an opportunity at least to comment on the penological implication of new maximum penalties in any future legislation reforming the substantive criminal law. This parliamentary reference to the Council's role in penal

---

[1] Our Chairman, Baroness Serota, is also a member of the Policy Advisory Committee which reports to the Criminal Law Revision Committee on the subject of sexual offences.

[2] In the Criminal Code (Indictable Offences) Bill of that year. It is interesting to note that Stephen's approach to the implementation of his penal code was similar to our proposals in Chapter 16 for implementing our own scheme of penalties—that practical experience of the new system should precede major legislation:

"Its form must be changed by private enterprise, and the public and the legal profession must be accustomed to it in a new and improved form, before legislation can be undertaken with much advantage."

A Penal Code by J. F. Stephen, *The Fortnightly Review*, Vol. XXI (New Series), page 362. 1 March 1877.

[3] Committee Stage. House of Lords Official Report, Vol. 316, Cols. 1256–60. 30 March 1971; Report Stage. House of Lords Official Report, Vol. 317, Cols. 509–15. 8 April 1971.

affairs prompted the then Chairman, Sir Kenneth Younger, to suggest the idea of asking the Home Secretary to refer to it the whole question of maximum penalties as a separate review. At a meeting of the Council on 20 July that year, Sir Kenneth was authorised to approach officials at the Home Office with a view to initiating, as a first step in any review, research into the system of maximum penalties. The following year, the Home Office agreed to the suggestion that Mr. David Thomas, Lecturer at the Cambridge Institute of Criminology, should be invited to undertake the necessary research, and a project was commissioned and funded by the Home Office Research Unit. Shortly after the subject of maximum penalties was referred to the Council in July 1975, Mr Thomas supplied us with the first part of his historical survey, and it was this which formed the starting point of our review. We wish to record our great indebtedness to Mr. Thomas, on whose research we have extensively relied in constructing Chapter 3 of this report. (Much of what appears in that chapter can be found in Mr. Thomas's occasional paper[1] on the subject.) His work has thrown a flood of light upon an obscure corner of our penal history.

Scope of the review

7. Our terms of reference limit us to a consideration of maximum penalties of imprisonment; we are not therefore concerned with maximum fines.[2] This has meant that for the most part our review has been concerned with sentencing practice in the Crown Court and not magistrates' courts. Certain of our recommendations, however, such as those on partially suspended sentences, are of relevance to the practice of magistrates and we have drawn attention to such points in the course of the report. In July 1975, the then Home Secretary, Mr. Jenkins, attended our first meeting and explained to us the objectives, as he saw them, of our review. We agreed with him that our main objective was to consider whether the principles governing the maximum penalties for the major offences were still valid in the light of current thinking about the purposes of sentencing, and it is this objective which underlies our central recommendation for a new penalty structure. When he met us, the Home Secretary also indicated that the review was bound to raise theoretical issues such as whether maximum penalties should leave room for exemplary sentences and whether long prison sentences were more efficacious than shorter ones. It was inevitable, therefore, that our review should have been set against the background of contemporary views about the nature and purpose of imprisonment. This was the subject of our interim report and features in many of the chapters of this one. Our main aim has been to produce a more rational and relevant penalty structure; if, at the same time, our recommendations can help with the burdensome problem of a rising prison population, this would be a bonus.

Structure of the report

8. For the convenience of readers, Chapter 2 provides a summary of our proposals. Our detailed recommendations are set out in Chapters 8 to 15, which form Part B of this report. The final chapter deals with the question of

---

[1] *The Penal Equation. Derivations of the penalty structure of English criminal law* by D. A. Thomas (University of Cambridge, Institute of Criminology, 1978).
[2] The Criminal Law Act 1977 has only recently upgraded many maximum fines to take account of inflation.

5

how our main recommendation for a new penalty structure might be implemented. Chapters 3 to 7 (Part A of the report) provide the historical and contemporary background to our recommendations.

Assessors and Secretariat

9. Throughout the two and a half years of our review of maximum penalties we have been assisted by a variety of officials. Mr. John Chilcot, Mr. Clifford Hindley and Miss Margaret Clayton (in chronological order) served as assessors. Mr. Michael Moriarty, who had been our assessor during the Young Adult Offender inquiry and was promoted in 1975 to head the Criminal Policy Department at the Home Office, remained available to us for consultation and advice. To all four we express our great indebtedness for the expert knowledge that they injected into our deliberations.

10. We have been served successively by two secretaries in Mr. Nigel Varney (until autumn 1976) and Mr. Chris Scoble, supported throughout respectively by Miss Tessa Marston and Mr. Ian Jones. The conventional language of gratitude does not suffice to express how much we owe them. Without their dedication to the task, and administrative skill in preparing our memoranda, organising and recording our meetings, and drafting our report (including the interim report to which we devoted much time and hence delayed our final recommendations), our work would have been the poorer. No independent body such as ours can have been better served by its secretariat.

11. Criminal statistics formed an essential ingredient of our review and of the scheme that we are proposing. Since none of us is a professional statistician, we have been particularly grateful for the assistance and guidance so willingly given by both Miss Stella Cunliffe, until recently Director of Statistics, and successively Dr. Charles Glennie, Mr. John Williams and Mr. Lawrence Davidoff. But for their help we might so easily have become submerged by the sophisticated techniques for handling statistical material.

12. Mr. Alex Stephen of the Scottish Home and Health Department has attended our meetings as an observer and has helpfully illuminated the Scottish system whereby the judges sentence offenders to imprisonment without guidance from Parliament. Although our terms of reference were restricted to England and Wales, we have nevertheless taken particular note of Scottish law and practice.

13. We wish finally to record our thanks to all those in the Home Office who assisted with the task of typing, copying and distributing the mass of paper we generated. Mrs. Joan Sakkas, who arranged our meetings and organised our papers, deserves our special thanks for her consistent efficiency.

CHAPTER 2

SUMMARY OF OUR PROPOSALS

The historical background (Chapters 3 to 7)

14. On looking into the history of maximum penalties of imprisonment in this country, we discovered that they have grown up largely as a result of historical accident. The structure of the present penalty system was first formulated in the five criminal law statutes of 1861, which consolidated the existing law in relation to the major offences. The periods selected at that time for maximum sentences of imprisonment largely followed the periods traditionally chosen as fixed sentences for transportation, which by that time had given way to penal servitude. The 1861 Acts did not attempt to reform the law, and the structure they created was no more logical than that which had preceded them. Parliamentary activity since the 19th century has added further penalties to the statute book, but normally as the result of transient concern with a particular offence. Not until the establishment of the Criminal Law Revision Committee and the Law Commission has there been a concerted attempt to rationalise the penalty structure, but even this has not been as extensive as it might have been.

15. The maximum penalties created in the 19th century were in general set too high to influence the daily practice of the courts. Even following the setting up of an appellate court in 1907, there has been little case-law to affect the manner in which the courts have regarded them; the only really significant case, *R* v *Harrison* in 1909,[1] merely established the principle that maximum penalties are designed to cater for the worst offences, and in recent years even this principle has been diluted. Maximum penalties have thus scarcely influenced at all the important question of what should be the appropriate period of imprisonment for the majority of cases which come before the courts. In the absence of any guide from the penalty system, courts began in the late 19th century to establish their own normal range of penalties in an attempt both to assimilate disparities in sentencing practice and to shorten sentences which were generally held to be too long. It is this system of a normal range of penalties, rather than the system of maximum penalties, which guides sentencing practice today.

16. The system of penalties imposed in court and the system of imprisonment have a close relationship, each influencing the other. The origins of the modern system of imprisonment, like the modern penalty structure, can be traced back to the mid-19th century, when both were in a state of flux and some confusion. The prison system of the latter half of the 19th century was almost wholly informed by principles of deterrence. When this ultimately gave rise to public concern, the Gladstone Committee in 1895 ushered in a new era, of deterrence combined with rehabilitation, which probably reached its apogee

---

[1] (1909) 2 Cr. App. R. 94.

he high days of the borstal system in the 1920s and 30s. In the last 20 years, the emphasis has changed as the old faith in the ability of custodial institutions to reform offenders has been eroded, largely by the results of criminological research. Prisons are now seen by many as institutions primarily of containment, where some assistance can be given to offenders in various ways. It is the change to this new, less idealistic, philosophy which has given rise to the view, which we expressed in our interim report of June 1977, that imprisonment should be used as little as possible, and that the case for a reduction in the length of prison sentences passed on the ordinary offender is as strong today as it was in the late 19th century.

Other countries (Appendix C)

17. Like all committees charged with a wide remit, we looked to the position in other countries to see what guidance they might give us. A résumé of what we found is set out in Appendix C. We were interested to note that many of the countries of the old Commonwealth, whose penalty structures have been modelled on English lines, are, like this country, still subject to high maximum penalties bearing little relationship to the day-to-day practice of the courts. We were even more interested to note that in some cases the continuance of this system has given rise to expressions of dissatisfaction and to pressure for reform. In particular, the recent report of the Law Reform Commission of Canada on *Imprisonment and Release*, with its call for restriction in the use of imprisonment and the establishment of a more realistic system of penalties, expresses views which are very much akin to our own. We were impressed by the evidence we received of countries with lower maximum penalties than our own whose courts pass prison sentences which are on average considerably shorter than in this country. The Netherlands is the prime, and most often quoted, example. We looked at the various penalty systems current in the different jurisdictions of the United States, and noted in particular the recent legislative moves away from indeterminacy in sentencing towards a more fixed and rigid penalty structure. The system of sentencing guidelines, now making headway in the United States as a compromise between indeterminate sentencing and a system of more or less fixed penalties, was of special interest to us, both because the philosophy of steering a middle course between a wide and a narrow discretion in sentencing was the one which most appealed to us, and because the practical solution of adopting a penalty system based on the existing practice of the courts was that which we ourselves ultimately decided to recommend.

Our approach to maximum penalties (Chapters 8 and 9)

18. We are conscious that at the present time there is no overall view of the system of penalties of imprisonment. The work of the Criminal Law Revision Committee and the Law Commission in updating penalties, though extremely valuable, has been piecemeal in its effect—concerning itself with one set of offences at a time. This has been true too of the discussion of penalties in Parliament. But the system of penalties as a whole can become the subject of public debate only if it is a readily identifiable structure, based on principles that can be understood, and bearing some relationship to what actually happens in the courts. Although debate on the present system has been extremely limited, we nevertheless considered the two alternative views that had been

8

expounded at various times. The view of the Criminal Law Revision Committee, in its Eighth Report on *Theft and Related Offences*, was that the present system of high maxima, catering for the worst cases and leaving a wide discretion for dealing with less serious cases, works well and should not be disturbed. On the other hand, there is the view represented by the 1959 report of *Justice* on *Legal Penalties* that there should be a closer link between the system of maxima and the common run of penalties actually imposed by the courts.

19. Our study of the historical growth of the penalty system and the way in which it operates today led us to endorse the views expressed by *Justice* in its report. High maximum penalties do not act as a guide to the courts in their sentencing practice and it is our belief that they should. If Parliament in legislating penalties can provide such a guide, the roles of Parliament and of the courts in the sentencing system will become more clearly defined, and a more fruitful relationship is bound to develop. We also believe that a more formal structuring of sentencing practice within a new system of penalties will make it easier for courts to monitor their own practice and, in particular, to operate the policy we have advocated in our interim report of reducing the length of sentences in run-of-the-mill cases.

20. We were faced with the difficult question of what shape a new system of maximum penalties might take, and the method by which we might construct it. The most obvious course which we first considered was to adopt the traditional method of the law reform bodies and of Parliament and proceed through the statute book fixing new penalties offence by offence. There are, however, inherent difficulties in such a proceeding. To begin with, we knew it was unlikely that the 18 of us would be able to agree on the precise relativities of the hundreds of offences on the statute book; we could only hope to produce a very broad consensus, the result of a large number of compromises based upon differing value judgments. However useful such a result might have been, it would itself have been the subject of further discussion and compromise in Parliament, where doubtless fresh value judgments would have been brought to bear upon the question. We doubted, therefore, whether there was anything to be gained by this traditional approach, when the courts themselves already operate a system which distinguishes the relative seriousness of offences in line with contemporary values and which, generally speaking, works well. Our intention was to use the current practice of the courts as the basis for the new penalty system, not to attempt to pluck a whole new system of values out of the ether.

A new scheme of penalties (Chapter 9)

21. Having decided to eschew all value judgments in our approach to the relativities of different penalties, we had to consider the fundamental shape of the new structure we wished to build upon the existing sentencing practice of the courts. We looked at the two extremes of the possibilities which faced us—on the one hand, the abolition of maximum penalties altogether, permitting the courts to operate with an almost unlimited discretion; on the other, a system of almost fixed penalties, reducing the sentencing task of the court merely to matching a predetermined sentence to the particular crime which came before

it. We rejected both extremes, and decided to steer a middle course between a system of unlimited discretion and one of inflexible fixed sentencing. We were conscious that the sentencing system as it operates today deals broadly with two classes of case: the ordinary case where a penalty can be fixed within the normal range; and the exceptional, very serious, case, where the task of sentencing is made difficult by a number of complex considerations. The penalty system we now propose attempts to reflect this distinction by creating a two-tier sentencing structure, in which the degree of flexibility in passing a sentence is made proportionate to the seriousness of the case and the sentencing problems it poses. For the ordinary case, we have proposed a narrowing of sentencing discretion, fixing our projected new maxima at a level which, we hope, will comprise all such cases. For the exceptional case, we propose a broadening of the existing discretion which is now confined within the limits of the present maximum penalties.

The new maxima (Chapter 9)

22.   We resolved the problem of how to narrow the discretion in the case of the ordinary offender by a study of sentencing statistics in recent years. Looking at the figures, we concluded that a working distinction between the ordinary and the exceptional case might be achieved by fixing a cut-off point between the top 10% of longest sentences and the remaining 90% of sentences (which we felt could be equated with the "ordinary" cases) which fell below them. One case in ten conforms, in our view, to what the ordinary person would commonly regard as exceptional. This said, we recognise that any cut-off point of this kind must to some extent be arbitrary, but we do not consider the proposition is any the worse for that.

23.   The maximum penalties we propose in this report are therefore fixed at the point below which 90% of prison sentences have fallen for each individual offence in the last three years for which criminal statistics are available (1974–76). The new maxima are set out in Appendix A to this report, and a summary of how they have been calculated is at Appendix B. The most noticeable feature of the new penalties is the substantial reduction they make upon the existing maxima; it is important to recognise, however, not only that they represent current court practice in at least 90% of cases, but also that they are intended for the ordinary, and not the exceptional, case. We considered whether we should make an exception to our scheme in the case of those maxima which are now commonly held to be too low—principally the offences of cruelty to or neglect of children, indecent assault on a girl of 13 and over, corruption offences and fraudulent trading. We concluded, however, that our proposals should apply to these offences as to others on the statute book. We also concluded that existing statutory maxima should not be reduced below two years. The new maximum is not to be regarded as in any way a standard or "average" sentence. Rather it is the point which marks the upper limit for the ordinary cases.

24.   Our interim report on *The Length of Prison Sentences*, proposing the reduction of sentences for the ordinary offender, appears to have been well received by the public and by the courts. The new maximum penalties in this report could assist the implementation of this philosophy by clearly distinguishing the ordinary from the exceptional case. We recognise that a policy

10

of shorter sentences could lead to a marginal increase in offences, in that prisoners who are likely to re-offend will be released to the community at an earlier stage. We do not think, however, that this is a substantial problem when set against the totality of offending, and we believe that it is a price that society should be prepared to pay.

Exceeding the new maxima (Chapter 10)

25. The other purpose of our proposed new system is that the passing of an exceptional sentence upon an offender should become a more explicit act than it is today. In our view, exceptional sentences should be designed for the protection of the public rather than for any other purpose, such as deterrence, and thus should be passed only in cases involving the threat of serious harm in the future. We define serious harm as normally comprising serious physical injury, serious psychological effects, exceptional personal hardship, or damage to the security of the State or to the fabric of society. We have proposed a detailed criterion which we believe courts should follow when imposing a sentence in excess of the new maxima. The imposition of such a sentence would be a serious matter; accordingly, courts should always give prior indication to the defendant that they propose to invoke the exceptional powers, and whenever such a sentence is imposed it should carry with it a right to legal aid for the purposes of appeal.

26. We considered at some length the form the exceptional sentence might take. We rejected the idea of retaining the present maxima, which we had already found to be irrational, and also of fixing an arbitrary new level of penalty, since this would have involved applying value judgments which we had decided to avoid. In the event, we decided that at this level of sentencing there should be no limits. When exceeding the new maxima, courts should have power (as they do at present in the case of those offences where the maximum penalty is life imprisonment) to impose a determinate sentence of any length. As a disincentive to inordinately long prison sentences, we propose a relaxation in the provisions governing eligibility for parole: a person receiving an exceptional sentence should be eligible for parole after serving a third of it, or the maximum ordinary sentence he could have received under our proposed new maxima, whichever is the less. The period of his parole licence, during which he would be subject to supervision by the probation and after-care service and to recall to prison at any time, should last until his total nominal sentence has expired.

Extended sentences (Chapter 5)

27. We traced the history of attempts to deal with the recidivist offender, from the early experiments of the 19th century, through the two 20th century versions of preventive detention, to the present-day power of passing an extended sentence. We concluded that none of these provisions had succeeded in fulfilling its objective, and that extended sentences, which are now only rarely used, should be abolished. We do not intend that the unlimited powers that would be available to courts when exceeding the new maxima should be regarded as in any way a substitute for the extended sentence; they are intended broadly to deal with the exceptional, but not necessarily the persistent, offender.

11

Consecutive sentences (Chapter 10)

28. We recognise that the power to impose consecutive sentences could be used as a means of passing the equivalent of an exceptional sentence without meeting the strict criterion laid down for such a sentence. We have set out some basic ground rules to prevent such an occurrence. They merely apply the existing principles which today govern consecutive sentences: namely, that the offences should relate to more than one transaction, and that the total of consecutive sentences should not be excessive in the light of all the circumstances.

Life imprisonment (Chapter 11)

29. We share a common dislike of the wholly indeterminate sentence, such as the present sentence of life imprisonment, principally because of its deleterious effects upon the individual prisoner. We regard the idea of the "merciful" life sentence as a contradiction in terms; the essential uncertainty which the sentence creates in the prisoner's mind, and the innate conservatism of executive release procedures, produces the reverse of a merciful result. The rapid increase in life sentence prisoners in recent years, from just over 100 in 1957 to more than 1,300 today, places an especially heavy managerial burden upon the prison service; the system of review and release of such prisoners is complex and demanding of resources. We recognise, however, that the life sentence will need to be retained for cases of homicide, to mark out unlawful killing as a crime apart, and for the really serious non-homicide cases where the release date of an apparently dangerous prisoner cannot safely be predicted at the time of his trial. We therefore propose that life imprisonment should be the maximum penalty for murder and manslaughter. We also propose retention of life imprisonment (as an additional power when exceeding the maxima) for the 10 non-homicide offences for which the sentence has actually been imposed during the last 10 years. Where life imprisonment is not imposed for a period of 10 years for a particular offence, it should lapse in the case of that offence. Although we have thus reluctantly proposed the retention of life imprisonment as an additional power when exceeding the new maxima, we also propose that the practice of the courts in passing life sentences should be restricted. In recent years the essential criteria for passing life sentences have been relaxed; we advocate a return to the stricter criteria of 20 years ago.

Implementation of the new scheme (Chapter 16)

30. The proposals outlined above comprise our new scheme of penalties. Assuming that Parliament and the judiciary find acceptable changes along these lines, we would envisage a short experimental period in which the courts would operate the new maxima for ordinary offenders and the criterion for exceeding the new maxima on a non-statutory basis. During this period, the Home Office should conduct research to monitor the effects of the experiment and assess its practicability. If the experiment is successful, and once any necessary adjustments have been made, the new system of penalties (including the provisions for exceeding the new maxima) could become law.

The penalty for murder (Chapter 12)

31. We have made a number of other recommendations which, though peripheral to our new scheme of penalties, arise directly out of our terms of reference.

After consideration of what is a highly complex issue, we propose the abolition of the mandatory element in the penalty of life imprisonment for murder. We consider that there is a need for flexibility at the point of sentence to express the great variety of cases of murder and to ensure that the penalty does not bear too heavily upon the less serious crimes—such as mercy killings. This, in our view, can only be achieved by the power to impose determinate sentences, within a maximum penalty of life imprisonment. If the mandatory element in the penalty is abolished, with it could disappear the confusing complexities caused by the special defences of provocation and diminished responsibility, and by the statutory power to make recommendations as to the length of the prisoner's period in custody. We hope that such a change will not lead to inordinately long determinate sentences for murder; we are confident that the Court of Appeal (Criminal Division) will insist upon setting reasonable limits to such sentences. We also propose more flexibility in the provisions for parole eligibility in murder cases, in line with our proposals for exceeding the new maxima. We envisage a new sentencing system for murder cases where courts may impose determinate sentences up to, say, 20 or 25 years, and reserve the maximum penalty of life imprisonment for the really serious or unpredictable case. This will have the effect of reinforcing the gravity of the life sentence which is today commonly, but erroneously, regarded as equivalent to imprisonment for nine years.

Suspended sentences (Chapter 13)

32. We reviewed the system of suspended sentences of imprisonment, but do not have any major recommendations to make. As regards wholly suspended sentences, we recommend that there should be power to vary any financial order made at the time of imposition of the sentence when that sentence comes to be activated. Our own proposal for partially suspended sentences has already been enacted, in section 47 of the Criminal Law Act 1977. While we have some reservations about recent public descriptions of the new sentence as akin to a "short, sharp shock" (which was far from our original intention), we hope that the provision will work well. We see its principal utility in the case of the serious first offender or person receiving his first prison sentence, where the imposition of imprisonment is regarded as unavoidable. We set out in this report some guidance to courts on the possible use of the sentence.

Combined sentences (Chapter 14)

33. Early in our review, we thought there might be scope for the greater use of combined penalties (that is, non-custodial penalties in combination with sentences of imprisonment) to help reduce the length of prison sentences imposed in any particular case. We looked at a number of new ideas in this field, but eventually concluded that the most realistic combinations were the conventional ones of imprisonment with a financial penalty, such as a fine, a compensation order or an order for costs. We see, however, strong objection in principle to the imposition of a financial penalty at the same time as a prison sentence since, unless the offender is known to have assets (such as the hidden fruits of his crime), such a combination of penalties will bear heavily upon him on his release from prison at a time when he is struggling to rehabilitate himself. We see the combination of the financial penalty with imprisonment as generally more appropriate where the prison sentence is wholly suspended.

13

Criminal bankruptcy (Chapter 15)

34. Finally, we reviewed the system of criminal bankruptcy orders which the Council proposed in 1970 in its report on *Reparation by the Offender*. Although they have been in force for only a few years, the provisions have not proved successful in releasing money to the victims of crime. They need tightening up and their objectives redefined. For the long-term prisoner, where co-operation with the bankruptcy order has been noticeably lacking, we recommend that his response to the order should be taken into account at the time of his consideration for parole. Otherwise, the securing of his assets can be achieved only by careful follow-up on his release from prison. We see, however, more hope in the application of the provisions to less serious offenders. We propose that the provisions should be applied to a wider range of offenders, and that accordingly the financial limit on the loss caused by the crime in order to qualify for the imposition of an order should be reduced from £15,000 to £10,000. In the case of the less serious offender (convicted of non-violent crime, for example), criminal bankruptcy could be used in conjunction with a non-custodial penalty, a suspended sentence or a short prison term. Where the order is made in conjunction with a suspended sentence, we propose that failure to co-operate with the bankruptcy proceedings should become a ground for activating the suspended sentence. We also propose the use of the power to attach future earnings in criminal bankruptcy cases. In this way, we hope that the criminal bankruptcy provisions will be able to make some contribution to a general reduction in the use of imprisonment.

Research

35. If all, or some, of the recommendations in this report are implemented, the need will arise for detailed research to be undertaken from the beginning. *We recommend that our new system of maxima, if adopted, should be closely monitored, both to determine what effects it is having on sentence lengths and to indicate what adjustments may need to be made in the future.* It will be particularly important to review the effects of the new system upon court practice, in particular the question of how the criterion for exceeding the maxima is interpreted. Since our proposals are built on a statistical base, it is essential that they continue to be monitored statistically.

36. A similar monitoring process will be highly desirable in relation to our other proposals regarding life imprisonment, partially suspended sentences and criminal bankruptcy. The change in the penalty for murder that we propose will throw up some important questions: what will be, for example, the distribution of determinate sentences for the different types of murder, and to what extent will defences of diminished responsibility and provocation be made redundant? Criminal bankruptcy has not to date been closely monitored and we consider that a revitalisation of the experiment on the lines we propose would merit a separate research project. It will, for example, be important to record the consequences of the lowering of the financial limit in its effects upon the number of orders made and the type of offender in respect of whom they are made. The effectiveness of our proposal for combining criminal bankruptcy orders with suspended sentences can only be assessed by the frequency of its use and the financial returns it will produce. Partial suspension of sentences is already a part of the law, and its operation will no doubt be

14

closely monitored, as all new disposals are. We foresee a large number of practical issues on which such research might focus: the proportions of sentences both suspended and unsuspended; the types of offender and offence considered to be appropriate; the rate of activation of the suspended portion; and whether the sentence is used (as we advocate) strictly as an alternative to imprisonment or as an alternative to full suspension.

37. These are some of the issues upon which future research will, we hope, be concentrated. We are conscious that, in the past at least, sentencing practice and the conventions of the courts have not been given the degree of attention devoted to some other areas of criminological research—such as the effectiveness of different disposals following their imposition by the courts. We hope that a new structure of penalties will help to turn the eyes of the researcher more directly towards the many important questions of sentencing practice and policy.

PART A

THE BACKGROUND

"Penal legislation hitherto has resembled what the science of physic must have been when physicians did not know the properties and effects of the medicines they administered."

Samuel Romilly, commenting on Bentham's *Théorie des peines et des récompenses* (1811)

CHAPTER 3

THE HISTORY OF MAXIMUM PENALTIES

38. Imprisonment has a long history. As a punishment, however, it is almost entirely a modern social phenomenon. When Plato wrote in the fourth century BC:

> "Let there be three prisons in the city, one for the safe keeping of persons awaiting trial and sentence: another for the amendment of disorderly persons and vagrants, those guilty of misdemeanours . . . a third to be situated in the country away from the habitations of man, and to be used for the punishment of felons . . ."[1]

he was not merely anticipating the penal systems of modern western Europe; he was also unconsciously predicting the stages through which imprisonment would go, culminating as a penalty for convicted felons only when the death penalty, outlawry and banishment from the realm were no longer viable instruments of the State. In mediæval times imprisonment had its place as a punishment, but it was infrequently used by comparison with other forms of penal disposal such as mutilation, flogging, branding and public exposure as a miscreant. Prisons did not hold the mass of offenders convicted of crime other than as a staging post pending some other, more fearsome, disposal. During Tudor times death was the usual penalty for felonies, and by the end of the 17th century some 50 crimes were punishable by death. By the beginning of the 19th century the number had risen to 200. Thereafter the number of offences that carried the death penalty progressively dwindled until by 1861 murder and a few uncommon crimes (that is, arson in Her Majesty's dockyards, piracy and treason) were the sole survivors of the campaign waged by Sir Samuel Romilly and others to abolish capital punishment for all offences other than those involving unlawful killing.

39. Transportation to the colonies proved to be another convenient method of disposing of convicts. It served as a lesser penalty for the less serious crimes as well as being used in commutation of the death penalty. The practice had grown up in the 17th century whereby the King granted Crown Pardons to certain felons on condition that they agreed to be transported to the colonies, a practice that was given express statutory recognition in 1679 when detention pending transportation was excepted from the application of the writ of habeas corpus.[2] But transportation proved an ephemeral solution to a continuing social problem. By the middle of the 19th century, most of the Australian colonies declined to receive any more convicts, though Western Australia was happy to accept them until 1867 when the British Government finally reconciled itself to abandoning this penal device.[3]

---

[1] *The Laws*, Book X, 908A, quoted in *The evolution of the prison* by Leslie Fairweather, in *Prison Architecture*, United Nations Social Defence Research Institute (Architectural Press, 1975), page 13.

[2] Habeas Corpus Act 1679 (31 Car. 2 c. 2, section 14).

[3] For a detailed history of transportation, see *Convicts and the Colonies* by A. G. L. Shaw (Faber, 1966).

40. The demise of transportation, coinciding with the rapid abolition of the death penalty for one crime after another within the decade 1827–37, added impetus to the search for the appropriate alternative penal sanction. By the middle of the 19th century, penal servitude had been accepted by the legislators as the next most severe sanction to the death penalty, the abolition of which was conceded unwillingly by many members of the public. Deprivation of liberty for long periods was coming into favour as a suitable punishment, for lack of anything better; prison seemed to be the ideal penalty since it contributed, so the argument ran, to the effective protection of society and to the improvement of the offender. Thus imprisonment, whether served in convict prisons by those sentenced to penal servitude or in the local prisons where the misdemeanants were sent, became a punishment in its own right and inevitably the core of the modern penal system. The questions that exercised the minds of administrators and legislators during the middle third of the 19th century were: what were to be the periods of incarceration, whether mandatory, minimum or maximum; and, where the penalties were not to be mandatory, what principles, if any, were to guide the courts in determining the periods of a prisoner's loss of liberty?

41. The modern structure of statutory maximum penalties can be traced to its origins in the five consolidating statutes of 1861. Those Acts, dealing with violence against the person, larceny, malicious damage, forgery and coinage offences, constituted a catalogue of crimes that forms the bulk of today's substantive criminal law. To date, only two of them have undergone contemporary refurbishment.[1] The 1861 legislation provided the yardstick against which newly created offences were to be evaluated as the criminal law expanded during the following 100 years, as well as the basic material upon which the principles of judicial sentencing were to develop. The penalties prescribed in the five statutes were formulated out of the confluence of three separate streams of penal thought: first, transportation and the piecemeal legislation of the early 19th century substituting alternative penalties to that of death; second, the various reports of the First and Second Criminal Law Commissioners, who in the 1830s and 1840s were appointed to

"digest into one Statute all the Statutes and enactments touching Crimes and the trial *and punishment thereof,* and also to digest into one other Statute all the provisions of the common or unwritten Law touching the same . . .";

and third, the Penal Servitude Acts of 1853 and 1857 which replaced transportation by the sentence of penal servitude.

Transportation and the repeal of the capital statutes

42. The pattern established in the five consolidating Acts of 1861 had been shaped in the second and third decades of the 19th century when capital punishment gave way to judicially imposed transportation. It was in relation primarily to transportation that the first legislative attempts were made to measure the gravity of offences in units of time forfeited to the State; the quantities then chosen formed the basis of the scheme adopted as transportation evolved into penal confinement in the 1850s. Several statutes of the late 17th century had

---

[1] The Theft Act 1968 replaces all the old law of larceny; the Criminal Damage Act 1971 modernises the various crimes of malicious damage. The Law Commission in 1973 produced its *Report on Forgery and Counterfeit Currency* (Law Com. No. 55) and the Criminal Law Revision Committee is currently working on offences against the person.

already authorised courts to order transportation in non-capital cases, but the period of transportation was generally not specified, and when it was, the period was either seven years or life. By an Act of 1717[1] courts had been authorised to order the transportation of persons convicted of larceny or other felonious taking of property and entitled to benefit of clergy, as an alternative to burning in the hand. The court was given the discretion whether or not to exercise the power to order transportation, but the term of transportation was fixed at seven years in all cases, except that of a person convicted of knowingly receiving or buying stolen goods, who might be transported for a period fixed at 14 years. The Act of 1717 was not only of major significance in the history of transportation; it also marked the legislative preference for the seven times table that Parliament was later to adopt in fixing the maximum penalty of imprisonment and that was to characterise all legislation long after transportation had vanished. Seven years became the common term of incarceration, much as in biblical times it symbolically denoted completion or perfection, and became the favoured period in Talmudic law. After 1750, many transportation statutes repeated the formula of mandatory transportation for a fixed period of seven years, while others opted for 14 years. In the chaotic jumble of criminal laws enacted in the 18th century, the model for fixing penalties was always the 1717 Act and, until its repeal in 1827, the occasion for the exercise of judicial discretion in fixing the term of transportation rarely arose.

43. Two statutes of 1808 and 1811 mark the first successful attempts to abolish the death penalty. Under the 1808 Act[2] the offence of larceny from the person ceased to attract the death penalty and became punishable by transportation for life, or for any period of not less than seven years. The 1811 Act[3] which abolished capital punishment for stealing from bleaching grounds, employed a similar formula in relation to transportation but provided the alternative of a period of imprisonment not exceeding seven years. These two Acts were notable also for extending the scope of judicial discretion in sentencing. The formula of the 1812 Act, empowering courts to order up to seven years' imprisonment, or transportation for life, or for any period not less than seven years, was repeated in subsequent statutes. The process of reducing the scope of capital punishment gathered pace and was largely achieved within the period from 1827-37. The penalty structure that emerged, and was to provide the raw material for the 1861 legislation, was devoid of any appearance of system or principle. The Commissioners on the Criminal Law, surveying the law relating to punishment as it stood in 1843, commented that it

> "presents a vast variety of punishments which are not however adapted to corresponding gradations or shades of guilt, but are of an arbitrary and sometimes of a capricious character . . . in annexing penalties to offences from time to time, no endeavour has been made to frame them according to any systematic rules."[4]

The Criminal Law Commissioners

44. Initially the Commissioners did not include in their programme the revision of the law governing punishments, but in their First Report in 1834 they alluded

---

[1] 4 Geo. 1 c. 11.
[2] 48 Geo. 3 c. 129.
[3] 51 Geo. 3 c. 41.
[4] Seventh Report (1843), page 100.

to the close connection between the substantive criminal law and the control of the sentencing process, observing that the law

> "in the assignment of punishments, often exhibits a remarkable degree of inconsistency. This has, apparently, arisen in most instances from the circumstance that new statutes have been passed, without sufficient reference to the antecedent state of the criminal law."[1]

In the course of their subsequent Second, Fourth and Seventh Reports the Commissioners discussed the illogicality of the existing penalty structure and the proper ambit of judicial discretion in awarding punishment (which they considered should be severely restricted), and attempted to construct a scale of punishment, varying from the most trivial offence to the most heinous crime, against which all offences could be measured.

45. The prototype of this graduated scale of punishment, allowing only a restricted scope for judicial discretion, consisted of 15 classes of punishment. By the Seventh Report it had grown to 45 classes, descending from death to a fine of £40. The 45 classes were reduced to 13 by the Second Commissioners in their Second Report in 1846, which omitted some of the classes relating to minor penalties and amalgamated several of the others. (The number of classes was varied again upwards and downwards in the Third and Fourth Reports.) The proposals for a single scale of penalty provisions independent of the definition of offences was never translated into legislation, but the arguments advanced for it undoubtedly influenced the thinking of the 1861 draftsmen. Parliament was, however, in no mood for rationalising the structure of penalties, and very few of the draftsmen's arguments found favour. One proposal which did was taken from the Seventh Report of the First Commissioners, who had recommended that maximum terms of imprisonment (as distinguished from penal servitude), whether authorised as alternatives to transportation in felony cases, or as the primary sanction in cases of misdemeanour, should not normally exceed three years. This maximum term of imprisonment—the period eventually chosen was two years rather than three—was adopted in the 1861 legislation; it remained a legislative convention until imprisonment was assimilated with penal servitude in the Criminal Justice Act 1948.[2]

Penal servitude

46. By the early 1850s the end of transportation was in sight. While the numbers being transported were declining severely, Parliament passed the Penal Servitude Act 1853—which in fact did little more than confirm administrative practice. It provided that no person should be sentenced to transportation for terms of less than 14 years, and persons previously sentenced to terms of less than 14 years' transportation would instead be given penal servitude. The Act provided the following scale by which terms of penal servitude were to be substituted for transportation:

---

[1] First Report (1834), page 32.
[2] The maximum could be evaded by consecutive sentencing, and cumulative sentences of four, and even six, years' imprisonment were occasionally passed, particularly where the alternative of penal servitude was not available (see Statement B in the Du Cane letter of February 1884, reproduced in Appendix D).

Transportation	Penal servitude
7 years or less	4 years
Over 7 and up to 10	Not less than 4 and not exceeding 6
Over 10 and up to 15	Not less than 6 and not exceeding 8
Exceeding 15	Not less than 6 and not exceeding 10
For life	For life.

In the Penal Servitude Act 1857, which formally abolished the sentence[1] of transportation, the scale was repealed, and it was enacted that a person should be liable to penal servitude for the same period (though subject to remission and licence) as the term of transportation to which he would have been liable under the former laws. But at the same time it provided that a sentence of not less than three years' penal servitude might be inflicted in cases where seven years' transportation might previously have been given. The third Penal Servitude Act in 1864 (see paragraph 51) established the *minimum* sentence of five years' penal servitude, or seven years after a previous conviction (the latter was repealed in 1879 leaving the minimum in all cases at five years, but demonstrated that the septimal system continued to pervade the sentencing structure in the 1860s). Meanwhile Parliament had passed the five consolidating Acts of 1861.

The consolidation Acts of 1861

47. The 1861 Acts were a consolidation of the existing criminal law and the punishments it prescribed, and were not a codification. They incorporated, therefore, a penalty structure that bore all the marks of earlier legislative activity and outdated penological thought. The legislation consisted chiefly of re-enactments of the former law with amendments and additions.[2] While the consolidation owed much to the work of the Criminal Law Commissioners, the Acts do not in any way reflect the views of the Commissioners, either on the penalty structure or on the scope of judicial discretion in sentencing. The Acts inclined towards relatively broad definitions within specific branches of the criminal law but there was still a multiplicity of punishments for analogous crimes. They also reflected a very wide measure of judicial discretion in sentencing by providing maxima according to the severe penalties fixed in even harsher penal times. Despite the many and vigorous criticisms by the Criminal Law Commissioners of the disorderly nature of the penalty structure of the early 19th century, no significant rationalisation was achieved. Improvements were limited to minor amendments. The two of any significance were: that periods of 15 years' penal servitude were reduced to 14 years so as to conform to the preponderance of legislation loyal to the septimal system established in 1717; and the establishment of a general maximum sentence of imprisonment (the lesser penalty, as distinct from penal servitude) of two years, whether as an alternative to penal servitude or as the primary sanction for misdemeanours. The

---

[1] For a further 10 years, some offenders were still sent overseas, to serve their sentence of penal servitude in the colonies (see paragraph 39).

[2] Describing the 1861 Acts, James Fitzjames Stephen wrote in 1877 in a letter to the Attorney-General:
"Their arrangement is so obscure, their language so lengthy and cumbrous, and they are based upon and assume the existence of so many singular common law principles that no one who was not already well acquainted with the law would derive any information from reading them."

parliamentary opportunity held out by the Criminal Law Commissioners for a coherent new penalty structure had been lost. Instead, Parliament persisted in prescribing penalties for specific offences dealing with closely related subjects. The result was often a wide variety of penalties within the same field, derived from different statutes enacted at different times and usually without regard to the existing state of the criminal law. The principal draftsman of the legislation, Charles Greaves, wrote in 1861[1]:

> "I have long wished that all punishments for offences should be considered and placed on a satisfactory footing with reference to each other, and I had at one time hoped that that might have been done in these Acts. It was however impracticable . . . The truth is, that whenever the punishment of any offence is considered, it is never looked at, as it always ought to be, with reference to other offences, and with a view to establish any congruity in the punishment of them, and the consequence is that nothing can well be more unsatisfactory than the punishments assigned to different offences."

48. The statutory maxima established in 1861 as the foundation of the modern sentencing structure were thus based on an incongruous analogy with the periods of transportation fixed in the 18th century, as adapted to terms of penal servitude fixed in the middle of the 19th century. Only the terms of imprisonment, as the primary sanction for misdemeanours or as an alternative to penal servitude, possessed any coherent rationality. Nothing that has happened since 1864 has disturbed the basic structure of the 1861 legislation. Indeed all legislative activity (save the most recent) has built upon the foundation of the irrational and inconvenient penalty system of the 1861 Acts.

49. The penalty structure of the 1861 legislation was substantially modified within three years of its inception. Following the garottings in London in the latter half of 1862 there was a panic reaction.[2] Apart from the hasty passing of the Security from Violence Act 1863 (known as the Garotters Act) empowering courts to order the whipping of adults, in addition to any sentence of penal servitude, in cases of robbery with violence, a Royal Commission was set up to inquire further into the workings of the Penal Servitude Acts. The Commission came to the view that the recent changes in the penalty structure of the criminal law were in part responsible for the apparent increase in crime that had taken place since 1860. The new system, it considered, was a less potent deterrent than transportation. The majority of the Commissioners reported that penal servitude "appears not to be sufficiently dreaded, either by those who have undergone it, or by the criminal classes in general", and they ascribed its want of efficacy as a means of deterring from crime mainly to the shortness of the sentences commonly inflicted upon convicts and only in a minor degree to defects in the discipline to which they were subjected.[3] Sentences of penal servitude for only three or four years were being passed where transportation for seven years

---

[1] In his preface to *The Criminal Law Consolidation and Amendment Acts of the 24 & 25 Vict. with notes and observations* (V. & R. Stevens, 1861), page xlv.

[2] The Home Secretary of the day, Sir George Grey, described the Parliamentary reaction as "panic legislation after the panic had subsided". Parliamentary Debates, Third Series, Vol. 169, Col. 1311. 11 March 1863.

[3] Report of the Commissioners appointed to inquire into the operation of the Acts relating to Transportation and Penal Servitude. 20 June 1863.

would probably have been given. The main recommendation of the Commission was that short sentences of penal servitude should not be passed, and that it would be advisable to return to the standard term of seven years used for transportation as the minimum term of penal servitude. Under the Commission's proposals such sentences would still carry an element of indeterminacy; a convict would be able (under the system of remission and licence) to gain his discharge from a sentence of seven years' penal servitude after serving a little short of five years, as opposed to the two and a half years which a convict sentenced to three years' penal servitude would normally serve.[1]

50. One of the Commissioners who entirely dissented from the majority was the Lord Chief Justice, Sir Alexander Cockburn. He discounted the importance of the recent apparent increase of violent robberies, and opposed the policy of extending the length of sentences and incorporating an element of indeterminacy. His answer, which has a contemporary ring about it, was: short sentences of a more rigorous character—"in proportion as the severity of the punishment is increased, so may its duration be abridged". The Lord Chief Justice argued that the system of remission and licence should be abolished: "the sentence of the judge once pronounced, the punishment should be suffered for the full and entire period of the sentence".

51. The Commission recognised that its proposals would involve considerable amendment of the consolidation Acts of 1861; many offences under those Acts had specified three years' penal servitude as the minimum terms; in a small number of cases three years was the maximum. As the proposals would have involved a substantial increase in the maximum penalty for this second group of offences, the Commission suggested that the increase should be applied selectively. This was ignored by Parliament which provided in the Penal Servitude Act 1864 that in all such cases the maximum, and in fact the only, terms of penal servitude would be five years; the minimum term was raised from three years to five years. It further provided that after a previous conviction, the least sentence that could be awarded was seven years' penal servitude. One effect of the 1864 Act was to disfigure further the already disjointed structure of the 1861 legislation.

52. A more profound effect of the 1864 Act on the penalty structure was to open up a wider gap between the maximum term of two years' imprisonment for misdemeanours and the minimum term of five years' penal servitude for felonies. This gap was not closed until the Penal Servitude Act 1891 (under which the minimum period of penal servitude was reduced to three years). In the meantime

---

[1] Changes in the system of remission and licence at this time were as frequent as the changes in penalties. In transportation days, convicts found unfit for removal to the colonies had been released unconditionally from the hulks after serving a little over half their nominal sentence. After 1853, convicts subject to the new sentence of penal servitude could be released on ticket-of-leave for the same period as under the transportation system, but it was only done in the case of those already under sentence of transportation. Following the 1857 Act, a sliding scale of remission was introduced, ranging from one sixth for three-year sentences up to one third for 15 years and over. After the 1864 Act, the scale was abolished and male convicts could earn a maximum of one quarter (female convicts, one third) of the balance of the sentence remaining after the first nine months (later eight months) of separate confinement. Until 1891, no remission could be earned on the period of recall to prison when a licence was revoked, In that year, when the rates of one quarter and one third were applied to the *whole* of the convict sentence, the complexity of the earlier system led a Home Office official to remark: " . . . Judges very often do not know the exact effect of the sentences they pass, and though Circulars containing tables of remission have been issued several times by the Home Office, the Circulars get lost and the tables are too complex for anyone to bear in mind".

the judges were beginning to formulate the normal levels of sentence that, under the influence of a powerful official lobby to cut sentence lengths, were eventually articulated in the Alverstone Memorandum of 1901, which we describe in paragraph 59. There can be little doubt that the existence of five years and seven years as *minimum* terms of penal servitude powerfully influenced the development of judicial concepts of the appropriate level of sentencing, and that the conventions which they helped to establish continued to influence the sentencing process long after the statutory minima were removed from the statute book.

The reduction of sentence lengths

53. With the consolidation in the legislation of 1861–64 of the system of high maximum penalties, the sentencing role of the judges had changed considerably since the early years of the 19th century when the choice before them had been a relatively simple one between a fixed penalty of transportation and death. The exercise of a new and wide discretion was inevitably to take time to settle down. The succeeding 50 years were marked by a dual concern, shared equally in governmental and judicial circles: first, that sentences were on average too long and second, that there was too wide a disparity in sentencing between one court and the next.

54. After the panic reaction to the "crime wave" of the early 1860s had subsided, doubts began to grow as to the justification for longer deterrent sentences. The prison population was already declining when in February 1884 Sir Edmund Du Cane, the first Chairman of the Prison Commissioners, sent a letter[1] to the Permanent Secretary at the Home Office suggesting a reduction in the length of sentences, principally by the fuller use of the complete scale of penalties available to the courts. He observed that the statistics indicated that the bulk of sentences of penal servitude were for either five, seven or 10 years, and that very few were for six, eight or nine years; a similar picture emerged from a study of the range of sentences within the limit of two years' imprisonment. Du Cane argued that it was possible to cut sentence lengths and thus reduce the amount of unnecessary hardship to prisoners and their families without any loss in the efficiency of the law. His letter was forwarded to the Lord Chancellor by the Home Secretary[2] who, in December 1884, wrote a further letter to his Cabinet colleague which concluded:

> "I must express to you, and ask you to communicate to the Judges in the most respectful manner my concurrence in the opinion of Sir E. Du Cane, that the deterring and reformatory effect of imprisonment . . . would be as well and even more effectually accomplished if the average length of sentences were materially shortened."

---

[1] This followed upon an article on the same theme which Du Cane had published the previous year in *The Fortnightly Review*. In that article, entitled *The Duration of Penal Sentences*, he had commented:

> "On the whole, then, it is quite clear that every year, even every month and every week to which a prisoner is sentenced beyond the necessity of the case, entails an unjustifiable addition to the great mass of human sorrow, and that those who have the duty of apportioning those sentences incur very serious responsibilities in the execution of the duty which they have undertaken."

The Fortnightly Review, Vol. XXXIII (New Series), pages 856–63. 1 June 1883.

[2] Then Sir William Harcourt, who had a strongly liberal reputation. John Bright once described him as the most humane Home Secretary he had ever encountered. It was probably the knowledge that he was likely to have the sympathetic ear of the Home Secretary that decided Du Cane in taking this initiative.

This was followed up in March 1885 by a memorandum on the same theme prepared by Du Cane[1] especially for the Lord Chief Justice. Sir Edmund's covering note to the Home Secretary stated:

"I hope the enclosed memorandum may be of some service to Lord Coleridge. I do not suppose that any definite rules could be laid down for apportioning sentences, but a common agreement on certain principles might lead in that direction, and these principles being adopted by the Judges might in due course be followed by the Courts of Quarter Sessions etc . . ."

The Home Secretary wholeheartedly endorsed the memorandum and ordered it to be sent in confidence to the Lord Chief Justice. This initiative was of particular interest to us as a striking historical parallel to our own action in the interim report of June 1977. Accordingly, we have reproduced the principal documents in Appendix D.

55. The reaction of the courts in the succeeding years was noted by a number of commentators including the Gladstone Committee which, in 1895, remarked[2] upon the reduction of sentence lengths, rather than on reduction in recidivism, as the principal cause of the decline of the prison population.[3] An illustration of how the policy was adopted in the field was given in 1892 when the Recorder of Liverpool, Charles Hopwood QC,[4] who had been appointed to that part-time judicial office in 1886, wrote a letter to *The Times* indicating that he had successfully reduced the length of prison sentences without any consequent increase

---

[1] Probably at the request of Harcourt who had written to the Lord Chief Justice in January urging "the cause of mercy at the bar of the judges". Harcourt believed that five years was the maximum sentence of penal servitude a prisoner should receive: "Few judges I believe realize what ten years' penal servitude mean . . . Still less is it understood what a tremendous penalty is two years' hard labour in the ordinary prison." See *The Life of Sir William Harcourt* by A. G. Gardiner (Constable, 1923), Vol. 1, pages 534–5. Harcourt declared his position to the House of Commons at this time in a debate on law and justice initiated by Charles Hopwood QC (see footnote [4] below):

"There is, I think, a disposition on the part of those who administer the Criminal Law to mitigate its severity. I believe that the time has arrived when it may be more considerably done—when the sentences may be less severe and less protracted, with equal security to life and property in this country."

Parliamentary Debates, Third Series, Vol. 296, Col. 1125. 31 March 1885.

[2] Report from the Departmental Committee on Prisons, C. 7702, 1895, paragraph 15.

[3] In 1899 an internal Home Office memorandum (see paragraph 58) recorded:

"Sentences passed by criminal courts have of late years shown an undeniable tendency to leniency, and in its action the Home Office has marched with the times."

[4] Member of Parliament for Stockport 1874–85 and for Middleton, Lancashire 1892–95. A life-long campaigner for libertarian causes, he was described at his death in 1904 as "the last of those Liberals who were all for freedom". In 1882, he introduced a Criminal Law Amendment Bill designed to establish a court of appeal in criminal cases and, among other things, to limit judicial powers of consecutive sentencing, but it did not make progress (see Parliamentary Debates, Third Series, Vol. 267, Cols. 402–10. 8 March 1882). He attempted to give statutory form to his policy of shorter sentences by pressing forward reforms in the summary jurisdiction of magistrates to reduce the frequency and length of imprisonment. Confronted with his radical sentencing policy, the local magistrates in Lancashire made every effort to by-pass his court, wherever possible by dealing with offenders summarily or committing them to the Assizes. In 1893, one of his cases, where he had imposed a fine on a man convicted of keeping a disorderly house, even provoked a local petition and questions in Parliament (see the extract from Parliamentary Debates also reproduced in Appendix D). In spite of the contemporary view that his indulgence was probably at times misplaced, it was nevertheless recognised that he had played a leading role in spreading the gospel of shorter sentences in the last quarter of the 19th century. As one judge remarked, "Charles Hopwood has taught us all. We are all his pupils, though some of us don't admit it".

in recorded crime. He noted that there were chairmen of quarter sessions, recorders and magistrates who had resorted to unnecessary imprisonment and disproportionately long sentences, but that the Lord Chief Justice, who was then still Lord Coleridge, the recipient of the Du Cane memorandum seven years earlier, had set an example of moderation in sentencing. The Recorder of Liverpool concluded that his experience was that moderate sentences were as effective as excessive ones in containing the level of crime. His letter is also reproduced in Appendix D. It is true that such practical experiments in the restriction of imprisonment coincided with a time when recorded crime was decreasing,[1] but they do, we think, provide a useful historical instance to support the view that the length of prison sentences can be reduced without apparently affecting adversely the rate of crime.

The emergence of the "tariff"

56. The other major concern, which Du Cane also expressed in his 1884 letter,[2] was the wide disparity in sentences imposed in different parts of the country; a concern which led, with the help of close governmental interest, to the establishment of judicial conventions in sentencing. One of the earliest public advocacies of a "tariff" system was made by Lord Penzance, himself a judge,[3] when in 1870 he inaugurated a debate in the House of Lords, the ostensible purpose of which was to seek from the Home Office a return showing the recent use of the Prerogative of Mercy. In moving the motion, he commented on the contemporary disparities in sentencing and said:

"This inequality of sentences is due to the absence of any standard; for if there were a standard laid down, still leaving the Judges the utmost liberty of increasing or diminishing it, it would be felt that in nine cases out of ten the Judges would not disturb it; for the circumstances of cases really differ very little. I venture to say that such a standard would be gladly adopted by the Judges in the large majority of cases, and we should thus obtain something like uniformity of sentences . . . When I first had the honour of a seat on the Common Law Bench I was struck with the desirability of such a standard:—which might be obtained either by Act of Parliament, by an Order in Council, or even by agreement among the

---

[1] Though this was disputed in some quarters, notably by the Rev. W. D. Morrison. The Hopwood correspondence in *The Times*, to which Morrison contributed, seems to have been the inspiration of the later exchanges between Morrison and Du Cane in *The Nineteenth Century*; see *The Increase of Crime* by W. D. Morrison in *The Nineteenth Century*, Vol. XXXI, June 1892, pages 950–7, and *The Decrease of Crime* by E. F. Du Cane in *The Nineteenth Century*, Vol. XXXIII, March 1893, pages 480–92. For a discussion of the statistical evidence of a trend in shorter sentences at this period, see *Crime and Industrial Society in the 19th century* by J. J. Tobias (Batsford, 1967), pages 216–22.

[2] Du Cane had originally written:

" . . . it is impossible to doubt that the practice in different localities varies very widely, and that, if those, who, from custom and tradition, are in the habit of awarding longer sentences than necessary, were fully aware of the practice in other localities, where shorter sentences are quite as effective, they would find they could frequently shorten the duration of their sentences. This variation in the practice in different localities is less justifiable, now [*that is, since the enactment of the Prison Act 1877*] that the punishment inflicted is the same in all, and it seems very desirable that the improvement in the latter respect should now be followed up by the introduction of some approach to agreement in principle and uniformity of practice among those who fix the duration of the sentence."

These sentiments were omitted from the copy of the letter which the Home Secretary eventually forwarded to the Lord Chancellor—see Appendix D.

[3] As Sir James Wilde, he had been from 1860 to 1863 a Baron of the Court of Exchequer, and subsequently a Probate and Divorce Court judge.

Judges themselves. There would be no reason why it should not be altered from time to time, as the prevalence of a particular crime or other circumstances might render advisable."[1]

The earliest official context in which the expressions the "tariff"[2] and "range" of sentences are known to have been used was in a Home Office inquiry in 1874 into the adequacy of penalties for wife-beating. One correspondent[3] to the inquiry actually used these expressions in the exact modern sense to describe his standard sentencing practice in ordering floggings for garotters. Although these precise expressions did not pass into common use immediately thereafter, the idea of a "normal range" soon became accepted[4].

57. In the 1890s, the expression of judicial concern at the disparity of sentences became more concerted. In 1892, in a report[5] to the Lord Chancellor, the Council of Judges of the Supreme Court[6] put forward a firm recommendation for the establishment of a court of criminal appeal to remedy the problem. It commented:

"There is a great diversity in the sentences passed by different Courts in respect of offences of the same kind, where the circumstances are very similar. It is much to be desired that this diversity should be, if possible, avoided . . . After full consideration, the institution of a Court is recommended, having full jurisdiction to review and alter sentences, and a limited jurisdiction to assist the Home Secretary in reconsidering sentences or convictions at his request. As to sentences, the great object is to procure a greater uniformity than exists. A series of decisions by one Court would, by examples and the reasons given for them, tend to secure uniformity . . . the punishment inflicted on a convicted prisoner should, if justice requires it, be diminished, and the Court, on the hearing of such an application, should have power to increase the Applicant's sentence when the facts seem to need it."

The recommendation was not immediately taken up.

58. In the absence of such a court, sentences that were patently over-severe were adjusted by the Home Secretary through his exercise of the Prerogative of Mercy. In 1899 the Home Office drew up a memorandum describing the standards that had been followed in equalising sentences and this was passed

---

[1] Parliamentary Debates, Third Series, Vol. 200, Col. 1153. 4 April 1870.

[2] There are, of course, earlier references to the tariff in unofficial sources. James Fitzjames Stephen, proposing in 1856 a judicial system for review of sentences, wrote:

"Judgments would be delivered, laying down the principles upon which punishment ought to be allotted; and by degrees the discretion which the judges exercise would be guided and regulated by *a sort of tariff* formed by the ablest men in the country."

Classification of Punishments, an article in *The Saturday Review*, Vol. II, page 438. 13 September 1856.

[3] Mr. Justice Lush. See Reports to the Secretary of State for the Home Department on the state of the law relating to brutal assaults, &c., C. 1138, 1875, page 8.

[4] The Alverstone Memorandum (see paragraph 59), for example, referred to a "normal standard of punishment"; the Dove-Wilson Report on *Persistent Offenders* in 1932 referred to "certain general standards"—Cmd. 4090, paragraph 20.

[5] Return of Report of the Judges in 1892 to the Lord Chancellor, recommending the Constitution of a Court of Appeal and Revision of Sentences in Criminal Cases. 24 May 1894. The moving force behind the publication of the report, two years after it was written, was Charles Hopwood QC, then Member of Parliament for Middleton, Lancashire.

[6] Section 75 of the Supreme Court of Judicature Act 1873 (now section 210 of the Supreme Court of Judicature (Consolidation) Act 1925) established a Council of High Court judges to hold annual meetings to discuss matters relating to the administration of justice.

on a confidential basis to the Lord Chief Justice. There was talk in judicial circles at the time (later revived by Churchill in 1910) of a Royal Commission to lay down the standard principles governing maximum penalties and sentencing practice, but this never reached the realms of practical policy.

59. The Home Office memorandum appears to have been the inspiration of the deliberations of the judges that led up to the Alverstone Memorandum of 1901 (reproduced in Appendix E), in which the High Court judges indicated the range of penalties that ordinarily ought to be passed for specific offences. In its introduction, the Memorandum specifically discounted public fears of discrepancies in sentencing as exaggerated, pointing to the danger of a strict adherence to a tariff system:

"Any attempt to mete out punishment to offenders in the same class of crime at a rigidly uniform rate could result only in the frequent perpetration of injustice."

In spite of this disclaimer, the judges nevertheless regarded it as desirable to promulgate what they called a "normal standard" of punishment:

"At the same time, the Judges of the King's Bench Division are agreed that it would be convenient and of public advantage in regard to certain classes of crime to come to an agreement, or, at least, to an approximate agreement, as to what may be called a 'normal' standard of punishment: a standard of punishment, that is to say, which should be assumed to be properly applicable, unless the particular case under consideration presented some special features of aggravation or of extenuation."

In considering this list of "normal" penalties, it is interesting to note how often the penalty for the more serious offences is couched in terms of three to five years', or five to seven years' penal servitude—a direct reflection of the influence of the statutory minimum terms. The Alverstone Memorandum is a remarkable document, representing, as it does, the first, and only, emergence in public of the tacit tariff, which is communicated today either through the decisions of the Court of Appeal (Criminal Division) or through the periodical sentencing seminars and conferences organised for judges since the mid-1960s. After 1901, the judges followed the lines set by the Alverstone Memorandum, but it was never formally disseminated among the recorders or chairmen of quarter sessions. The Home Office compiled at the time a more detailed memorandum of its practice in Prerogative of Mercy cases, intended as a follow-up to Alverstone, but the idea was lost in the more pressing concern of equalising the sentences passed on habitual criminals—the proposals that were eventually to reach the statute book in the Prevention of Crime Act 1908.

60. The question was not revived until Winston Churchill came to the Home Office in 1910. In the enthusiasm of the early days of a new office, he put forward a number of suggestions for his officials to pursue: the enactment of new reduced maxima, the establishment of a court to assimilate sentences, and the possibility of a Royal Commission on the whole subject. He even drew up his own scale of offences, graded in descending order of gravity, which is reproduced in Appendix F. He was swiftly reminded by officials that

"It is impossible to arrange crimes in the abstract in order of gravity: almost every designation of crime covers a very wide range of criminality . . .

30

to graduate crimes according to their real gravity we must look to the actual facts of each case and not to the legal designation of the crime or the maximum punishment that the law imposes."

This was a view which (as we indicate in paragraph 164) we came ultimately to share ourselves after initially contemplating the compilation of a subjective list of this kind. Churchill pondered the issues for a further year, but had reached no conclusion on what action to take when he finally left the Home Office in 1911.

61. In 1910, the idea of a reduction of the statutory maxima was specifically rejected in official circles on the grounds that Parliament would concentrate on the penalty for the normal offender and leave insufficient room for the adequate sentencing of the exceptional case. It was, therefore, hardly surprising that an attempt by a private member the following year to scale down the maxima should have ended in failure. The Criminal Law (Mitigation) Bill, introduced in 1911, was designed to remove the death penalty for all remaining capital offences except murder, raise the minimum age of execution to 21, abolish the death penalty for infanticide and restrict corporal punishment to boys between the ages of 10 and 16. It also proposed a complete revision of existing maximum terms of penal servitude. Two new scales of maxima were proposed, one for adults and another for juvenile adults (persons aged between 18 and 21). Existing maxima of penal servitude for life would have been reduced (with the exception of manslaughter) to 10 years, or in a few cases to 15 years. Existing maxima of 14 years were to be reduced in almost all cases to seven years. For a series of other offences, including larceny, it was proposed to limit penal servitude to persons previously convicted on indictment. The effect of this would have been to reduce the maximum of five years' penal servitude to two years' imprisonment for many offenders. The Bill never received a second reading, being engulfed in the impending constitutional crisis over the powers of the House of Lords. It was reintroduced the following year[1] but still made no progress, and nothing more was seen of it or its proposals. It attracted no discernible public interest and aroused no parliamentary controversy.

62. By that time, however, judicial conventions of sentencing had already been established. Very early in the life of the Court of Criminal Appeal, set up in 1907, it had been decided, for example, that a trial judge's sentence would be interfered with only if he had erred in principle and not simply where the Appeal Court thought the sentence too long or (since there was then power to increase a sentence) too short.[2] And in 1909 the Court declared that the maximum penalty prescribed by statute should be reserved for the "worst cases" of a particular offence.[3]

The structure of maximum penalties today

63. The combined effect of the consolidation Acts of 1861 and the Penal Servitude Act 1864 was to establish a series of conventions relating to maximum terms of confinement, to which virtually all legislation since has conformed.

---

[1] With additional provisions, including a rudimentary form of community service for fine defaulters; the offender would have been required "to perform in a casual ward such task as may be prescribed by rules made under this Act for such number of consecutive days as the court may order . . ."
[2] *R* v *Sidlow* (1908) 1 Cr. App. R. 28.
[3] *R* v *Harrison* (1909) 2 Cr. App. R. 94.

At present, for offences triable on indictment, one finds nine maximum terms scattered around the statute book: one year, two years, three, five, seven, 10, 14 and 20 years and life. Of these, three years and 20 years are limited to a small number of offences. The majority of offences commonly triable on indictment are punishable with imprisonment for two, five, seven, 10 or 14 years or life, and all those terms are to be found in the Acts of 1861 as amended by the 1864 Act. Detailed studies of the legislative history of several criminal law statutes show that the maximum penalty allotted to new offences has rarely been the subject of any discussion in or out of Parliament. In general the approach has been to allocate one of the conventional terms on a rule-of-thumb basis, drawing on the maximum penalty prescribed for an analogous offence. Little or no consideration of contemporary sentencing practice or penal policy is discernible.

64. The general tendency, although not consistently so, has been to favour the shorter maximum terms. Two years' imprisonment has remained a popular figure, probably because for so many years it marked the boundary line between imprisonment and penal servitude. But it has also, in relation to a few crimes, been the one maximum term that has come in for sustained judicial criticism. Five years has been an infrequent legislative choice, despite the fact that it was established in the 1864 Act as the maximum term of penal servitude associated with some of the most common offences, such as simple larceny, malicious wounding and assault occasioning actual bodily harm. It has had a slight revival in recent years in the new offence of causing death by dangerous driving (in 1960) and in the Firearms Act 1965. Seven years has recently begun to lose its traditional popularity, although it found favour as the maximum for immigrant smuggling under the Immigration Act 1971 and in the Misuse of Drugs Act 1971. While maximum penalties of more than seven years were not uncommon in the 1861 legislation, only a few examples have since been added to that list. Life imprisonment was infrequently adopted for new offences at the end of the last century, but in this century it has been applied to new offences of genocide, hijacking and certain offences in connection with firearms. The effect of the broad-banding of offences in the Theft Act 1968 and the Criminal Damage Act 1971 has been to extend the ambit of the maximum term of life imprisonment that appeared in their 1861 precursors. Maximum sentences of 14 years which are found in the 1861 legislation have only rarely been applied to new offences;[1] for example, some of the offences in the Explosive Substances Act 1883, the Official Secrets Act 1920 (for spying) and the remaining offences relating to suicide under the Suicide Act 1961. Ten years has recently become the most popular maximum. It was used extensively in the Firearms Act 1965 and the Dangerous Drugs Act 1965, although in the Misuse of Drugs Act 1971 there was a reversion to the traditional seven and 14-year legislative syndrome. But since the Theft Act 1968 10 years generally has become the standard choice in place of both seven and 14 years as the highest maximum short of life imprisonment.

65. Once a new offence has been assigned a maximum penalty it has tended to retain it. Changes in maxima are relatively rarely made and then only in

---

[1] As recently as August 1976, the Criminal Law Revision Committee has proposed a maximum penalty of 14 years for a new offence of causing death recklessly—*Working Paper on Offences against the Person* (HMSO, 1976), paragraph 91.

response to some emergency prompted by an apparent wave of some particular criminal activity; but changes do occur as and when the offence is either re-enacted or redefined. The Prevention of Corruption Act 1916 raised the maximum sentence for corrupt practices in relation to government contracts from two years' imprisonment to seven years' penal servitude as a result of public feeling about widespread corruption and dishonesty over the supply of military equipment. The Official Secrets Act 1920 doubled the penalty for spying following the experience of the First World War. Other indictable offences whose maxima have been raised are living off the immoral earnings of prostitution, indecent assault on a girl under 13 and certain offences in connection with possession of firearms and the use of drugs. The recent Criminal Law Act 1977 increased the penalty of 20 years for explosive substances offences to life imprisonment. Only one offence appears to have had its maximum decreased; buggery with a male person of 16 and over, originally punishable with life imprisonment, became punishable with various shorter maxima in the Sexual Offences Act 1967. Apart from the recasting of the law of theft in 1968, of criminal damage in 1971, and of dangerous drugs in 1971, no general reconstruction of maximum penalties has been undertaken.

66. This short historical review sufficiently indicates the lack of any rational system of maximum penalties. The extent to which the pattern of maximum penalties has been governed by historical accident and not by any rational penal or sentencing policy is perhaps best exemplified by the variety of penalties for theft that have emerged over the years. Simple larceny (as the crime was dubbed by the legislators of the 18th century) under the Transportation Act 1717[1] carried a sentence of seven years' transportation, with the alternative of one year's imprisonment; under the consolidating legislation of 1827 that became seven years' transportation or two years' imprisonment. Lord John Russell, as Home Secretary, thought that transportation was too severe for this offence and secured its removal in 1849, leaving the maximum at two years' imprisonment. This was later thought to be too low. The Larceny Act 1861 imposed a maximum penalty of three years' penal servitude, or two years' imprisonment. The Penal Servitude Act 1864 increased the maximum, and indeed the minimum, term of penal servitude to five years. The penalty for larceny between 1864 and 1891 was for any term not exceeding two years' imprisonment, or five years' penal servitude. The Penal Servitude Act 1891, following the recommendation of the Royal Commission on Penal Servitude 1879, reduced the minimum terms of penal servitude to three years, but left the maximum alone so that from 1891 until the Larceny Act 1916 the penalty structure was imprisonment for any period not exceeding two years, or penal servitude from three to five years. Five years' penal servitude was thus the maximum sentence provided when the law of larceny was consolidated for the third time in 1916. It remained the maximum term until the law of dishonesty was reconstructed in the Theft Act 1968 when the redefined offence of theft (including various aggravated forms of larceny up until then punishable with maxima of 14 years' imprisonment or life) was given a maximum of 10 years' imprisonment. This changing of the penalty for the most common crime was achieved without any reference to any other branch of the criminal law, except aggravated forms of theft and related dishonesty offences, and with scarcely any consideration of the demands of penal policy.

---

[1] 4 Geo. 1c. 11.

CHAPTER 4

MAXIMUM PENALTIES AND THE COURTS

The powers of the courts

67. The maximum powers of imprisonment are limited according to the type of court and crime. Magistrates' courts are limited to six months' imprisonment in the case of an indictable offence tried summarily, with an overriding maximum of 12 months for consecutive sentences; in the case of purely summary offences, the power to order two or more sentences to run consecutively is subject to an overriding limit of six months. In the Crown Court it is the maximum penalty prescribed by Parliament for the specific crime that alone limits the judge's powers of imprisonment (since the Criminal Law Act 1977 there are very few common law crimes for which there is now no maximum penalty). The maximum penalty provided for the offence will rarely have any direct relevance to magistrates; it is likely to be relevant only in respect of the minor offence for which the maximum is expressed as imprisonment for a term of six months or less and then, more often than not, for the sole purpose of determining the right to trial by jury.[1] While the vast majority of all those who are convicted before the criminal courts are sentenced by magistrates' courts, it is the Crown Court which passes the larger number of sentences of imprisonment. Out of approximately 40,000 sentences of immediate imprisonment in 1976, 57% were imposed by the Crown Court. And, by definition, most of the 43% of sentences of immediate imprisonment imposed by magistrates' courts were the shorter ones. We have, therefore, inevitably concerned ourselves primarily with sentencing in the Crown Court. (In Appendix G, we indicate the relative powers of imprisonment of the two types of court and the manner in which they are exercised.)

The appellate process

68. The patchwork of statutory penalties we have traced in the previous chapter left the judges with a wide discretion, which was reduced first by the unique formulation of a normal range of penalties in the Alverstone Memorandum of 1901 and second, by the establishment of the Court of Criminal Appeal in 1907. Apart from the establishment of the important principle that the Court would intervene in a sentence only if the trial judge had erred in principle, the impact of appellate review has been marginal, at least until the last ten years. The number of sentences that came up for review were few, and trial judges were largely left to their own devices in determining the appropriate length of sentences of penal servitude or imprisonment. The normal range of penalties imposed at the turn of the century was simply perpetuated by the absence of an appellate corrective. It was in the early years of the life of the Court that the

---

[1] Under section 25 of the Magistrates' Courts Act 1952, only offences that carry a maximum penalty of more than three months' imprisonment at present give the accused a right to trial by jury. This provision will disappear when section 15 of the Criminal Law Act 1977 is brought into force and the new category of offences triable either way comes into operation.

case-law, sparse as it is, on maximum penalties was established and it has persisted down to our present day.

69. It was not surprising that few prisoners took the risk of an appeal since there were powerful disincentives to appealing at this time. Even so, a few prisoners did appeal initially, but soon after the establishment of the Court a warning note was sounded. In January 1909, the appeal of a prisoner with an extremely bad record of crime against his conviction and sentence of 18 months' imprisonment with hard labour for stealing a shawl was dismissed by the Lord Chief Justice with the warning that

> "If these frivolous kinds of appeal continue it will be necessary to consider whether some step cannot be taken to prevent them. Such cases involve much unnecessary expense and preparation of documents. The appellant, who was convicted upon the clearest possible evidence, merely repeats what any man of his class would say in the circumstances."[1]

There was no need for the Court to take special steps; the law was sufficiently daunting to discourage any but the supreme optimist. Prison sentences did not begin to run until the case was finally disposed of, and this "automatic loss of time" was a powerful factor in stopping appeals in their tracks. The Court furthermore had power to *increase* sentences, and was not averse to exercising it. The Criminal Justice Act 1948 had some effect on this position by limiting the amount of the "automatic loss of time" to 42 days; but the Court was also given power to order whether more or less than the 42 days should be lost, and where an application for leave to appeal was refused by the single judge the standing direction from the Court was the loss of 63 days. These controls effectively stifled the number of appeals and hence reduced the influence of the appellate process on the principles of sentencing.

70. The business of the Court of Criminal Appeal until the late 1950s was dispatched by three judges sitting on one day in the court week (often disposing of the cases in the morning session). Today the Court of Appeal (Criminal Division) sits, often in three divisions, four days a week; and much of its work is dealing with sentence applications and appeals alone, not in conjunction with convictions. The increase in the Court's workload led to the establishment of the Donovan Committee to review the Court's work and its functions. It recommended in its report[2] the abolition of a separate Court of Criminal Appeal, the transfer of its functions to a new Criminal Division of the Court of Appeal (with the Lords Justices of Appeal for the first time sitting to preside over the divisions of the Court) and the abolition of the power to increase sentences. Effect was given to these recommendations by the Criminal Appeal Act 1966, consolidated in the Criminal Appeal Act 1968. But even before the Government had indicated its acceptance of the recommendations, the Court announced that it would not in future increase sentences. The abolition of the power to increase sentences and the replacement of the "automatic loss of time" by a rule that time pending appeal would be lost only if the single judge or the Court so directed, impelled another period of great expansion in the Court's work. It was short-lived. In March 1970 the Lord Chief Justice

---

[1] *R* v *Baker* (1909) 2 Cr. App. R. 2.
[2] Report of the Interdepartmental Committee on the Court of Criminal Appeal, Cmnd. 2755. August 1965.

indicated that single judges might properly exercise more frequently their power to order loss of time.[1] The effect was dramatic; within a fortnight the rate of notices from prisoners of applications for leave to appeal was reduced by half. As Appendix H shows, immediately before the direction, the rate was about 800 a month; thereafter it fell to 400 a month and the annual rate has not been above 6,500 since.

71.   The important factor to note in the Court's workload over the 70 years of its existence is the almost unbroken rise in the number of appeals against conviction and sentence, as opposed to applications for leave to appeal. Unless the convicted person has a point of law, which is rare, he must first obtain leave to appeal from the Court. On the prisoner giving his notice of application for leave to appeal, the case is normally referred to a single judge of the High Court who scrutinises the papers and decides whether leave to appeal should be granted. If he refuses leave, the prisoner may renew his application before the full Court, which will hear the matter in open court and deliver a reasoned judgment. The hearing of an appeal is an acknowledgement that there is an arguable point for consideration by the judges which is therefore worthy of the full treatment of the appellate process—a hearing before a court of three (as opposed to two) judges in open court, with counsel appearing on legal aid, if necessary. The volume of all the other business of the Court—the applications for leave to appeal—is governed by the individual decisions of offenders and their legal representatives and affected by changes in the law and practice of the Court itself, irrespective of any legal merits the case might possess. It is thus mainly the appeals that have increased in recent years the influence of the Court on the criminal law and, incidentally, on sentencing policy and practice.

Sentencing principles

72.   The existing sentencing practice of the trial courts has been primarily and decisively influenced by the authoritative rulings of the Court of Appeal (Criminal Division) and, to a much less extent, its predecessor, the Court of Criminal Appeal. While from the outset it has been consistently recognised that the Appeal Court is there to ensure the legality of any sentence and that the principles and guidelines of sentencing that it lays down from time to time are observed, the court will not generally interfere with the discretion of trial judges. This fundamental role of the Court was probably best expressed in recent times by Lord Justice Widgery, the present Lord Chief Justice, in *R* v *Newsome and Browne*[2] when presiding over a five-judge court, which held that a court so constituted could review such principles and guidelines previously laid down by a court constituted (as it normally is) of three judges. But the growth of the number of appeals against sentence, the greater sense of the importance of the sentencing aspect of the criminal law and the increase in serious crime, with inevitably longer sentences, have all conspired to stimulate a re-statement of the sentencing principles and even some statements of new ones.

---

[1] The change in the prison rules in 1973, whereby certain privileges (such as unlimited letter-writing and visits in connection with the appeal) were taken away from aspiring appellants had a short-term impact on the rate of applications in the following period.

[2] (1970) 54 Cr. App. R. 485 at page 490.

73. We have not ourselves felt it necessary, or even useful, to the purposes of this report to embark upon an examination of the principles of sentencing. Whether retribution, deterrence, prevention or rehabilitation (or any single one or more of them in combination) govern sentencing policy and practice is the subject of consistent controversy and debate. Attitudes change over the years. Rehabilitation, once a key factor in determining both the question of imprisonment and the length of any custodial penalty, is now seriously questioned, simply because research has largely failed to show that prisons can reform those sent to them. Retribution is now also questioned as a valid function of the sentencing process but may still retain its role under other guises, such as denunciation. While most commentators admit the role of deterrence in some disposals, such as the fine, criminological research has raised questions about the general effectiveness of deterrent sentencing and, in particular, the existence of any greater deterrent effect in longer sentences. The preventive role of the sentencing process probably arouses the least controversy; only the degree to which public protection can justify long incarceration causes debate. We mention these four principles here only to observe that all have at one time or another played their part in the sentencing process. That they continue to play their part is evident from judicial pronouncements, the latest and most explicit example of which came recently from Lord Justice Lawton in R v Sargeant,[1] reproduced in Appendix I. Recent instances of guidance on the length of sentences for particular crimes have been in R v Turner,[2] quoted at length in Appendix M, concerning grave offences of robbery, and in R v Rathbone,[3] dealing with the approach to sentencing men convicted of unlawful sexual intercourse with young girls. The construction by the courts of a normal range of penalty for all the more common crimes is a constant process that has accelerated in recent years as the result of the increased impact of the Court of Appeal.

74. It is against the background of the fundamental principles of sentencing, as enunciated by the courts themselves, that the role of maximum penalties both in theory and practice must be seen. In the past, the fundamental objectives of sentencing were regarded as being adequately served by the passing of a "tariff" sentence: that is, one which was designed essentially to give the offender his deserts in the form of a punishment proportionate to the gravity of the offence and to his own culpability. Today, the wide variety of different penalties at the disposal of the court, varying from the predominantly punitive to the almost wholly reformative, has made the task of the sentencer enormously more complex. He is now frequently faced with the question of choosing between a "tariff" sentence based upon the circumstances of the criminal event and what has come to be known as the "individualised" sentence, based upon the needs of the offender and designed primarily to control future events by, for instance, assisting the offender to keep out of trouble. This can, and does, lead to a choice of sentences based upon quite different, and often conflicting, objectives. In this development of the theory and practice of sentencing the part played by maximum penalties has become increasingly irrelevant. Given the variety of non-custodial penalties, the discretion of the sentencer has widened to the point where the

---

[1] (1975) 60 Cr. App. R. 74.
[2] (1975) 61 Cr. App. R. 67.
[3] [1976] Crim. L.R. 521. See also R v Taylor, Roberts and Simons (1977) 64 Cr. App. R. 182, quoted in footnote [2] on page 85.

dilemma he faces in choosing the appropriate penalty has greatly increased. The important issue for the court in imposing a sentence of imprisonment inevitably must be the length of term selected, and because the majority of maximum penalties are set so high, they have never been able to play a formative role in deciding that question. Only in a very few instances is the maximum penalty for an offence set sufficiently low so as to exercise any influence upon the sentence passed, and those have occurred largely as a result of historical chance. Because the offences at the time they were enacted were regarded as insufficiently grave to be labelled felonies, they automatically attracted the traditional maximum term of two years' imprisonment prescribed for misdemeanours. It is hardly surprising therefore that the occasions upon which the courts have explicitly considered the role of maximum penalties in the sentencing process have been few in number.

The function of maximum penalties

75. One view of maximum penalties is that they represent a scale by which the gravity of different offences can be measured. If such a scale could be accepted as reliable, it would be reflected in the penalties imposed for everyday examples of offences; that is, if the maximum penalty were high relative to other maxima, so therefore would the penalty imposed in the "normal" case be higher than for most other offences. Something akin to this view of the penalty system was expounded in 1877 by Edward Cox in *The Principles of Punishment*, the first systematic textbook on sentencing. The maximum penalty was treated by Cox as fixing the parliamentary standard for a particular crime—the starting point for sentencers from which mitigation would then proceed:

> "The law affixes the punishment to the crime and gives to the Judge power to mitigate that punishment, as in his judgment he may deem to be right, upon consideration of all the circumstances attending the particular case. The *law* looks at the *crime* and imposes the punishment which it deems appropriate. The consideration of the *Judge* is for the *criminal*. He has to determine to what extent—tempering justice with mercy and consulting the interests of the public as well as the character of the prisoner—he may properly *reduce the penalty*."[1]

Although such a theory is not inconsistent with the idea of maxima as appropriate to the worst cases,[2] it is essentially the creation of a period before the emergence of the concept of the tariff. With the promulgation of the Alverstone Memorandum in 1901, it was inevitable that the starting point of the sentencing process should cease to be the maximum penalty and become the tariff itself, which the sentencer could exceed as well as undercut, according to circumstances of aggravation as well as mitigation. As the tariff thus usurped the "guideline" function of the maximum penalty, the role of the latter began to be seen as relevant only to those few cases which could be designated "the worst". It is evident from any review of the historical growth of maximum penalties such as we have undertaken in Chapter 3 that the idea of "steering by the maximum" could have survived only in a relatively unsophisticated system of sentencing.

---

[1] *The Principles of Punishment, as applied in the administration of the criminal law, by judges and magistrates* by Edward W. Cox (Law Times Office, 1877), page 18.

[2] In certain contexts, Cox himself points out that "the worst cases will demand the highest measure of punishment"—*ibid.*, page 95.

The truth is that maximum penalties do not reflect any consistent scale of the seriousness of offences, but rather the transient concern of Parliament with particular offences and values which change rapidly over time. Only in a very broad way can they be said to reflect a scale of gravity. The theory is not in itself deficient; it merely requires, if it is to operate successfully, a more consistent framework of maximum penalties, such as that which we ourselves recommend in this report.

76. Another view is that maximum penalties should act as a deterrent upon the potential offender.[1] It is one that the Criminal Law Commissioners themselves put forward in their Second Report in 1836 when arguing that penalties, both maximum and actual, should be distinct and known:

"It may be hoped that the law, in the annexation of severe and appropriate penalties to heinous offences, may operate not only on the fears, but also on the consciences and feelings of mankind, and serve to impress their minds with just conceptions of the comparative enormity of crimes."[2]

We doubt, however, whether this is a function to which much weight can in reality be attached. The average offender does not consult the statute book before committing an offence; many offenders do not know the maxima to which they may be liable even by the time they reach court. Those offenders who could claim knowledge of sentencing practice are more likely to base it on the normal range of penalty; if deterrence has a valid role in this context, it is the risk of the sentence likely to be imposed which might affect the behaviour of the potential offender rather than the known maxima, which in the vast majority of cases will never be imposed.

77. The fundamental approach of the courts to maximum penalties was established in the very early days of the Court of Criminal Appeal. The simple and straightforward proposition was that the maxima (and not surprisingly in the particular case it was a low maximum of two years' imprisonment) are "reserved for the worst cases".[3] The case of *R v Harrison*[4] in 1909 entered the law books as the authority for that proposition, and has remained unsullied by any judicial pronouncement for more than half a century; and when it did come up for consideration it was endorsed (in another case involving a two-year maximum penalty[5]) with only a minor modification. Harrison had been indicted at Warwick Assizes with three others for rape, but was convicted of the lesser offence of indecent assault largely because the complainant, a woman of known bad

---

[1] Support for such a view is implied by Cox in his suggestion that the maximum penalty for the offence should be read out in court at the time of passing sentence—*ibid.*, page 20.

[2] Second Report (1836), page 28.

[3] It is interesting that *Harrison* has often been colloquially cited as authority for the proposition that the maxima are designed to embrace "the worst *possible* case", but this precise phrase was never used. Other phrases have been used from time to time in applying the *Harrison* principle: for example, in *R v Mackintosh and Hughes* (1917) 12 Cr. App. R. 41 the Lord Chief Justice described the offence as "as bad a case as can be imagined".

[4] (1909) 2 Cr. App. R. 94. The report indicates that Harrison's three co-accused had not appealed, although the Court's remarks applied equally to them. The Court said that, since the Home Secretary had a power of revising sentences, an appeal to the Court was unnecessary. Despite this (maybe because there was a certain sensitivity about using the prerogative powers to interfere with the sentences of the courts after the advent of the Court of Criminal Appeal), the three did later appeal successfully: see *R v Boxall, Hammersley and Marston* (1909) 2 Cr. App. R. 175.

[5] *R v Ambler and Hargreaves* [1976] Crim. L.R. 266 (see paragraph 79).

character, failed to appear as a witness. On appeal, his counsel argued that the judge, in passing the maximum sentence of two years' imprisonment with hard labour, had been biased by the circumstances of vice disclosed in the evidence and by the depravity of the area in which the offence took place. It was freely admitted by the members of the court that there were many worse cases than Harrison's. Mr. Justice Jelf observed that

> "There are cases of old men committing indecent assaults upon little children with circumstances of great brutality, and yet they can only receive two years' imprisonment. The badness disclosed here is the badness of immorality."

In substituting a sentence of 12 months' imprisonment with hard labour, exceptionally to date from the moment of conviction (Harrison had spent four months in prison), Mr. Justice Channell said that

> "It was admittedly a very bad case, but there was the fact that the prisoners had on previous occasions had relations with the prosecutrix, and an indecent assault with a view to such relations is different in the case of a woman of her character."

and he added

> "The maximum sentence must, *as presumably the law intended*, be reserved for the worst cases."

78. It is perhaps ironic that a case decided upon the basis of a low maximum of two years' imprisonment should have been used to justify the retention of very high maxima, where the case that merits the highest penalty is rarely, if ever, met. For an offence with a maximum as low as two years it is difficult for the courts to distinguish in their sentencing between a serious and a more serious offence, let alone between the worst possible case and the rest.[1] The Court in *Harrison* was concerned only with imprisonment and never alluded to the high maxima for sentences of penal servitude, which was still in 1909 clearly distinguishable from imprisonment for the lesser offences. As the Lord Chief Justice said in *R v Thornton* in 1909, when an offender was sentenced to three years' penal servitude for stealing a coat at a club for members of the Baptist congregation at Shipley in the West Riding of Yorkshire:

> "Three years' penal servitude is not twice as heavy as eighteen months', hard labour. In view of the prisoner's record of ten previous convictions the sentence was a perfectly proper one. There comes a time when the sentence of imprisonment with hard labour must cease, and a longer term and a different treatment must be tried."[2]

79. The principle enunciated in *Harrison* was only recently considered in *R v Ambler and Hargreaves*[3] and subjected to a modification that provided a little more elbow room for the judge sentencing an offender for an offence that

---

[1] A hint of this dilemma was given by Lord Coleridge when applying the *Harrison* principle to reduce to 12 months a maximum sentence of two years' imprisonment for larceny:
"This Court has often pointed out that if very severe sentences are imposed for small crimes, it leaves no heavier sentence for graver crimes . . ."
R v Edwards (1910) 5 Cr. App. R. 229.

[2] (1909) 2 Cr. App. R. 284 and 315.

[3] [1976] Crim. L.R. 266.

40

carried a two-year maximum. The two appellants had been found guilty on three counts of corruption; while serving prison sentences in Leeds Prison, they bribed two prison officers to smuggle into the prison unauthorised articles, such as whisky, brandy and two hacksaw blades. The maximum sentence for offences of corruption has remained at two years' imprisonment since the original legislation of 1889 and 1906 (an amendment in 1916 increasing the penalty to seven years for corruption in relation to government contracts followed a spectacular case relating to army property—see paragraph 65). The trial judge passed the maximum sentence on each count, but made them concurrent. The Court of Appeal considered that the offences amply justified the imposition of the low maximum penalty and courts were advised not to strain their imaginations in conjuring up the worst possible case. Giving judgment, Lord Justice Lawton said

> "It is of course a principle of sentencing that maximum sentences should only be passed for the worst kind of offence. But it is to be borne in mind that when judges are asking themselves whether they should pass the maximum sentence, they should not use their imaginations to conjure up unlikely worst possible kinds of case. What they should consider is the worst type of offence which comes before the Court and ask themselves whether the particular case they are dealing with comes within the broad band of that type."

Again the Court was clearly influenced by the fact that the maximum was exceptionally low to accommodate the more serious offences committed. Lord Justice Lawton added

> "When the maximum is low, the band may be wide. In our judgment it is for this crime. The maximum is probably far too low."

The decision in *Ambler and Hargreaves* has greatly diluted the "worst possible case" principle; given a penalty range of only two years within which to distinguish offences, courts might be forgiven for treating many, if not most, cases as the "worst possible".

80. The broadening of the concept of the "worst possible case" in *Ambler and Hargreaves* was adopted in one of the few decisions specifically[1] applying the principle to a crime with a high maximum. In *R v Sholanke*[2] in 1977 an 18-year

---

[1] The *Harrison* principle has, of course, frequently been applied to cases involving high maxima, but without the Court citing directly the original principle—see, for example, *R v Myland* (1910) 6 Cr. App. R. 135 (where a maximum sentence of five years' penal servitude was reduced to one year) and *R v Moran* (1910) 5 Cr. App. R. 219 (where the maximum sentence of 10 years' preventive detention was quashed).

[2] No. 1786/B/76, 4 July 1977. For another example of the application of the *Ambler* formula to a case involving a high maximum, see *R v Byrne* (1976) 62 Cr. App. R. 159, where sentences of 15 to 18 years for offences carrying a maximum of 20 years under the Explosive Substances Act 1883 were reduced to 14 years. In that case, Lord Justice Lawton referred to "the general sentencing principle that the maximum sentence provided for by statute should be reserved for the most serious type of case". Another recent case where the maximum has been specifically referred to is *R v Faulkner and Thomas* (1976) 63 Cr. App. R. 295, where a four-year sentence was passed for assisting in the commission outside the United Kingdom of an offence (drug smuggling) under a corresponding law abroad (in this case Denmark), for which the United Kingdom maximum penalty is 14 years. The Court rebuked the trial judge for having taken as a useful guide the fact that the maximum sentence for the importation of drugs into Denmark is six years, and held that maximum penalties in foreign countries for drug smuggling were irrelevant. The court should have regard only to the maximum penalty under English law.

old forced his stepmother to swallow a large quantity of tablets of digoxin, a poison; he also threatened to strangle her with a piece of wire and placed a pillow over her head. Although he desisted from suffocating her, she nearly died from the poisoning. He pleaded guilty to unlawfully administering a poison so as to endanger life. That crime, under section 23 of the Offences against the Person Act 1861, carries a maximum of 10 years' imprisonment, which the trial judge imposed. Countering counsel's argument that the maximum sentence must be reserved for the worst possible case, and this being a bad, but not conceivably the worst possible, case, the Court adopted the *Ambler* formula by saying that

"the present offence was *well within the band* of the worst type of case."

81. The fact that the theory of maximum penalties has been ruled on by the courts almost exclusively in cases where the maxima are low speaks for itself.[1] The courts' attitude has been highly coloured by the fact that the principle was proclaimed where the low maxima gave insufficient scope to the discretionary power of the sentencing court. Maxima are often seen by the judiciary as the final limit placed by Parliament upon the court's discretion. Courts believe that the maxima are (with rare exceptions) set appropriately high to give the courts the amplest discretion in differentiating cases. The contrary view is that maxima should be fixed at a point where they directly influence the sentencing policy and daily practice of the courts. We have considered the conflicting views as to the level of maximum penalties in greater detail in Chapter 8. We wish here to add only some further general points.

82. The penalty structure provides only a very few exceptions to the fixed maxima catering for the worst possible case. There are, for example, the fixed maxima within which the sentence is indeterminate and release from custody is decided by the Executive aided by the Parole Board. Life imprisonment and borstal training are the two notable examples. They operate as maxima in wholly different ways: borstal training offers courts in sentencing young adult offenders a sentence that means a minimum of six months and a maximum of two years[2] within which the court has no discretion at all. Similarly, once a court selects life imprisonment it surrenders all discretion as to time of release to the Executive, but up to the maximum of life imprisonment it can select a determinate sentence of any length, and thus enjoys the widest possible discretion. Extended sentences for the persistent offender provide another variation, enabling courts to sentence, within limits, beyond the existing maxima. We deal with extended sentences in the next chapter and with life imprisonment in Chapter 11.

83. Maximum penalties have not prompted any concern in the courts save for the few instances where, by historical chance, they have been set deliberately

---

[1] Two significant cases in which the Court described the circumstances where the imposition of the maximum penalty would *not* be appropriate both involved two-year maxima. In *R v Bradbury and Edlin* (1920) 15 Cr. App. R. 76, the Court developed the view that when restitution has been made for an offence, the maximum penalty should not be inflicted; and in *R v Welch* (1920) 15 Cr. App. R. 102, it gave a judgment implying that a maximum penalty should not be imposed where a considerable interval of time has elapsed since the last conviction.

[2] The maximum period of two years in custody for a borstal sentence overrides any lower maximum penalty for the offence in question—see *R v Amos* (1961) 45 Cr. App. R. 42.

low. The most commonly quoted examples are corruption offences (as in the case of *Ambler and Hargreaves*), cruelty to children, indecent assault on a girl of 13 and over and fraudulent trading under the Companies Act. We deal with all four examples in Chapter 9. Apart from these cases, the maxima do not affect the normal range of sentences passed by the courts, and thus scarcely have any bearing, let alone influence, upon the vital question of the relative severity of sentences. We observed in the last chapter how sentence lengths were decreasing in the last two decades of the 19th century, in part at least as a direct result of a deliberate policy by the courts to cut sentences. The Du Cane correspondence in Appendix D shows the breakdown of sentence lengths as it appeared in 1883. There were many very short sentences; in 1883, almost a quarter of the prisoners serving sentences of imprisonment had been given terms of one month or less. Throughout this century the trend has been in the reverse direction: the proportion of long sentences has increased (as the figures in Appendix J clearly demonstrate), often as the direct result of legislative changes, such as the reduction in the number of fine defaulters by the Criminal Justice Administration Act 1914 and, since the last war, the substitution of a wide variety of non-custodial penalties for the short and very short term of imprisonment. It does, however, appear that the length of sentences in the upper ranges has increased since the last war, independently of what has been happening in the lower ranges, and this must be seen in the context of changes in social patterns and in criminal activity over the period. Our belief is that a more consistent penalty structure will produce a greater awareness of trends in sentencing and particularly those relating to sentence lengths. The scheme that we propose in Chapter 9 should make it easier for courts to adjust their sentencing practice where such a course is seen to be appropriate.

CHAPTER 5

SENTENCING THE RECIDIVIST

The historical background

84. A subsidiary, but by no means minor, problem for all penal systems is the offender who continues to offend after experiencing penal measures. Measures which were eliminatory in effect—such as hanging and transportation for life—did not raise this problem; the felon who illegally returned from transportation was normally disposed of on the gallows. But the less severe penalties which were imposed for misdemeanours, and gradually extended to an increasing number of felonies, did not eliminate the possibility of further offences.

85. On the assumption that an important function of penalties was to deter offenders from repeating their offences, and that those who did had demonstrated the inadequacy of the deterrent, it seemed logical either to increase the severity of the penalty or to eliminate the offender. Several mediæval statutes provided heavier penalties for repetition of a misdemeanour. An Elizabethan rogue who was not "reformed of the roguish kinde of lyfe" by whipping and the house of correction was sent to the galleys or the colonies.[1] A statute[2] of James I made certain minor forms of witchcraft misdemeanours on the first occasion, felonies if repeated.

86. These, however, were piecemeal provisions for specific forms of conduct. There was no demand for a general statute dealing with the habitual offender. The gallows or the colonies disposed of all but a few convicted felons, and not until these measures became unpopular or impracticable was the need recognised. The Act of 1827,[3] which replaced death with transportation or imprisonment for most felonies, contained the first general provision dealing with recidivist felons. Anyone previously convicted of a felony and later convicted of a non-capital one was to be liable, at the court's discretion, to transportation for life or at least seven years, or to imprisonment for not more than four years, with or without whipping.

87. It was the Victorians, however, who became seriously concerned about recidivism. The rapid growth of industrial towns and commercial seaports in Britain and continental Europe was producing a new kind of human being, the urban rogue and vagabond. French sociologists and English legislators began to talk of "the dangerous classes", "the perishing and dangerous classes" and eventually "the criminal classes". The Commissioners of 1863 who considered the Penal Servitude Acts advocated the passing of longer sentences to deal with the persistent criminal.

---

[1] 39 Eliz. 1 c. 4.
[2] 1 Ja. 1 c. 12.
[3] 7 & 8 Geo. 4 c. 28, section 11.

88. A technical difficulty, however, had to be overcome. Before a man could be treated as a persistent criminal he must be recognised as such. This was not a problem for small static mediæval communities in which a man's misdeeds, proved or suspected, were recorded in his neighbours' memories. But the increasing mobility of the Tudor era, coupled with the widespread evasion of penalties through "benefit of clergy", made the identification of convicted felons a serious problem. The Tudor solution was the infliction of an indelible mark on the offender: his ears were cropped, his nose was slit open, or his face was branded. When Henry VIII limited benefit of clergy to a first conviction for a felony, the felon was branded on the thumb. All these served not only as warnings to the public that a potential criminal was amongst them, but also as a substitute for a card-index.

89. By the 19th century these methods had long since become obsolete. Even branding on the thumb, which was abolished in 1799, had become a ritual farce, in which a slice of raw bacon protected the felon's hand from the red-hot iron. But more sophisticated, if less efficient, techniques were now possible. Under the transportation system there had been a crude register of felons who were shipped to Australia, and—like so many other features of transportation —this was perpetuated. The Habitual Criminals Act of 1869 provided for registers of "all persons convicted of crime" to be kept by the London and Dublin police, and to be fed with information about known criminals by prison governors and police forces. The development of photography had made it possible to produce recognisable likenesses of criminals. In the early 1850s, the Governor of Bristol Prison, on his own initiative, began to circulate to other prisons photographs of prisoners suspected of having undisclosed previous convictions. This yielded some results, and the Prevention of Crimes Act of 1871 provided for the compulsory photographing of prisoners; but at the turn of the century, photography was replaced by fingerprinting.

90. Unfortunately the legislators had not realised how large the category of persons convicted of "crimes" would be. Although "crimes" were defined so as to include only certain serious offences, the registers rapidly became un-manageably bulky, so that searches in them were impossible. In 1876 they were therefore limited to a special category. The Prevention of Crimes Act of 1871 had enacted that persons convicted of a "crime" for the second time should be liable to police supervision for seven years after the end of their sentence, and it was this group to which the index was now restricted. Moreover, they became liable to arrest and a year's imprisonment if it merely appeared to a summary court that there were reasonable grounds for believing that they were "getting their livelihood by dishonest means", or if they were found in a public or private place in suspicious circumstances. Parts of this measure of social defence still survive.

91. None of these steps seemed to prevent the number of criminals with previous convictions from increasing, although it was appreciated by the more sophisticated that at least part of the increase must be due to improved methods of identification. The Gladstone Committee in 1895 published alarming statistics[1]

---

[1] C. 7702, paragraph 28.

showing how the probability of a further prison sentence increased with each term of imprisonment:

after first imprisonment   30%
after second imprisonment 48%
after third imprisonment   64%
after fourth imprisonment 71%
after fifth imprisonment   79%.

This is as smooth a curve as any modern statistician could produce.

Preventive detention in 1908

92. The Committee was concerned at the substantial number of offenders for whom crime seemed to be their normal means of livelihood. It believed that most habitual criminals acquired this way of life between the ages of 16 and 21 —a range which happily coincided with certain existing legal distinctions. For these young criminals it proposed a special prison regime; a proposal which eventually developed into the borstal system. For confirmed recidivists, however, it recommended "segregation" for "long periods of detention during which they would not be treated with the severity of first-class hard labour or penal servitude, but would be forced to work under less onerous conditions".[1] This proposal embodied an important new principle. Hitherto, courts which fixed the lengths of custodial sentences had been circumscribed by statutory maxima which were related to the nature of the offence, and although their sentences had been regarded as deterrent as well as retributive they were expected to keep within the limits of severity merited by the nature of the offence. The increased maxima for "twice convicted" criminals were not really a breach of this principle, since the argument which justified them was that such criminals had shown their need for stronger measures of deterrence. But what the Gladstone Committee was in effect proposing was a measure of prolonged elimination based on the assumption that some recidivists were incapable of being deterred. These were to be detained for longer than could be justified by the nature of their offence, but since this was retributively unjustifiable their conditions of detention were not to be quite as hard as those of punitive imprisonment. To carry this argument to its logical conclusion, the Prevention of Crime Act which eventually reached the statute book in 1908 created in its provisions for preventive detention[2] what became known as the "double-track" sentence. The unlucky "habitual criminal" could receive what were really two sentences: one for the offence itself, and one for the protection of society. Moreover, the latter was to begin when the former ended! The intention of Herbert Gladstone —who was now Home Secretary—had been that the second part of the sentence should be indeterminate, so that the habitual criminal would be released at the discretion of the Executive, in the same way as a "lifer". Parliament, however, forced him to substitute a provision under which the second part of the sentence was subject to a limit fixed by the judge, which must not be less than five years, nor more than 10, but within which the Executive could release the offender when it thought fit.

---

[1] C. 7702, paragraph 85.
[2] Not to be confused with the 1948 version; see paragraph 97.

93. More important, however, were the precautions taken in the statute and by administrative procedures to make sure that the new sentence was restricted to "habitual criminals" who were a "real danger". The police had to obtain the consent of the Director of Public Prosecutions to charge the offender with being an "habitual criminal" (unless he himself were ill-advised enough to admit this); and the jury had to be persuaded to find that he was. In the short period before Winston Churchill succeeded Herbert Gladstone at the Home Office (in 1910)

134 such applications by police had been refused by the Director of Public Prosecutions;

298 persons had been indicted as habitual criminals;

9 had been acquitted of the offence itself;

54 had been acquitted of being habitual criminals;

28 had been found by the jury to be habitual criminals but had not been given preventive detention;

173 had been given preventive detention;

66 had appealed to the new Court of Criminal Appeal, who quashed seven sentences and slightly reduced six others; and

37[1] outcomes were still awaited.

94. Churchill disliked the idea of preventive detention, and after considerable discussion with his officials wrote to the Director of Public Prosecutions to tell him that police forces were being asked not to submit applications unless (apart from statutory qualifications) the offender was at least 30 years of age[2] and had already been sentenced to at least one term of penal servitude. He also suggested to the Director that in judging applications first, the criminal record should "be such as to show, except in unusual cases, that the offender was not merely a nuisance but a danger to society. Violence conjoined with other crimes would appear to be an adverse factor"; second, "his general mode of life should be surveyed" and not only the period between his last release and new arrest; any spell of honest work should count in his favour ("*Hopelessness* is a very important element in justifying preventive detention"); third, "the new crime ought in itself to be a substantial and serious offence"—not, for example, mere pilfering.[3]

Preventive detention in 1948

95. This excellent advice had a severely restrictive effect. Out of the steady flow of recidivists through the courts, only a tiny trickle was diverted into

---

[1] The sources for the information in this paragraph are papers in the Public Record Office which Mr. David Thomas uncovered in the course of the research commissioned by the Home Office. It will be noticed (though it does not seem to have been at the time) that the figures add up only approximately!

[2] The Court of Criminal Appeal took specific note of the Home Secretary's informal age qualification when faced with appeals on grounds of age: "It is true that a circular has been drawn up by the Home Office with regard to the ordinary practice, but on the other hand, the Director of Public Prosecutions may take a different view for strong special reasons"—*R* v *Saunders* (1912) 7 Cr. App. R. 271; and in *R* v *Hooper and Hardy* (1913) 9 Cr. App. R. 5, it stated: "there is no law which prevents a person from being convicted as a habitual criminal before he is thirty, but it is a matter on which we ought to be careful." The conclusion was that the imposition of preventive detention on an offender under 30 should be regarded as exceptional.

[3] See also the Home Office memorandum of 16 February 1911 cited in paragraph 34 of the Report of the Departmental Committee on *Persistent Offenders* (Cmd. 4090) and reproduced in full in Appendix 4 to that report.

preventive detention. In the next 20 years only 40 men a year, on average, actually began sentences of preventive detention, and the average was falling in spite of the steady increase in convictions.[1] This comparatively small use of the 1908 provisions resulted in the appointment of the Dove-Wilson Committee on *Persistent Offenders* in 1931, whose report[2] led eventually (after the delay caused by the War) to the new form of preventive detention embodied in the Criminal Justice Act of 1948. Two kinds of recidivist were distinguished. For the younger one, who might still be redeemable, there was to be an adult counterpart of the borstal sentence,[3] called "corrective training". To be eligible for this, the offender must be at least 21 years of age (and so outside the scope of borstal); he must have been convicted of an offence punishable with at least two years' imprisonment; and he must have been convicted on at least two occasions since his 17th birthday of offences punishable with at least two years' imprisonment. The sentence, which could be imposed only by a higher court, could be of any length from two to four years, and it was intended to consist of a more positive form of training than the ordinary prison regime provided. Real efforts were made by the Prison Commissioners to ensure this, and the courts used the new power with a will. In the first three years, over 3,000 men were sentenced to corrective training, although as its novelty wore off its popularity declined; the corrective trainee was automatically placed under supervision on his release and this provision contributed to the unpopularity of the sentence with those who received it.

96. The results of corrective training were disappointing; eventually, and usually within three years, about 60% of corrective trainees were again found guilty of an indictable offence. What was not realised at the time was that this rate ought to have been compared with the reconvictions of men with comparable penal histories who had been sentenced to shorter terms of ordinary imprisonment; but no such comparison was ever made. Meanwhile, training had become a feature of other medium sentences of imprisonment, and during the 1950s the difference between the two types of sentence diminished; indeed, before long, corrective trainees and ordinary prisoners were being mixed in the regional prisons. The White Paper of December 1965[4] announced that corrective training as a sentence would be abandoned. Nevertheless, what it undoubtedly achieved was the introduction of a more constructive regime for adult medium-term prisoners.

97. For the older recidivist whose penal history suggested that there was little chance of reforming him, the Dove-Wilson Committee recommended, and the 1948 Act provided, new powers of preventive detention. These could be used in

---

[1] Certain aspects of the habitual criminal legislation had in any case placed the courts in considerable difficulties, best exemplified by the case of *Norman* in 1924—[1924] 2 K.B. 315. This appeal case, which turned on the apparently simple issue of the status of an habitual criminal who re-offends on release from a sentence of preventive detention, was first heard by the Lord Chief Justice and two judges, adjourned for 11 days to a court of five judges, and finally, in an unparalleled constitution of the Court of Appeal, to a court of *thirteen* judges. The final judgment of the Court was supported by eight of the judges, four others dissenting and one failing to deliver a judgment at all!

[2] Cmnd. 4090, May 1932.

[3] Section 21(1) of the Criminal Justice Act 1948. In an important judgment soon after the Act came into force, the Lord Chief Justice, Lord Goddard, described corrective training as "extended Borstal treatment"—*R v Barrett* (1949) 34 Cr. App. R. 3.

[4] *The Adult Offender*, Cmnd 2852.

the higher courts if the offender was past his 30th birthday (Churchill's rule); had been convicted of an offence punishable with at least two years' imprisonment; had been convicted or sentenced for offences in this category on at least three previous occasions since his 17th birthday; *and on at least two of those occasions had actually been sentenced to imprisonment (or corrective training or borstal)*. Thus the prosecution no longer had to decide whether to charge him with being an habitual criminal, and the jury had no say in whether he should be eligible for the special sentence. Only the judge still had discretion. The length of the sentence was still to be fixed by him, but the minimum was now to be five years, and the maximum 14. The sentence was a *substitute*[1] for an ordinary prison sentence, and not an addition to it; the double-track system was a thing of the past (although copies of it survived abroad).

98. In practice, although the numbers of such sentences shot up to an average of more than 200 a year for men, the judges were still using their discretion and being sparing. Research by Dr. Hammond of the Home Office Research Unit[2] showed that in 1956 although 1,384 men who came up for sentencing were eligible for preventive detention, only 13% of them (178) were actually sentenced to it, and in spite of the raised maximum few of the terms of preventive detention were for more than the old limit of 10 years. Moreover, although the Director of Public Prosecutions' pre-war practice of treating 30 as the minimum age had now been embodied in statute, in practice men under 40 were unlikely to get preventive detention.

99. Dr. Hammond's figure of 1,384 men who were eligible for preventive detention in 1956 was probably a considerable under-estimate. It was based on the number of men who had been committed to quarter sessions or assizes for trial or sentence and who had been given the required notice by the prosecution that it was intended to prove them eligible for preventive detention. It is possible that some men were committed for trial and sentence without such a notice; and it is quite certain that some men who would otherwise have been eligible for preventive detention were simply tried and sentenced summarily. Although the section dealing with preventive detention seemed to insist that the accused must be convicted on indictment, the Criminal Justice Act 1948 contained a general section (29(3)(*a*)) which made it possible for a person to be convicted summarily but committed to quarter sessions and there dealt with as if he had been convicted on indictment; and the same is true of the extended sentence today.

100. Judges and recorders became even more cautious in their use of preventive detention towards the end of the 1950s. In 1958 a man called Grimwood[3] was sentenced to eight years' preventive detention after being convicted of the theft of 14 shillings from a gas meter in his house. The Court of Criminal Appeal reduced his sentence to two years, and said that "a sentence, particularly one of preventive detention, ought really to have relation to the gravity of the crime itself". Although the Court of Criminal Appeal did not always hold to

---

[1] In quality but not in quantity—it was, of course, longer than an ordinary sentence would have been.
[2] See *Persistent Criminals* by W. H. Hammond and E. Chayen (HMSO, 1963).
[3] *R v Grimwood* [1958] Crim. L.R. 403.

this principle, it had some effect on the percentage of prison sentences in higher courts which took the form of preventive detention; these fell from just over 2% in 1957 to about 1·7% in 1961.

101. Even so, the following year a practice direction[1] of the Court of Criminal Appeal said that preventive detention was still being used too often, and should be regarded as a last resort. It went on to make three other points: first, preventive detention should not be imposed until a recidivist was "nearing 40 years of age or over" (thus raising Churchill's minimum); second, it should not be imposed if a man had "held down a job" for a substantial period immediately before the offence for which he was being sentenced—and the practice direction made it clear that 12 months or more was a substantial period; and third, if the crime were a serious one, "a sentence of imprisonment of sufficient length may often properly be given which will give adequate protection to the public".

102. Finally, towards the end of the same year, the Advisory Council on the Treatment of Offenders, which had been asked by the Home Secretary in 1961 "to review the working of the preventive detention system", reported unfavourably on it.[2] In this adverse climate, the use of preventive detention fell again to 0·6% of prison sentences in 1963, and to 0·3% in 1964.

103. The unpopularity of the post-war form of preventive detention was due to a number of features—for example, the slowness of progress through the stages of the sentence and the general feeling that the difference between it and an ordinary prison sentence was not as marked as it should have been. It was due also to two criticisms, one of them rational, and the other irrational. The irrational criticism was that the reconviction rate of men released from it was very high indeed: 77% within five years of release in Dr. Hammond's sample. Since the sentence was intended for the offender who had demonstrated his inability or unwillingness to respond to penal measures, this can hardly be regarded as evidence of failure; on the contrary, it can be argued that it shows how right the courts were in 77% of the cases. Preventive detention should have been judged by what it prevented. It would have been more logical to blame the system for mistakenly subjecting to preventive detention the 23% who were not reconvicted, but even this depends on the not very safe assumption that they really had not committed further offences, instead of merely escaping detection.

104. But *what* had preventive detention been used to prevent? A more legitimate criticism was that the typical preventive detainee was not a skilled professional robber or burglar, nor a sexual molester, nor a man of violence, but an incompetent petty swindler or pilferer, whose dishonesties cost society little more—and in some cases less—than his maintenance in prison.[3] It is true that the losses which he caused were not borne by society as a whole, but fell at best on organisations and at worst on uninsured individuals of slender means, to whom they were serious. But our increasingly affluent and insurance-minded

---

[1] [1962] 1 W.L.R. 402. It was issued after consultation with the Prison Commissioners, and dealt also with the sentence of corrective training.
[2] *Preventive Detention*, Report of the Advisory Council on the Treatment of Offenders (HMSO, 1963).
[3] See Hammond and Chayen *op. cit.*, page 35.

society seemed to be generating a feeling that there were less drastic and more economical ways of protecting its members against unlawful petty acquisitiveness than a 10 year incarceration.

Extended sentences

105. Reasoning of this sort—some of it rational, some of it based on misconception—led to several proposals for revised legislation on recidivists. In 1963 the Advisory Council on the Treatment of Offenders produced its proposals for a new form of sentence. They did not meet with immediate acceptance, and the Home Secretary of the day put forward ideas of his own. Eventually, however, the White Paper of 1965[1] proposed something very like the Advisory Council's sentence and this has been in operation since 1967. Both preventive detention and corrective training were replaced by the "extended sentence".[2] For an offence carrying a maximum of two, three or four years, an extended sentence can be anything up to five years. For offences carrying maxima of five to nine years, an extended sentence can be anything up to 10 years. For offences carrying higher maxima, those maxima are the limit (the point of an extended sentence in such cases is explained in paragraphs 111–13).

106. More important, however, is the question: who and what is to decide whether an offender is a persistent offender? The latest legislation was intended (according to the White Paper)

"to apply only to delinquents whose character and record of offences are such as to put it beyond all doubt that they are a real menace to society, and to exclude the petty criminal who commits a series of lesser offences."

This was to be achieved by insisting that the offender must be sentenced by a superior court for an offence punishable with two years' imprisonment or more *and committed within three years of a previous conviction or completion of a custodial sentence for an offence similarly punishable*; and have been convicted on indictment on at least three previous occasions since reaching the age of 21 (not 17 as before) of offences punishable on indictment with imprisonment for two years or more; and have been on at least two of those occasions given a custodial sentence.

107. The italics reveal the respects in which the conditions of eligibility differ from those of the 1948 Act, and how minor these differences are. Indeed, the Minister of State at the Home Office (Lord Stonham) agreed during the passage of the provision that in the form in which it was introduced it would have excluded only 1% of the men who actually received preventive detention in 1957[3]. To meet this point, the Bill was later amended in the Lords so as to add a third proviso *that at least one of the offender's previous sentences must have been for not less than three years, or at least two for not less than two years each.* Even so, only 10%—15% of those who had received preventive detention in 1957 would be excluded.[4]

---

[1] *The Adult Offender*, Cmnd. 2852.
[2] In the Criminal Justice Act of 1967. The provisions are now to be found in the consolidating Powers of Criminal Courts Act 1973, sections 28 and 29.
[3] It would have excluded 20%–30% of those eligible for preventive detention, not all of whom received it.
[4] But it would have excluded 40%–50% of those who had been eligible for preventive detention.

108. The remarkable feature of the whole discussion was that although one of the express objects of the Bill was to confine the extended sentence to the "real menaces" and exclude the "petty criminal" (to use the words of the White Paper), it tried to do this without expressly defining the sort of harm which "real menaces" cause. Instead of scheduling a list of offences or types of behaviour, it provided—as before—that there should be offences carrying at least two years' imprisonment (very few kinds of real crime carry less) and then tried to restrict eligibility by stipulating that the offender should have a minimum number of convictions and prison sentences of a certain length.

109. The courts received the extended sentence with no great enthusiasm. In the first complete calendar year after the Act came into operation only 27 such sentences were pronounced—not much more than the 20 sentences of preventive detention imposed in the last calendar year before the Act. It is possible that procedural difficulties made the police or the courts cautious. Not only must the defendant (as before) have been given notice of the intention to prove to the court the previous convictions needed for a protective sentence (an obligation which usually fell on the police), it was also necessary to provide the court with a prison governor's certificate dealing with the date of the defendant's release from his last custodial sentence. At first the police were asked by the Home Office to serve notices on all defendants who appeared eligible for extended sentences (although in practice there must have been quite a few whose eligibility escaped unrecognised, so complex are the criteria). But, in August 1970, the Home Office issued a new circular saying that the use of the new sentence had been so slight that the service of notices in every case was involving the police in a good deal of nugatory work. As an experiment, in the busier courts, notices were served only when the court had indicated an intention to pass an extended sentence; and this experimental procedure was applied to all courts in March 1972.[1]

110. In fact, as Table 1 in Appendix K shows, the use of extended sentences was increasing until 1970, when it reached a peak of 129. Thereafter began a decline which has continued until in 1976, the last year for which we have figures, only 14 such sentences were passed. It is unlikely that procedural difficulties account for more than a small part of this decline, and more likely that it is attributable to a hardening of the attitude of the courts against long sentences for offences which did not seem to be at the highest degree of gravity. As Table 2 of the Appendix shows, the great majority of extended sentences are imposed for property offences, chiefly burglaries. (The fact that they are seldom imposed for sexual or violent offences does not necessarily reflect a disproportionate solicitude for property on the part of the courts; violent or sexual offenders seldom have the penal records necessary to qualify for the sentence.)

111. It is true that the extended sentence has two functions instead of preventive detention's one. Like preventive detention, it could be used to make possible a period of detention longer than an ordinary sentence would have been allowed to do (having regard to the statutory maximum or the normal range appropriate to the type of offence). But the 1967 Act which created the extended sentence had also introduced parole, and had moreover provided that, whereas the normal

---

[1] See Home Office Circulars 150/1967, 158/1969, 189/1970 and 43/1972.

parolee should be under licence only until he would in any case have been released on remission (that is, in normal cases, for the middle third of his sentence), prisoners with extended sentences could be released under a licence which lasted until the very end of the nominal sentence. Unlike an ordinary prisoner who was refused parole but released on remission, therefore, the extended sentence prisoner could be put under licence.[1] This was an important consideration because it was expected that the Parole Board would not parole many extended sentence men; an expectation which was to be borne out by the figures: in the three years 1974–76, 17% of extended sentence prisoners considered for parole were granted it—a total of 64 men. Thus it was possible for courts to impose an extended sentence no longer than the ordinary term which they would have specified, with the sole intention of ensuring that the offender remained longer under supervision and the threat of recall.

112. The principle of imposing extended sentences for this purpose was established in *D.P.P.* v *Ottewell*,[2] an important case which defined the relationship between extended sentences and maximum penalties. Ottewell had pleaded guilty to two counts of assault occasioning actual bodily harm, and was sentenced to consecutive terms of two years' imprisonment on each. The total sentence of four years was less than the maximum penalty for the offence— five years under section 47 of the Offences against the Person Act 1861. In passing sentence, the judge indicated that he was invoking the extended sentences provision of the Criminal Justice Act 1967 and issued an extended sentence certificate. The Court of Appeal, although confirming the length of sentence imposed, was faced with the issue whether an extended sentence could be passed if it did not, as in Ottewell's case, exceed the maximum penalty, and concluded that it could not. It interpreted the provisions in the 1967 Act as providing for sentences that could only be extended beyond the maximum penalty, and not merely beyond the ordinary sentence that might otherwise have been imposed. It specifically rejected the contention that one object of the provision was to confer a power to ensure that a persistent offender should be kept under a measure of control after his release.

113. On a further appeal, the House of Lords rejected the Court of Appeal's interpretation, and held that an extended sentence could be passed within the maximum penalty. Lord Donovan in his judgment made clear his view that an extended sentence embraced the purpose of ensuring release on licence[3]:

> "at present the only way for a judge to ensure some supervision after a person's release is to pass an extended term of imprisonment under the Act of 1967 which then brings into effect the release on licence provisions to be found in section 60. If this be the case then, again, it would seem a little incongruous that a sentence exceeding the statutory maximum should have to be passed by the judge in order to procure that effect."

---

[1] Strictly speaking, an extended sentence prisoner who is not released before his remission date is not under licence unless the Home Secretary makes an order under section 60(3)(a) of the Criminal Justice Act 1967, which he does in every case.

[2] [1969] 1 Q.B. 27 and [1970] A.C. 642.

[3] The Home Secretary had already indicated, in response to the Court of Appeal decision, that he would not be making any direction to release Ottewell on licence.

The Court of Appeal has applied the decision of the House of Lords in *Ottewell* and has upheld relatively short extended sentences, especially in recent years.[1] As Table 3 of Appendix K shows, the lengths of extended sentences have tended to decrease, until now more than two thirds are for five years or less.

114. In short, what seems to have happened is that, after an initial period of caution owing to the complexity of the criteria and the new procedural requirements, the courts used the new sentence to a limited extent. The hardening of attitudes, however, against long sentences for the less serious type of offence discouraged them from using it to prolong the period of detention, leaving on the whole those few cases in which they wanted to ensure a substantial period on licence for the released prisoner. Now even these cases seem to be petering out.

115. The story of anti-recidivist legislation in England has several lessons. First, the draftsmen have been preoccupied with persistence and incorrigibility rather than serious harm. That being so, their laudable attempts to restrict eligibility and to do so by hard criteria of the kinds that could be proved to the satisfaction of courts were unnecessary, since courts have been far more selective than the statutory criteria. On the other hand, where serious harm is involved the offenders have usually been excluded by the statutory criteria, and the courts have been quite content to use ordinary sentences or life sentences. The hardening of courts' attitudes towards long sentences for less serious offences seems to be leading to the virtual obsolescence of genuinely "extended" sentences. Even the shorter special sentence which makes it possible to put the persistent offender on licence for longer than usual is no longer in demand. *In our view, the extended sentence is demonstrably inappropriate to the problem it was intended to solve and unwanted by the courts who have been empowered to use it. It should be abolished.*

---

[1] It approved of the use of the sentence to ensure a period on licence in such cases as *R* v *Johnson* (1975) No. 4183/B/74, 13 February 1975. We are indebted to Mr. David Thomas for information about this unreported case.

CHAPTER 6

IMPRISONMENT AND THE PENALTY STRUCTURE

116. In Chapter 3 we traced the growth of the 19th century penalty structure which forms the foundation of our penalty system today. But the judicial exercise of sentencing powers in any age can only properly be understood against the background of how the sentence is translated by the Executive into penal practice; the true effects of sentencing practice can only be found in the prisons themselves. The growth of the penalty structure in the 19th century was essentially an interaction between ideas about the powers appropriate to the courts and strongly held views of how a prison system should treat those who are subjected to it. The influence of existing prison practice upon the penalty structure was strong. For example, in the scale in the Penal Servitude Act 1853 (see paragraph 46) by which penal servitude was substituted for transportation, the shorter periods of penal servitude were a direct reflection of the amounts of the transportation sentence normally served in custody. Similarly, the maximum penalty of imprisonment[1] was fixed at two years because, given the existing prison regime, a longer term could not have been borne (see paragraph 120).

117. The emergent prison system of over 100 years ago was as confused and uncertain in its origins as the sentencing system which it helped to form; for a system of penal imprisonment was as much a novel phenomenon as the exercise of a wide judicial discretion in sentencing, and was as much, if not more, the subject of philosophical controversy. It grew out of two strands both separately identifiable in their historical growth: the prison system of the central government, which gradually replaced the transportation system and became the custodian of the new sentence of penal servitude; and the local authority system, based upon the local prison, which housed the less serious offenders, mostly those convicted of misdemeanours.

Prisons in the 18th century

118. Although imprisonment as a penalty in its own right existed in mediæval times, it was comparatively rarely used. As we have already indicated in Chapter 3, until the middle of the 19th century the prison was first and foremost a place of safe custody for those awaiting trial. For convicted prisoners, it was only a staging post on the road to the colonies or the gallows—in the famous 18th century phrase "the ante-room to either the New World, or the Next". Since their population was, in theory at least, a transient one, the growth of prisons as institutions was haphazard and almost unconscious. The common gaol of the 18th century was not the purpose-built fortress of Victorian England which has formed our image of the typical prison today; it was often merely one or two rooms in an already existing building—the gate-house to a castle, a municipal building, a public house. The conditions prevailing in prisons at

---

[1] As distinct from penal servitude which, towards the end of the sentence, was less rigorous.

this time have been well documented. Prisoners of both sexes and of all ages and all degrees of criminality were herded into open rooms where they lived and slept in common. Security was maintained by irons; otherwise little control was exercised by the gaoler who lived by the fees he was able to extract from the wretched inmates. In the overcrowded, insanitary conditions, disease was rife; it was not uncommon for more prisoners to die of gaol fever in the course of a year than suffered the death penalty. A more conscious development had taken place in the case of the houses of correction, established first in the 16th century as places for the relief of destitution, where the idle and the vagrant were set to productive work. As such they were more precursors of the Poor Law work-house than the local prison, but gradually became places of containment for petty, and then more serious, offenders, so that by the end of the 17th century they were almost indistinguishable from the common gaols. This was finally recognised in the Prison Act 1865 when both institutions were amalgamated under the generic title of "local prison".

119. Little public concern had been expressed over the scandalous state of the prisons until John Howard appeared on the scene in the 1770s. The Howard programme of reform, which, like the man, was essentially pragmatic, had four main aims—the provision of secure, sanitary prisons; the transformation of the gaoler from a private profit-maker to a public servant; the introduction of a reformatory regime based upon a controlled diet, work and religious exercises; and the inauguration of a system of public inspection. Although Howard was an advocate of cellular confinement, his regime was not based on the Separate System which was to have so much influence over prison conditions in 19th century England. On the contrary, he proposed a system of cellular confinement by night and profitable work in association by day.

The convict prisons

120. We explained in Chapter 3 the genesis of the two 19th century custodial penalties—penal servitude and imprisonment—which were to run in double harness from the 1850s until 1948. It is important to recognise from the outset that penal servitude was by far the more important sanction, and, as the ancestor of medium and long-term sentences today, is really the historical equivalent of what many people commonly think of as "imprisonment". Because of the graver nature of their crimes, convicted felons, or "convicts" as they came to be called, had a special mystique, much in the way that "lifers" or "Category A" prisoners may have today. Even as late as 1897, the journalist G. W. Steevens, on a visit to Wormwood Scrubs, speaks of them in awed tones as almost a race apart:

> "And the convicts proper—the penal servitude men, that is—exercise by themselves. They alone wear knickerbockers and stockings; they alone are shaved. I only looked in at their yard for a moment, but there seemed a sullen desperation on their coarse faces that made the short-sentence men look very happy".[1]

---

[1] *Things Seen: Impressions of Men, Cities and Books* by George Warrington Steevens (Blackwood, 1900), page 271. The original article entitled *During Her Majesty's Pleasure* appeared in the *Daily Mail* in November 1897.

By contrast, imprisonment (in spite of its name) was a lesser penalty—from the 1860s carrying a maximum penalty of only two years, which in view of the harshness of its regime of separation was recognised by the mid-Victorians as the maximum period that could safely be served.[1] It was treated very much as the poor relation of penal servitude. When a crisis arose in the penal system, as with the supposed "crime wave" of the early 1860s, it was to reform of the sentence of penal servitude that attention was immediately turned; concern about imprisonment generally followed in the rear.

121. Penal servitude, the immediate successor of transportation, was served in the central government convict prisons which, like the hulks, had originally housed the "transports" in the early days of their sentence. The central government prisons were the first to take up on a wide scale the reforming programme put forward by Howard and his successors; and the history of 19th century imprisonment is marked by the gradual spread of these reforming principles to the local prisons as central government increased its control over them. The Howard programme, as developed by Blackstone and Eden, was first statutorily enunciated in an Act of 1779[2] which proposed the erection of national penitentiaries to house those convicts who, since the loss of the American colonies, could no longer be transported and were now temporarily quartered in the hulks at Woolwich. The Act contained a detailed code of prison discipline consisting of cellular confinement at night, and work in association by day, on labour of "the hardest and most servile kind, in which drudgery is chiefly required". The course was set for the emergence of the treadwheel and the crank in later days. The Act of 1779 did not, however, bear any immediate fruit, for the transportation crisis eased with the opening up of Australia, and the building of the first National Penitentiary had to wait another generation, until the completion of Millbank Prison (on the site of the present Tate Gallery) in 1821. The National Penitentiary was designed to replace the hulks in holding convicts in the early days of their sentence awaiting transportation. The theory was that convicts would be reformed in the penitentiary before they were transported. It was evident throughout this period, however, that transportation as a secondary punishment was breaking down. In the 1840s, as the Australian colonies began to refuse to accept more convicts, a second transportation crisis arose to be met in the same way by the building of more national prisons, beginning with the new model prison at Pentonville in 1842, designed by Colonel

---

[1] In his memorandum of dissent to the report of the Royal Commission of 1863 already quoted (see paragraph 50), Lord Chief Justice Cockburn commented:

"The severity of prison discipline in modern times, the complete isolation of the prisoner, the obligation of perpetual silence, the separation from his fellow men—which in some prisons has been carried so far as that, when necessarily brought into the presence of his fellows, the prisoner has been compelled to wear a mask—the severity of the labour required, in addition to its being carried on within the dreary walls of a prison, and the wearisome monotony of such a life, are found to produce so depressing an influence that, if protracted beyond a limited period, fatal consequences to health both of body and mind ensue. Under these circumstances the period of imprisonment to which criminals are sentenced has been gradually reduced. The maximum allowed by law has been recently fixed at two years. In practice, the period of 18 months is not, except in rare instances, exceeded. Under the system of discipline existing in most of our prisons, 18 months of solitary imprisonment is found to be as much as, with proper regard to humanity, can with safety be inflicted."

It is a clear example of how the nature of a prison regime can influence the level of a maximum penalty.

[2] 19 Geo. 3 c. 74.

Jebb, who two years later was to become the first Surveyor-General of Prisons. The importance of the national system, which assumed responsibility for those convicts previously sentenced to transportation, was its development of the code of 1779 into one of completely separate cellular confinement, both by day and night.

122. The central government was strongly influenced by the principles of imprisonment developed by the two American systems, the Pennsylvania, or separate confinement system (complete cellular separation throughout the prison day), and the Auburn or Silent System, which required the prisoners to sleep in separate cells but to work together under a rule of silence. In reaction to the excesses of the "mediæval" local prisons, the Government became early committed to the Separate System and to hard labour, and growing centralisation was to ensure the eventual triumph of this particular regime. Its purpose was that of Howard's followers: the religious and moral regeneration of the prisoner, by meditation upon his faults undistracted by other criminal company. Once the initial expense of building cellular accommodation had been met, the system was convenient to administer, for a prisoner confined to his cell all day required the minimum of supervision. Intimations from America and from the experiments carried out in some local prisons in England that solitary confinement could cause loss of health, mental depression, and an increase in cases of insanity[1] and suicide were overlooked in the zeal of reform.

123. The Penal Servitude Act of 1853 was the final statutory recognition of the breakdown of the system of transportation. The new sentence of penal servitude,[2] whose name was chosen no doubt to convey the maximum effect of horror and gloom, followed the general pattern of the transportation sentence, being served in three parts: first 18 months' solitary confinement with hard labour in a penitentiary (the full rigours of the Separate System); then a period in a public works prison, usually adjacent to a dockyard where the convicts would be employed on public works; then a period on ticket-of-leave (a kind of 19th century parole) under police supervision.

The local prisons

124. The development of penal theory in the local prisons, where those sentenced to imprisonment (mostly for misdemeanours) were incarcerated, was far less assured than in the Government's convict prisons. The Howard philosophy of cellular confinement and profitable labour made little impact on the generality of common gaols and houses of correction in the late 18th and early 19th centuries. A handful of local authorities, notably Gloucestershire,[3] developed the ideas of the Separate System from Howard and the 1779 Act, but by and large the building of cellular prisons was too expensive for most authorities to

---

[1] As late as 1890, the Medical Inspector of Prisons could blithely boast:
"Among the probable causes of the unsoundness of mind are mentioned business worries, drinking, injury to head, sunstroke, attending revival meetings, ill-usage, epilepsy, grief, overwork, speculation on the stock exchange, domestic trouble, fear of 'Jack the Ripper', privation and irregular life; but imprisonment is not suggested as the cause of the insanity in a single instance."
Thirteenth Report of the Commissioners of Prisons, C. 6191, Appendix 18.
[2] It was originally the period spent on public works in the colonies.
[3] For a recent account of the work of Sir George Paul in Gloucestershire, see *Prison Reform in Gloucestershire 1776–1820* by J. R. S. Whiting (Phillimore, 1975).

contemplate. With the advent of Peel to the Home Office in 1822, however, a new era began. The Gaol Act of 1823, which he promoted, was the first measure of general prison reform to be framed and enacted on the responsibility of the national Executive. It provided for the uniform adoption of Howard's principles and the furnishing of reports to the Home Office, but it promised rather more than it could fulfil since it did not extend to all the local gaols, and omitted to provide a system of inspection by which its provisions might be enforced. Surprisingly, in view of the Government's commitment to cellular confinement in its own prison at Millbank, the Act proposed a system of classification, rather than separation, of prisoners, but this was probably only a recognition of the heavy cost of erecting cellular prisons. Pressure to adopt a system of separation increased, however, in the 1830s as news came from America of the successful experiments there. The Whig Government increased its control over the local system: in 1835 a system of government inspection of the local prisons was inaugurated, and in 1839 the adoption of the Separate System on a permissive basis was legalised. The stage was set for the establishment of the uniform system of the second half of the 19th century.

125. The principles laid down by the 1823 Act were those of safe custody, the maintenance of prisoners' health, deterrence combined with reform and, informing all of these, economy of expenditure. Prison as a punishment was, however, still a novel concept and for the first half of the 19th century there was little common agreement as to the validity of such principles or how they might be put into practice. In the 1830s and 40s, when the Criminal Law Commissioners were debating the principles upon which statutory offences and penalties were to be based, a debate of no less consequence was going on inside the prison system. At this period began the enduring controversy as to the proper balance between deterrence and reform, focusing on such narrow questions as the prison diet. Battle was joined between those who contended that dietaries should be sufficient to maintain good health and the advocates of a strictly penal diet which must compare adversely with that of the poor, but honest, labourer. The central controversy, however, concerned the regime and the nature of the work provided. In the common gaols, the less costly system of classification and association, which gave prisoners the freedom of social intercourse and yet reduced some of the dangers of contamination, was still the most popular. The proponents of the American cellular system were critical of classification, which they claimed was too unsophisticated to prevent contamination. But even amongst the advocates of cellular confinement, there was controversy between those who supported the Separate System and the proponents of the Silent System. Similar arguments arose as to whether prison labour should be penal or productive. Hard labour on the treadwheel and the crank was seen by some as a danger to health and to the reformative purpose of prison, whilst others regarded productive labour of the manufacturing kind as an over-indulgence, which threatened the livelihood of the honest worker outside prison. The issues of work and regime could not be entirely separated, since work which could be carried out in cellular confinement was difficult to find and purely penal measures, such as the crank, tended to be the most suitable.

126. The result of all this debate was a local prison system marked by a wide variation in practice. The maximum penalty of two years' imprisonment imposed

by a court in one county might represent, in its general severity, a quite different penalty from that of a similar sentence imposed by a court in a neighbouring county. Some indication of the extent of this variation (and incidentally also some flavour of the minuteness of contemporary concern about the nature of imprisonment) was given by Lord Carnarvon in the Lords debate on prison discipline which led to the establishment of the Select Committee of 1863:

> ". . . in some the labour system was based upon association, in others upon separation, and elsewhere, again, the mixed system was employed. The treadwheel was resorted to in some, in others, cranks, pumps, and oakum picking; in some there was no labour at all, while others seemed to be a sort of industrial school, and the prisoners were set to work as tailors, shoemakers, carpenters, tinmen, matmakers, weavers, and so forth. In some 56 steps on the wheel were required per minute; in others, 30 steps. In some the crank made 14,000 revolutions, in others 6,000. There was no uniformity in speed or in the construction of machines. As to the dietaries, some were higher, some lower than the Government scale. In some there were three meals, in some only two a day. Some had only one scale for all prisoners, whether committed for a few days or for months. In some the prisoners had the same diet every day; in others they had a variety of food, as at Wakefield, where they received pudding, treacle, and Irish stew. In some the cells were warmed and lit; in others they were not. In some the prisoners were allowed to sleep for twelve or fourteen hours; in some only seven or eight. In some there was association in chapel; in others there was not."[1]

There was no mistaking which of these extremes found favour with Lord Carnarvon and it was his report which fashioned the stern, unbending system that followed to the end of the century and beyond.

The Select Committee of 1863

127. Just as the year 1861 (the year of the consolidating Acts described in Chapter 3) marks the source of the penalty system we have today, so in a sense does the year 1863 mark the origins of our modern prison system. Although the values expressed in 1863 are very different from those expressed today, the year marks the first concerted agreement as to the specific direction prisons should henceforth follow and the coming together of the two strands of penal servitude and imprisonment that was to lead inevitably to the "nationalisation" of the local prisons in 1877 and the final assimilation of penal servitude with imprisonment in 1948. It was also the year in which Edmund Du Cane became a Director of Convict Prisons.

128. We referred in paragraph 49 to the origins of the Penal Servitude Act of 1864 in the panic which followed the outbreak of garottings in London in the latter half of 1862. That panic was to have widespread repercussions. How far it was justified by the events that were supposed to have caused it is difficult to tell. A number of attacks and alleged attacks were given extensive publicity

---

[1] Parliamentary Debates, Third Series, Vol. 169, Cols. 481–2. 19 February 1863.

following a nocturnal assault upon a Member of Parliament.[1] While it is true that the recorded number of such attacks represented a considerable increase on previous years,[2] it is by no means certain to what degree this was the result of imitation or of increased police vigilance. What is clear, however, is that the wave of attacks was short-lived, and had subsided before the Government or Parliament (which was not sitting at the height of the four months' panic) took action. Twenty-four offenders were convicted[3] at the Central Criminal Court in the November Session of 1862 in well-publicised trials and from that point on the attacks appeared to cease. At the end of December, however, a Royal Commission was set up to investigate the operation of the Penal Servitude Acts (see paragraph 49); one contention had been that the garotters and those responsible for the recent general increase in crime were those convicts released on ticket-of-leave under the shorter sentences available under the Penal Servitude Act of 1857. It is interesting to note that the original concern should have centred on the primary sentence of penal servitude. It was not until Parliament returned in February 1863 that a number of peers put pressure on the Government to investigate the system of discipline in the local prisons, as a counterpart to the review of the Penal Servitude Acts. A Lords Select Committee was set up under Lord Carnarvon.

129. As we have already noted, the Royal Commission found that penal servitude (when contrasted with transportation) was insufficiently deterrent, and proposed not so much a toughening of the regime (which it held to be more severe than had been generally recognised[4]), but an increase in the standard lengths of sentences. It proposed a minimum sentence of seven years, which became five years in the Penal Servitude Act of 1864. The Lords Select Committee took a much tougher line on the question of imprisonment. It noted with strong disapproval the variation in practice from one local prison to the next, and proposed a regime that would be not only standard but punitive in its effect. The Committee came down firmly on the side of separation of prisoners:

> "the system generally known as the separate system, must now be accepted as the foundation of prison discipline, and . . . its rigid maintenance is a vital principle to the efficiency of county and borough gaols."[5]

---

[1] James Pilkington, the Member for Blackburn. Returning from the Commons in the early hours of 16 July, he was set upon in Waterloo Place and robbed of his watch, but not his money. An almost identical assault occurred the same night in Piccadilly. (See Parliamentary Debates, Third Series, Vol. 168, Cols. 425–7, 17 July 1862, and The Times, 18 July 1862). The alleged culprits, James Anderson and George Roberts, were convicted at the Central Criminal Court on 26 November of another identical street robbery. Two days later, Anderson was given a life sentence and Roberts 20 years' penal servitude.

[2] The cases of robbery with violence reported to the Metropolitan Police in the last six months of 1862 were 82; during the same period in 1860 and 1861, the numbers were 18 and 17.

[3] Of the 24, two were sentenced to penal servitude for life, four to 20 years' penal servitude and seven to 10 years' penal servitude. At this distance in time, it is impossible to tell what, if any, deterrent effect these sentences may have had.

[4] The Commission commented (paragraph 49): "A very general impression appears to prevail, that the system pursued in these prisons is not of a sufficiently penal character. It has been said, that but little work is done by the convicts, that their diet is excessive, that they receive unnecessary indulgences, that their material condition is in many respects better than that of free labourers, and that consequently the punishment cannot be severely felt. We consider that upon the whole this impression is erroneous."

[5] Report from the Select Committee of the House of Lords on the Present State of Discipline in Gaols and Houses of Correction, 24 July 1863, page v.

and in favour of hard labour:

> "It has been alleged in the course of the evidence, that the use of the treadwheel and crank degrades, irritates, and demoralises the prisoner; but the Committee, after full consideration, see no reason for entertaining this opinion, and, under certain conditions, they highly approve of the use of both these instruments of prison discipline."[1]

It advocated the use of the restricted diet as another important element of penal discipline, and specified new regulations of a particularly detailed nature —the withdrawal of mattresses during the early stages of a sentence, and the strict limitation of the period of sleep to eight hours. Its general philosophy was taken from the words of Sir Joshua Jebb in his evidence:

> "I think that the deterring elements of the punishment are hard labour, hard fare, and a hard bed".[2]

The Prison Act of 1865 gave statutory form to many of the Committee's recommendations. Every prison authority was expressly required by the Act to adopt the system of separate cellular confinement as laid down by the Government in a minutely detailed code of rules, and (in principle at least) the old local autonomy disappeared overnight. Although some local prisons still clung to the idea of productive labour and the instillation of habits of industry, the 1865 Act decided for the prison system in general the form of regime which was to last for the rest of the century; a regime of separation originally designed for reform had become one of uniform deterrence.

130. The centrally enforced requirements placed a heavy financial burden upon many local authorities who were now committed to large-scale prison building. Many of the smaller prisons were forced to shut down; between 1862 and 1877, 80 out of 193 local prisons were closed. It was gradually recognised that the proliferation of small but intricate prison structures in every local authority area was highly wasteful of resources, and pressure grew for the Government to assume financial responsibility. With the advent in 1874 of a new Government committed to reducing the burden of the local rate, centralisation became assured. The Prison Act of 1877 passed to the Secretary of State the ownership and control of all local prisons and transferred their cost to public funds.[3] On the day of transfer, 1 April 1878, 38 local prisons were closed. The convict prisons and the local prisons were now under the same central control and the principles which governed the two sentences of imprisonment and penal servitude became in a sense united. Control was vested in a board of Prison Commissioners, under their first Chairman, Sir Edmund Du Cane, who were now rigidly to enforce the detailed regulations of a deadening and defeating system which, with only slight amelioration, was to last well into this century. The principles of the system were those of the 1863 Committee: "hard labour, hard fare and a hard bed". The regime followed a system of progressive stages, which allowed, as a consequence of good behaviour, movement from the almost intolerable to the barely tolerable. The prisoner

---

[1] *Ibid.*, page vii.
[2] *Ibid.*, page ix.
[3] The only remnant of local administration was the Visiting Committee of Justices to supervise the prisons and to exercise disciplinary powers. Since the Courts Act 1971, all Visiting Committees are now Boards of Visitors.

began the first stage of his sentence with a bare, darkened cell, a plank bed and solitary confinement. The improvement of his lot as he passed through the stages was often scarcely discernible. Movement to a higher stage might mean as little as the enjoyment of a mattress for one additional night per week.

131. It is clear from Sir Edmund Du Cane's initiative in 1884 (see paragraph 54), which betrayed his anxiety to reduce needless suffering in prisons, that he was not a man devoted to inhuman practices.[1] He merely saw it as his duty to put into practice the principles that had been so clearly enunciated by the 1863 Committee. When suicides increased by prisoners leaping from the upper corridors into the well of the prisons, no attempt was made to alter the regime which produced that state of mind; the response was merely to put up safety netting so that jumping to destruction became physically impossible.[2] The trouble was that the new administration of prisons, in contrast to that of the local authorities, was ruthlessly efficient in the most minute and detailed manner. The principles of punitive deterrence through separate confinement and hard labour were rigidly and uniformly enforced. However much we may today decry the Du Cane system, it served as an invaluable experiment in penological principle. The idea that the solution of the problem of crime lies in deterrence by severity of punishment is always latent in the public mind, and the Du Cane administration tried out this idea to its ultimate limits. A more brutally deterrent system, more rigidly controlled, would not—at least in this country—be conceivable. And the most significant result of the regime was its failure in its self-appointed aim—the reduction of recidivism. The only clear result was that those subjected to it came out of prison brutalised, embittered, anti-social and in every way worse than when they went in.

The Gladstone Committee

132. By the early 1890s there was growing uneasiness among informed opinion about the nature of the prison regime and, largely as the result of a press campaign led by an ex-prison chaplain,[3] the Gladstone Committee was set up to enquire into the prison system. The Gladstone Report represents a new and decisive shift in the direction of the penal system, as significant as that of the 1863 Committee. It formulated the central principles of 20th century prison

---

[1] See, for example, his historical account of transportation in which he was at pains to contrast the harsh nature of certain aspects of that sentence with the philosophy of imprisonment of his own day:

"The very notion of reformation seems hardly to have entered into the thoughts of anybody able to give effect to it. The results produced by this kind of treatment . . . would be hardly credible if they did not stand officially recorded on the most indubitable testimony; and it will serve a useful purpose to recall them now, because at the present time there exists in some quarters a tendency to undervalue reformatory influences, and to rely solely on severity and repression in dealing with our criminals."

Experiments in Punishment by E. F. Du Cane, an article in The Nineteenth Century, Vol. VI, page 876. November 1879.

[2] "The railings around the galleries of many of the old prisons were not sufficiently high to be safe against violent prisoners who desired to throw over an officer, or themselves to jump over, and the Commissioners have had many of these railings raised, particularly at the old metropolitan prisons, such as Cold Bath Fields and Clerkenwell. It has recently been found, however, that a better prevention of suicide is the stretching of wire netting across the corridors between the galleries of the first floor, and this, having been tried at Clerkenwell, is being carried out at Holloway, Pentonville, and other prisons."
Thirteenth Report of the Commissioners of Prisons, C. 6191, Appendix 17 (1890).

[3] Rev. W. D. Morrison of Wandsworth; see footnote [1] on page 28.

administration, those of rehabilitation combined with deterrence, which have only been eroded in very recent years. The report condemned entirely separate confinement (although in deference to the entrenched views on the subject did not recommend its total abolition) and recommended the employment of all prisoners on useful industrial work. Most important of all, it laid down that the reformation of the prisoner should be a primary object concurrent with deterrence:

> "... prison discipline and treatment should be more effectually designed to maintain, stimulate, or awaken the higher susceptibilities of prisoners, to develop their moral instincts, to train them in orderly and industrial habits, and whenever possible to turn them out of prison better men and women, both physically and morally, than when they came in."[1]

Reduction in the prison population which had been cited by the Prison Commissioners as indicative of the success of the system was shown by the Committee to be due to the action of the courts in reducing the length of prison sentences (see paragraph 55).

133. The first of the Gladstone recommendations were put into practice at the turn of the century, the time that the judges under Alverstone were moving towards a formulation of the tariff. They found their first statutory form in the Prison Act of 1898 which swept away the detailed regulations of the 1865 Act governing the treatment of prisoners. Significantly, it conferred upon the Secretary of State the power to make rules for prison administration and allowed alterations to be made in treatment without seeking fresh legislation (there was no further legislation governing prisoners until after the Second World War). The treadwheel, crank and other forms of penal labour were abolished. The early period of isolation in a prisoner's sentence was reduced to a few weeks, finally to be abolished after the First World War. The Act also empowered the Secretary of State to make rules so that a local prisoner could, by special industry and good conduct, earn remission which was fixed in 1907, at a maximum of one sixth of the sentence. Loss of remission henceforth became one of the most important sanctions governing the conduct of prisoners.[2] Some of the other Gladstone reforms had to wait until the Prevention of Crime Act of 1908, resulting in the introduction of borstal detention (later borstal training), which heralded the first imaginative steps in the rehabilitation of offenders. The Act was also to create the sentence of preventive detention, described in paragraph 92, with more questionable results.

134. In spite of the new principles which Gladstone had injected into the system, reform was not translated into practice as fast as some had expected. The experience in prison of suffragettes and conscientious objectors in the period up to the end of the First World War was to produce a fresh and highly articulate indictment of the existing system, as forthright as Gladstone in its

---

[1] C. 7702, paragraph 25.
[2] Although the idea had been suggested at various times in the 19th century, it was not until after the Prison Act 1898 that remission (without the convict licence) was applied to sentences of imprisonment. The first rules provided for the earning of a maximum of one quarter remission on the balance of a prisoner's sentence over six months, and in 1907 this became a standard sixth of the whole sentence. Thus until the introduction of one third remission for all during the Second World War, there were three rates of earned remission—one sixth for prisoners, one quarter for male convicts and one third for female convicts.

condemnation. A report[1] initiated by the Labour Research Department in 1919 described the treatment of prisoners as founded on "retributory and deterrent factors, to the exclusion of truly preventive and educational principles". A quarter of a century after the Gladstone Committee Report the condition of the individual prisoner was little improved. Unshaven, with beard and head clipped, clad in shapeless garments marked with broad arrows, separated from his fellows except when at exercise or employed on punitive work, subjected to a rigid discipline with only limited access to "improving" books, it is difficult to discern in his treatment any expression of the aspirations contained in that report.

135. The appointment of Alexander Paterson at about this time as a Prison Commissioner under the benevolent eye of a new Chairman, Sir Maurice Waller, was to lead to new and sweeping reforms. The convict crop and broad arrows disappeared; the rule of silence was made less rigorous; the system of visiting became more humane and generally the range of educational and cultural activities for prisoners outside work was extended. The grudging and often unfair mark system which had measured a prisoner's earning of remission was abolished during the Second World War, and a flat-rate of one third remission became the normal expectation for all prisoners, to be forfeited only as a punishment—the first step to the present situation where available privileges are enjoyed as of right and forfeited only if abused. Educational classes were provided in all prisons; workshops and the quality of work were improved and prisoners were paid, albeit modestly, for work done. Training prisons were established for first offenders and selected prisoners of the ordinary class. The Prison Medical Service and medical facilities were extended; the psychiatrists and psychologists were to come much later. The Prison Service Staff College was built, and staff training developed from its concern with initial training designed for prescribed tasks to providing continuing support for staff engaged in a changing situation. The appointment of Paterson gave a new vigour to the borstal system, which became the vanguard of the rehabilitative principle, and passed on some of the newly generated enthusiasm to the training prisons. The borstal system was responsible for the major innovation of the open establishment (at Lowdham Grange in 1930) with a new attitude to the quality of institutional life. The adult system followed suit with the establishment of the first open prison at New Hall Camp near Wakefield in 1936.

136. In the 1920s and 30s, life was thus breathed into the rehabilitative principle formulated by Gladstone and the doctrine continued to hold sway after the Second World War in spite of the fact that problems were increasing. The strength of the reforming principle was to affect the attitudes of the courts in sentencing. As we have shown in paragraph 95, corrective training was initially greeted with much enthusiasm, an optimism which overspilled into other sentences. Courts accepted Home Office advice that short sentences denied a prisoner the possibility of reform and the result can only have been an increase in the length of the sentences which might otherwise have been imposed.

137. The amelioration of prison conditions continued after the war despite the great difficulties which arose from overcrowding; the prison population

[1] *English Prisons Today*, the Report of the Prison System Enquiry Committee, edited by Stephen Hobhouse and A. Fenner Brockway (Longmans, 1922).

continued to grow faster than new prisons could be built. By the Criminal Justice Act 1948, the sentence of penal servitude was finally abolished, and imprisonment became a single custodial sentence for adults.

138. Since 1968 all prisoners serving 18 months and over have been eligible for parole. This has introduced an element of indeterminacy into prison sentences which for the prisoner has the same quality of uncertainty that characterised the mark system that formerly determined his remission. In spite of this drawback, it has shortened periods of imprisonment that in the passage of time can be seen as unnecessarily long and has helped to reduce the pressure of the prison population. It has also, by providing for release on licence, contributed to that arm of the penal system which provides support and supervision throughout the sentence. Probation officers now operate in prisons as part of the prison team, and custody takes its place as *part* of the process of the treatment of offenders, and for some it is, sadly, a recurrent part of a circular process.

Humane containment

139. The rehabilitative principle, first coherently argued by Gladstone and developed in the borstal system in the 1920s and 30s, had become accepted in the "training" concept of adult prison regimes in the 1940s and 50s. The growth of criminological research in the last 20 years has, however, cast significant doubts upon the ability of custodial regimes to reform those who are subject to them; it is freely admitted that the old paternalistic principle of imposing a rehabilitative regime is neither successful nor socially justifiable. The Gladstone philosophy, which only a few years ago appeared unassailable, now no longer holds sway. The idea of "humane containment" has grown up to take its place, recognising that the primary task of prisons is safe custody, but that help can be given to prisoners within the normal interaction that occurs in everyday prison life. The recommendations in this report can only be understood against the background of this change in philosophy which we as a Council wholly endorse. The last word can best be left to the Prison Department in its latest annual report[1]:

> "Although the use of the phrase 'humane containment' to describe the primary aim of a prison is less popular than it was, it has the merit of truth. The primary task of prison service establishments is to accept and contain, for as long as necessary, those whom the Courts send to them; and although men are sent to prison for a number of different reasons, they are not sent for treatment or for training in the first place. For many prisoners a proven inability to benefit from either treatment or training has led to their being in prison, and it is against this background that the 'treatment and training' provided should be measured. It involves no less skill and dedication on the part of the staff because it is based on encouragement rather than coercion."

---

[1] Report on the work of the Prison Department 1976, Cmnd. 6877, July 1977, paragraph 55.

CHAPTER 7

THE PRISONS TODAY

140. It is a commonplace that those who are at the receiving end in any penal organisation find it difficult to reconcile their experience with the official description of it. A prisoner complaining about the food and being shown the not-inconsiderable variety in the menu says that it all tastes like stew. When radios are allowed and television provided, expressions of gratification are muffled by complaints that the concession is overdue. A comfortable view of historical progress in prisons by those who have a clear perspective on the past is not shared by those who live recklessly in the present.

141. The prisoner is not likely to share society's satisfaction with his conviction and sentence. He sees himself as a transient and cannot be expected to make great efforts in a situation he hopes soon to quit. He may be in open opposition to it, or accommodate himself to what he finds and according to his abilities seek what advantages are open to him. The prison situation is one of conflict: prisoner with prisoner over scarce commodities—status, tobacco and unofficial privileges; prisoners with staff in the area of control and discipline and the latitude allowed and expected; staff with the administration who are seen to complicate the task and fail to provide the additional resources for its execution. The Prison Department is at the centre of the confused debate, which we have already traced from its 19th century origins and which still continues, between those who think prisoners over-indulged and those who readily respond to prisoners' necessarily subjective expressions of their experiences.

142. It is expected of the prisons that they should provide safe custody for those committed to their care, whether convicted or unconvicted, and do this without exercising any control over the number or type of person admitted; that they should serve the courts by producing prisoners for trial; protect the public from the activities of criminals by containing them during the period of their imprisonment, and afterwards by deterring or reforming them; and, further, that they should provide a general deterrence to potential offenders. Less specifically, there is the general expectation that whilst being punished the prisoner should be treated well and made virtuous, so that any manifestation of misconduct in prison is seen to reflect adversely on the skills of those responsible for the prisoner's care. Some of these expectations are unreal, and few would now claim that there is any certain knowledge of how behaviour and attitudes can be changed by means acceptable to a civilised society. Great credit is due to the Prison Department and its staff in their success in dealing with these multifarious tasks in conditions of severe overcrowding.

143. The dominant element of imprisonment is safe custody. This can be achieved in a general application to all prisoners of those measures which would defeat the most resourceful and determined escaper. The fettering of all prisoners with irons was the cheap and generally-followed practice in the

common gaol. The Separate System relied on the strength of walls and bars, the safe keeping of all tools that might aid their penetration, and the close invigilation and regular searching of prisoners and their cells.

144. The irksomeness of prison routine is felt most in this close supervision, which has a limiting effect on prison activities. Because of the need for supervision, the prisoner's day is necessarily contained within the working day of the staff, whose interest is that this should be as compact as possible and correspond with the normal day of other workers. The traditional prison, manned by a single shift of staff, provided a short day characterised by constant movement of the staff in and out for meals and of prisoners to be fed, put to exercise and work, all impeded by movement in single file to facilitate counting and by searching, which formed the final stage of every movement. It provided almost complete security, about 14 hours' effective work in a week and a minimum of activities outside the working day. It is with an improvement on this basic pattern that in more recent times the increase in staff and the relaxation in supervision has been concerned.

145. The first change was in the establishment of the open prison, a development which now excites little concern but which represented a breathtaking departure from earlier practice, and was confidently extended after the Second World War by the adventitious, but reassuring, results of moving prisoners from the relatively secure conditions at Wakefield Prison to the freedom of Lowdham Grange Borstal as part of wartime expediency. In the open prison, prisoners are left to their own resources in attending to their toilet and bodily needs, and find their own way to work and evening activities.

146. Gradually the increase in staffing has enabled the closed training prisons to provide a similar extension of activities, but change in the local prisons has been limited. To preserve the conditions in training prisons, the local prisons bear the brunt of the overcrowding of the system. It has borne particularly heavily on the condition of the unconvicted prisoner which has changed little over the years. His condition is simple containment, against his next appearance in court or the change in status which a possible conviction or acquittal may bring.

147. Despite careful selection, there has always been absconding from open prisons—some little more than breaking bounds. The majority are quickly apprehended when the excitement of running away has disappeared in the miserable uncertainty of what to do next. Consequently, there have been few serious incidents following absconding from open prisons. In the closed prisons, the relaxation of the restrictions of the former regime, the expansion of prison workshops, the introduction of work which allows the clandestine manufacture of tools that might aid escape, the sheer weight of numbers, the increased resources and mobility available to prisoners' accomplices who may aid escapes, have all made the maintenance of security difficult.

148. In achieving change the emphasis placed on security had diminished, with consequences that were in turn to lead to further change. The public outcry which engulfed the Prison Department following the escape of notable prisoners in the 1960s had an immoderate and lasting effect. The flow of prisoners to

open prisons has continued at a lower rate in recent years, principally because of the diminution of the reception into prison of suitable people, but also in part because, in the interests of security, the selection has become more rigorous. Security has regained its pre-eminence in the prison regime.

149. Prisons are not simple reflections of society's intentions. While it is true that overwhelming official authority and the isolation of prisoners can ensure superficial compliance and the semblance of good order, the establishment of prisoners' rights in place of privileges, which may be granted as reward for acceptable behaviour and as easily withdrawn, and the admission of prisoners to free association instead of isolation in cells provide a fundamentally different problem in control. With the change in the pattern of prison life, the ordering of a prison had proceeded on an informal system, itself always changing but understood by staff and inmates and defended by the inmates themselves, quick to inform staff of any impending trouble that might disrupt the general state of détente. The reaction to escapes sharpened the conflict between prisoners and staff in those prisons where the new pattern of more rigorous control changed the previous order. Many of the prisoners designated as members of a special security class have become united in their rejection of ordinary codes of conduct and defiance of normal discipline.

150. In recent years, the prison system has been troubled by concerted disobedience and violence which, though attributed by prisoners to ill-treatment, is often inspired by the techniques of protest adopted in society at large by other groups which see themselves as oppressed. They relish the considerable publicity their activities attract. Prisoners in the special security wing at Durham Prison in March 1968, on seizing and occupying a section of the prison, immediately telephoned a local paper to say what they had done. This is not the place for us to argue the merits of giving instant and widespread publicity to extravagant gestures of protest. It is enough to say that the problem of containing such activities, directed as they often are at provoking the staff into the kind of behaviour which is the ostensible reason for the demonstration, is part of the general scene. It will be a slow process to re-establish in this situation the mutual confidence which alone makes possible the continued development of a liberal prison system.

151. Whilst overcrowding contributes to the problems of control and security, it presents the administration with practical problems which no amount of ingenuity will turn away. Victorian prison cells which were designed for sleeping and work make ample single accommodation, but shared by three they are grossly overcrowded and squalid. The presence of three chamber-pots makes the situation indefensible. The provision of water closets in prisons is not ungenerous; the problem is allowing access to them for prisoners who, in the interests of control and security, are locked up. The expensive solutions to this problem can be seen at Albany (with its system of electronic unlocking) and in the new Holloway Prison (where toilets are provided in every cell), but there is no general solution in sight. But overcrowding affects all prison services; water supply, drainage, cooking facilities, workshop space, time within the day to allow those activities which are not only desirable but necessary, all prove inadequate.

152. Prisoners face a loss of identity in this press of population. The effect is particularly marked in the case of life-sentence prisoners who in the past 20 years have increased in number from under 200 to over 1,300, and seem likely to increase even further. They depend very much on senior staff for support in the painful process of adjusting to the indeterminacy of their sentences and in the emotional climaxes that attend their recurrent hopes and disappointments about release. The increasing numbers are a threat to such relationships.

153. The effects on the prisoner are not completely adverse. There are many who, despite its inadequacy, find a shared cell not only tolerable but enjoyable. For those with few inner resources, the companionship of others is to be preferred to the solitariness of a single cell. But for most, enforced close and intimate association with other prisoners is an added hardship to prison life. The pain always is the absence of choice—the freedom to seek privacy or companionship.

154. The Victorian prisons, with their lofty halls, with cells opening on to lines of galleries narrowing in distant perspective, succeeded admirably in their unconscious purpose of reducing their occupants to insignificance. Whilst modern prison building attempts to counter this, it cannot remove the inevitable effects of imprisonment in diminishing those who are admitted. The monotony of the small-scale pattern of existence, and the lack of opportunities for acceptable expressions of tenderness in a rough masculine society are damaging, once the initial, perhaps salutary, effect of such a jolt to ordinary habits of living have passed. Separation from wife and family disrupts family relationships and makes resettlement on discharge difficult. The serious disadvantage is that to live in any community is to be affected by its standards and attitudes, and identification with a criminal community means a rejection of those of normal society.

155. For the recidivist prisoner, the continuing round of conviction, imprisonment, release and reconviction is a process both familiar and perhaps inevitable. For society, the essential task is to limit its defeating consequences, both in the prison setting and on release. Any satisfaction society may feel in imprisoning the offender has to be set against its true cost in suffering to the offender and to his family and the not inconsiderable cost in maintaining him—estimated to be just under £5,000 in the financial year 1977–78.[1] These, we believe, are strong incentives for limiting the use of imprisonment.

---

[1] House of Commons Official Report, Vol. 943, No. 51, Written Answers, Col. 267. 2 February 1978.

PART B

OUR PROPOSALS

"Society can hardly perform an act of greater moral significance than that of deliberately depriving a fellow creature of life or of liberty; and the reasons which may, in special cases, incline it to depart from ordinary rules ought to be . . . promulgated in the most authentic and authoritative manner available for the purpose."

James Fitzjames Stephen, in an article

in *The Saturday Review* (1856)

SECTION 1—A NEW SCHEME OF PENALTIES

CHAPTER 8

OUR APPROACH TO MAXIMUM PENALTIES

156. We described in Chapter 3 the way in which the present system of maximum penalties has grown up since the middle of the 19th century, as a result of quite fortuitous events such as the ending of transportation and transient parliamentary concern with a particular crime. The result is a penalty structure which more closely reflects the atmosphere and attitudes of Victorian England than those of England in the 1980s. Its principal defects are its irrational and haphazard structure and its lack of internal consistency. The work of the Criminal Law Revision Committee and the Law Commission over the past 20 years, particularly in the formulation of the Theft Act 1968 and the Criminal Damage Act 1971, has, by removing the worst anomalies, gone some way to making the structure more presentable. The approach of the law reform bodies is, however, limited by its piecemeal nature; penalties are altered merely as a by-product of the consolidation or creation of offences, and the opportunity to rationalise the penalty structure as a whole is missed. We have kept in touch with both bodies in the course of our review and know that they too appreciate this problem. This *ad hoc* approach has prevented Parliament also from taking a broad view of the total penalty structure which might promote greater consistency in the relation of one offence to another. As we noted in paragraph 63, the fixing of maximum penalties in legislation does not generally arouse much serious discussion, either in Parliament or elsewhere. So far as consistency in fixing penalties can be maintained within a system constructed on an irrational base, it is left to the Executive to maintain it in the course of its preparation of legislation. We believe that a new, more clearly identifiable, penalty structure would assist the political and public discussion of the main issues which it raises.

157. We have already observed that for the majority of offences the statutory maxima are too high to exercise an influence upon the range of sentences passed by the courts. In these circumstances, the discretion of the judges is, in theory at least, a wide one, and they receive little guidance in its exercise, either from the statute in which the penalty is fixed or from any general expression of Parliament's view about the system of penalties. As a result, the judiciary has been forced to regard the maximum penalty as no more than a distant (sometimes very distant) long-stop, and set about constructing its own more realistic guide to sentencing practice. In the course of the past 100 years, the courts have developed a common sentencing system, based upon a normal range of penalties of imprisonment which an individual offence instinctively attracts. The system is a flexible one, which takes account of the multifarious criteria relating to the circumstances of the offence and the offender, leading either to aggravation or mitigation of the penalty. But the normal range of penalty, known to judges and reinforced by the decisions of the Court of Appeal (Criminal Division), is the point from which the complex sentencing process begins. This system impinges on the statutory maxima only in the rare

case where the maximum penalty is itself low, or where the circumstances of the case are sufficiently serious to demand a sentence which comes within striking distance of the maximum.

158. Could such a system be improved? Since the question is rarely debated in public we had few statements of view to guide us in our consideration of the issues, and of where the strengths of opinion might lie. There are, in effect, two views on the subject: on the one hand, that the present structure works well enough in its limited aim of providing a broad intimation of the seriousness with which Parliament regards a particular offence and of placing a finite limit upon sentencing power; on the other, that the anomalies of the present system should be replaced by a new and rational structure with a more dynamic role to play in sentencing decisions. The first point of view is well represented by the passage in the Eighth Report of the Criminal Law Revision Committee on *Theft and Related Offences* concerning the principles which should govern maximum penalties.[1] The Committee recalled that in judgments made this century courts had interpreted Parliament's intention as reserving the maximum penalty for the most serious offence committed in that particular category— the traditional doctrine of "the worst possible case". In upholding that traditional view, the Committee stated that the factors which determined the seriousness of an offence were so numerous that it would be wrong to single out particular ones for the purpose of formulating maximum penalties:

> "It seems to us better, and more in accordance with modern theories of sentencing, to fix a maximum for each offence which will be high enough for the worst cases, even though it will rarely be imposed, and to leave a wide discretion to the courts, than to lay down scales related to particular aggravating features."

This expression of view must be seen, of course, in the context of that particular report which was concerned with demolishing the numerous and idiosyncratic penalties enshrined in the Larceny Acts (see paragraph 66). The Committee seems to have been more anxious to oppose a proliferation of maxima that were almost "fixed" penalties, than to denigrate the idea of lower maxima as such.

159. The other, more radical, approach found expression in a report on *Legal Penalties* produced by *Justice* as long ago as 1959. The main recommendation of this Committee, set up under the chairmanship of Sir David Cairns (until recently a Lord Justice of Appeal), that an "official committee" should enquire into the system of penalties, we are now ourselves fulfilling. The report concluded that statutory maxima could play a more productive role in the criminal justice system if they were based on simple, intelligent and consistent principles; if the relationship between the maxima for different crimes could be demonstrated as logical, their influence as an expression of Parliament's view of the seriousness of offences would be greatly enhanced. On the question of fitting the maximum penalty more closely to the actual penalty passed by the courts, the report took a directly opposite view to that of the Criminal Law Revision Committee:

---

[1] Cmnd. 2977, May 1966, paragraphs 10–12.

"It appears to us that certain matters to be taken into account by way of aggravation might with advantage be laid down by law so as to apply to criminal offences generally. Thus, in connection with previous offences, the present haphazard provisions for certain crimes to be more heavily punishable after a previous conviction might be swept away and some general rules laid down for higher maxima for persons previously convicted. One advantage of dealing in this way with this and other matters of aggravation would be to enable the ordinary maximum to be reduced so as to be more closely related to what should represent a fitting punishment for the crime in question. At present most maxima are fixed high simply because provision has to be made for the case which may arise only once in many years where the aggravating circumstances are such as to demand a very heavy punishment. It would, we consider, be more satisfactory that the matters which will justify an unusually severe sentence should be laid down by the law than that they should be left entirely to the discretion of the judge."[1]

160. Since sentencing can apparently function perfectly well in the absence of any direct guidance from the system of maximum penalties, and since the existing high maxima do no apparent harm, we were faced at the outset with the question whether there was any real need for a change. At a superficial level, we were given the answer to this question in our terms of reference. We had been asked to consider how far the present system of maximum penalties represents "a valid guide to sentencing practice", and we drew from this the inference that if the present system did not constitute such a guide, it was for us to attempt to devise a new one which *did*.

161. But, more positively, we sympathised with the view of *Justice* that there was a contribution which a more carefully and more rationally structured system of penalties might make to the criminal justice system. In the first place, as we have already indicated, we felt the need for a more consistent statement of Parliament's view of the relative seriousness of offences. This might not necessarily take the form of legislated maxima; it might, at least at first, simply be a statement of guiding principles for the courts to consider.[2] We have serious reservations about the utility of the traditional doctrine of "the worst possible case" as a useful expression of Parliament's will. Leaving aside the almost metaphysical question as to whether a worst possible case can ever be conceived, it is evident that only in a minority of cases does a judge need to look to the maxima and seriously ponder the constituents of a worst possible case. We believe that it would greatly benefit the criminal justice system to possess some formalised statement of the principles which govern sentencing policy, both in the interests of the sentencers and the sentenced. Such a statement would always be open to public debate, and that can only be healthy.

162. Secondly, we believe that there should be greater accord between the scale of seriousness with which Parliament views offences (expressed today through the statutory maximum penalties) and the scale of seriousness adopted by the courts, as shown in the actual sentences passed. Even if it could be claimed

---

[1] *Legal Penalties—The Need for Revaluation* (Stevens, 1959), page 9.
[2] See the proposals for the implementation of our recommendations set out in Chapter 16.

that Parliament, in formulating a maximum penalty for a new offence, paid conscious regard to a scale reflecting the comparative seriousness of all offences, the courts do not regard that maximum penalty as a reflection of the relative seriousness of offences as such but rather of the relative seriousness of worst possible cases, a quite different concept. It is inevitable, then, in a system where the maxima bear no consistent relationship to the average sentences passed, that the scale of seriousness used by the courts for the run-of-the-mill cases should differ from Parliament's scale, interpreted as defining the worst cases. We feel that on an issue so important as the relative seriousness of offences there should be some common scale to which both Parliament and the courts can adhere. If it is true that maximum penalties have a deterrent value, a maximum which bears some relation to the actual penalty imposed in court is more likely to be effective than one set so high that it is never regarded as a serious risk.[1]

163. Finally, we would hope that a system of maximum penalties in closer harmony with the practice of the courts might assist the implementation of our firmly held views about the use of imprisonment today. In our interim report, *The Length of Prison Sentences*, published in June last year, we spelled out our belief that many sentences of imprisonment imposed today on the ordinary offender are longer than necessary, and that nothing would be lost from the point of view of deterrence if they were to be significantly reduced. The reaction to that report has encouraged us to conclude that this objective can be attained, but a system of high maximum penalties will not aid the implementation of such a policy, which depends upon drawing a clear distinction between the ordinary offender and those who are a danger to the community. The new two-tier scheme of penalties we have devised would, we hope, assist the judiciary in focusing upon this distinction in such a way that the length of sentences could be reduced without fear of untoward consequences.

---

[1] An exemplary sentence may also fail because it is not regarded as a serious risk. The point is perhaps most eloquently made by Barwick Lloyd Baker, writing in 1861:

"A carefully considered sentence may indeed excite the approbation of the Bar, the bench of magistrates, or of the intelligent classes; but these are not the people on whom we require to make an impression. The weak in mind, the thoughtless, make up full three-quarters of our criminal class. They practically cannot guess at the deeply-sought arguments which govern the judge. They look on the severity of the sentence as a matter of chance, and they always hope to have the good luck of a light one; consequently, the impression made on those whom we seek to deter is less than the pain inflicted on the offender—the exact contrary of our object."

See *On assimilating the Systems of Punishment* by T. B. L. Baker, *Transactions of the National Association for the Promotion of Social Science*, 1861, page 407. The same considerations must apply *a fortiori* to a system of unrealistically high maxima.

CHAPTER 9

THE NEW MAXIMA

Devising a new system

164. Having formulated the principles upon which our approach to the review was to be based, we were faced with the practical problem of how to devise a system which would embrace those principles. The most obvious procedure that first sprang to mind was to work our way through the statute book, fixing the appropriate penalty offence by offence. This, of course, has been the traditional method adopted by Parliament over the last century as it gradually made common law offences statutory crimes, and that followed by the Criminal Law Revision Committee and the Law Commission in their gradual codification of the criminal law. Simple though the method may seem, we were not attracted by it. In the first place, we wished to devise a scheme which was not too different from current sentencing practice and would be acceptable to the courts. The relevant starting point was, therefore, the practice of the courts and not the formulation of an entirely new system from first principles. Secondly, the difficulties of making value judgments about every individual offence on the statute book were overwhelming. Even were we able to agree among ourselves about the precise relativity of different offences (and agreement could probably only have been achieved by wholesale compromise, submerging each of our individual judgments and proving satisfactory to no-one), we felt sure that the judges, the legislators, and the public at large would all take different views, both from ourselves and among themselves, and that the momentum for adopting a new system would be squandered in a welter of confused debate. We took our lesson from the failure of a similar approach by the Criminal Law Commissioners in the 1830s and 40s, which we describe in Chapter 3. As we see it, the essential strength of the recommendations in this report is that they eschew all fresh and controversial value judgments, but rest squarely upon the contemporary practice of the courts.

165. One question which was certain to inform our choice of a new scheme concerned the balance between penalties which give to the courts a wide degree of discretion and those which confine judicial discretion more narrowly. The traditional arguments for either course are simply stated. A wide degree of discretion has always been seen as conferring sufficient flexibility to ensure that all the circumstances relating to the offence and the offender, which in no two cases are ever exactly alike, can be adequately reflected in the sentence. On the other hand, a narrower sentencing discretion is justified on the grounds that it is more likely to ensure uniformity of sentencing practice between courts, and make the actual penalty imposed more certain, with a consequent enhancement of the deterrent effect upon the potential offender.

166. We considered the extremes of these two contrasting views as exemplified in the current systems in Scotland on the one hand, and in some parts of the United States on the other, as we have described them in Appendix C. In

Scotland, most of the principal crimes are common law offences with no specific maximum penalty attaching to them. This leaves the High Court of Justiciary with a virtually unrestricted discretion, not even minimally guided by legislative action. In practice, the discretion is not as wide as it appears: life imprisonment is almost exclusively reserved for murder,[1] and for all other offences a notional scale of appropriate sentence lengths is known, accepted and applied by the very small number of judges, who sit mostly in Edinburgh. But we do not favour a system in which courts are permitted an unlimited discretion in sentencing, without any guidance from Parliament. Indeed, as we have indicated, we are critical of the present situation in England whereby the existing maxima fail to provide an effective guide to sentencing policy.

167. At the other extreme, the "fixed" sentence as provided, for example, in the recent Californian law is far too inflexible to be acceptable to us. It involves the almost mandatory imposition of a "fixed" term of years, allowing only the minimum of discretion to the judge to deal with questions of aggravation or mitigation, and no discretion to the Executive in terms of early release. Such a system can only be constructed by a legislature on the basis of unacceptably dogmatic value judgments which ignore the subtleties of distinction which courts are bound to make in real life.

168. Having rejected these two extreme solutions, we determined to devise a system which would steer a middle course between them. Something of the approach we were contemplating we discovered in some remarks made by Lord Justice (now Lord) Scarman in an address to the annual general meeting of the Howard League for Penal Reform in September 1974:

> "Long sentences should become the exception—only to be imposed if it can be shown that an extended sentence is necessary for the protection of society. I would suggest that all maximum sentences allowed by law should be reviewed as a matter of urgency. Parliament should consider whether there is any justification for permitting a court to impose a sentence of more than five or seven years save in exceptional circumstances which should be specified by statute."[2]

While we could not subscribe to the idea of placing an arbitrary overall ceiling on sentencing of the kind thus proposed, we were nevertheless attracted to the idea of a two-tier system of sentencing—that is, one where ordinary offenders would be subject to a set of maxima closely relating to sentences actually passed, while the minority of offenders who are considered by the courts to present a risk of serious future harm would be subject to a much wider range of penalties appropriate to their case. This was the approach on which we eventually decided. At the present time, the Crown Court has in theory a wide-ranging discretion conferred by a system of high maximum penalties; in practice this breadth of discretion is curtailed by the judicial concept of a normal range of sentences. What we propose is the narrowing of the present discretion of the court for normal cases, but the retention of a broad discretion for the abnormal.

---

[1] On three occasions in the past 10 years it has been imposed for culpable homicide, and on one occasion for rape.

[2] *Control of Sentencing: the balance between the judge and the executive* (Howard League, 1974), page 10; reprinted in *Criminal Justice* by John Baldwin and A. K. Bottomley (Martin Robertson, 1978).

The new maxima

169. We had decided that the lower tier of our new system, that applying to the ordinary offender, should be close to the current sentencing practice of the courts. The natural starting point in the formulation of a system more closely related to the practice of the courts was, of course, a study of what the courts have actually been doing in recent years. We therefore considered in some detail the length of sentences of imprisonment passed by the higher courts for the major offences during the past 10 years to see to what level the maximum penalty could be reduced adequately to cover what we regarded as the ordinary case, and yet leave sufficient scope for the exceptional case to exceed the new maxima. After a lengthy consideration of the possibilities, we finally settled for a formula which we thought would work. We found that a two-tier system of penalties might operate successfully if the top 10% of prison sentences (that is, the longest ones) were hived off and we took the heaviest of the sentences in the remaining 90% as the new maximum penalty. An example may help to explain the operation. The following table shows the sentence lengths imposed upon persons convicted in the Crown Court of burglary (under section 9 of the Theft Act 1968) in the years 1974 to 1976 and sentenced to immediate imprisonment.

	Up to 6 months	Over 6 months up to 12 months	Over 12 months up to 18 months	Over 18 months up to 2 years	Over 2 years up to 3 years	Over 3 years up to 4 years	Over 4 years up to 5 years	Over 5 years up to 7 years	Over 7 years up to 10 years	Over 10 years	Total
					Length of sentence						
Number	2,154	4,444	3,713	2,086	1,720	364	156	77	12	8	14,734
Cumulative percentage	15	49	70	84	96	98	99	100	100	100	100

The current maximum penalty is 14 years and the highest sentence awarded in the three years fell somewhere above 10 years. The cumulative percentages show that 84% of cases had sentence lengths of up to two years and 96% had sentence lengths up to three years; hence the point below which 90% of sentences were imposed (which for convenience we have called the 90% level) fell in the range over two years and up to three years. The procedure we actually used was more complicated than in this example and is explained in Appendix B. The new maximum proposed for burglary is in fact three years.

170. We recognise, of course, that the choice of 90% as the appropriate level is to some extent arbitrary, and that another figure might have served just as well. We chose 90% as the appropriate level because we considered it a rough but reliable guide to the present practice of the courts in distinguishing between the ordinary and the exceptional offender and because one in ten, in our view, represents the common conception of what constitutes the exceptional.[1] The figure merely fixes a dividing line between the ordinary offender and the exceptional offender, as we conceived them, based on the length of sentences imposed in recent years. It does not, of course, mean that in future years a fixed 90% of those imprisoned will be ordinary offenders and a fixed 10% the exceptional cases. For any particular offence in any particular year, the

---

[1] See, for example, the reference to "nine cases out of ten" in the speech of Lord Penzance, quoted in paragraph 56.

proportion of exceptional cases exceeding the maximum may be more or less than 10%. *We recommend that a new system of maximum penalties should be constructed, fixing a new penalty for each offence at the level below which 90% of the sentences of immediate imprisonment passed for that offence by the Crown Court fell, in the most recent selected period of time.* The effect of our proposals is to place the majority of offenders subjected to terms of immediate imprisonment within the bounds of a substantially reduced maximum penalty, while at the same time not restricting the courts' powers in sentencing the small proportion of offenders whom they consider to be exceptional and to require lengthy sentences for the protection of the public.

171. The rationale for the two-tier system is not that the courts should be prevented from sentencing above the point fixed by the new maxima. It is merely that in the exceptional cases, represented by the top 10% of contemporary prison sentences, we believe there should be a more explicit justification of the resort to the higher penalty, which henceforth would constitute exceeding the maxima. We describe in the next chapter the criterion we propose for exceeding the new maxima, and the sentencing and release powers for dealing with the exceptional offender. In this chapter, we show what new maxima are produced by adoption of the 90% level procedure; indicate some of the problems that arise in constructing the new system, both of a policy and of a statistical nature; and consider the likely effects that the new system might have upon the average length of sentences passed by the courts and upon the periodicity of re-offending.

172. Using the techniques described in Appendix B, we worked through a list[1] of offences and obtained a proposed new maximum for each offence, either by determining the 90% level or (where few or no cases of an offence had been recorded) by an alternative procedure. By this means, we completed the two tables set out in Appendix A, one for the more common offences where our normal statistical method was technically viable and one for the less common offences. The new maxima fixed in both these tables are to be treated as of equal validity; we distinguish between them only in order to indicate that a different technique has been used.

173. For convenience, we have placed opposite an extract from the first table, which shows what our proposed procedure produces by way of new maxima for the more common and important offences. The apparently radical nature of the reduction in penalties for some offences may at first sight cause surprise. We need, therefore, to reiterate two points. First, the new levels are based on the current sentencing practice of the courts and are a faithful reflection of it. As we have already indicated, we ourselves rejected the idea of substituting our subjective judgments for what the courts are currently doing, on the grounds that we could not hope to achieve a consensus by such an approach. Second, the table is misleadingly dramatic in that it juxtaposes two maximum penalties which have very different purposes. The existing maximum is designed to embrace the worst possible case of an offence; the new maximum would be the upper limit for ordinary cases. A more realistic comparison with the existing maximum penalties would be the penalty levels available to the courts when exceeding the new maxima, and these we describe in the next chapter.

---

[1] Based on that in the Appendix to Archbold, *Pleading, Evidence and Practice in Criminal Cases*, Thirty-Ninth Edition (Sweet and Maxwell, 1976).

Present maxima, and proposed maxima (for ordinary cases) based on prison sentences imposed at Crown Court trials over the period 1974 to 1976

Description of Offence	Statutory Provision	Present Maximum	Proposed New Maximum (in years) (*not applicable to exceptional cases*)[1]
Murder	Murder (Abolition of Death Penalty) Act 1965, s.1	Life*	Life*
Manslaughter	Offences against the Person Act 1861, s.5	Life*	Life*[2]
Rape	Sexual Offences Act 1956, s.1	Life*	7
Aggravated burglary	Theft Act 1968, s.10	Life*	6
Robbery	Theft Act 1968, s.8	Life*	6
Wounding with intent to do grievous bodily harm	Offences against the Person Act 1861, s.18	Life*	5
Indecent assault on a man	Sexual Offences Act 1956, s.15	10	5
Blackmail	Theft Act 1968, s.21	14	5
Arson	Criminal Damage Act 1971, s.1(3) and 4	Life*	5
Drugs: Supply	Misuse of Drugs Act 1971, s.4(3)	14 or 5†	5
Possession with intent to supply	Misuse of Drugs Act 1971, s.5(3)	14 or 5†	4
Assisting an illegal immigrant	Immigration Act 1971, s.25(1)	7	4
Conspiracy to defraud	Common law	Unlimited	4
Drugs: Possession	Misuse of Drugs Act 1971, s.5(2)	7, 5 or 2†	3, 3 or 2†
Unlawful wounding	Offences against the Person Act 1861, s.20	5	3
Burglary	Theft Act 1968, s.9	14	3
Theft	Theft Act 1968, s.1	10	3
Obtaining property by deception	Theft Act 1968, s.15	10	3
Obtaining pecuniary advantage by deception	Theft Act 1968, s.16	5	3
Handling stolen goods	Theft Act 1968, s.22	14	3
Forgery	Forgery Act 1913	Life*	3
Indecent assault on a woman	Sexual Offences Act 1956, s.14	If under 13, 5 otherwise 2	3 2
Perjury	Perjury Act 1911	7	2
Assault occasioning actual bodily harm	Offences against the Person Act 1861, s.47	5	2
Unauthorised taking of vehicle	Theft Act 1968, s.12	3	2

* See recommendations in Chapter 11 on life imprisonment.

† The alternative maxima represent the penalties for the various classes—A, B, and C—of controlled drugs under the Misuse of Drugs Act 1971. Sentence length figures for each class of drug were not separately available.

[1] See Chapter 10 where we explain what penalties would apply in exceptional cases.

[2] Had we not been proposing life imprisonment for this offence, the new maximum based on court practice would have been 10 years.

Some technical problems

174. As already indicated, the precise statistical approach we have adopted is set out in Appendix B, and the technical problems which arise in the process are there described. A few of the problems are at least worth noting here. We have restricted the exercise to the practice of the courts in the last three years for which statistics were available to us, namely 1974–76. There are essentially two reasons for this. First, there are dangers inherent in carrying out such an exercise over too long a period because important trends can occur in sentencing, whether through the action of the courts or Parliament, the influence of public attitudes or quite fortuitous events, and aggregating figures which incorporate such trends would not faithfully reflect contemporary sentencing policy. Second, we were faced with a purely practical constraint. As we explain in Appendix B, to carry out such an exercise it is necessary to break down the published statistics into more detailed sub-classifications, and information on this basis is only available from 1974. We would emphasise that we do not wish to dictate to those who seek to implement our recommendations that they should use exactly the same basis for calculation. The levels of maxima we have proposed might, in the course of the years ahead, cease to reflect so closely the practice of the courts. We would expect that in the event of any legislation to implement our proposals, Parliament would adopt the technique of using statistics from a period immediately preceding the legislation, conceivably for a period longer or shorter than three years.

175. When Parliament enacts a new criminal offence, once the new system is in force, it will be faced with the problem that there will be no sentencing experience available for determining the penalty for that offence. In those circumstances, *we recommend that the maximum penalty should be determined by reference to the maximum penalty for existing analogous offences.* Since sentencing practice changes over the years, the new maxima would need to be reviewed from time to time, and *we recommend that the Home Secretary should do so in consultation with a standing body,* such as this Council.

176. In the same way, we do not regard as in any way sacrosanct the formula (also described in Appendix B) we have proposed when determining a penalty for offences where there have been too few, or no, cases in the relevant period. There are other solutions to that technical problem which may prove equally or more attractive.

177. Another technical problem is posed by the manner in which maximum penalties have in the past been fixed. Normally, the statute book does not fix a maximum penalty in half-years where the maximum is greater than six months, but the calculation of the 90% level does in general produce figures in fractions of years. Courts, on the other hand, do from time to time pass sentences involving fractions of years, for example, of 18 or even 30 months, though it is very unusual for them to pass sentences in smaller fractions of a year. On considering this problem, we resolved not to put forward any maxima involving half-years, and thereby retain the essential simplicity of the present system. In Appendix B we explain how we arrived at the whole-year penalties now proposed. We also decided that there would be no advantage for sentencing practice in reducing existing maxima below two years; and that existing two-year maxima should

82

not be disturbed. *We therefore recommend that two years should be the lowest level to which the existing maxima should be reduced.*

178. One other technical difficulty sprang directly from the nature of the procedure we adopted. One of the problems of providing new penalty levels for offences on the basis of statistical groupings is that the two do not always coincide. There are, for instance, some statistical categories, such as shop-lifting, which do not constitute a separate statutory offence. In these circumstances, a 90% level can be created which may be of value in a system involving non-statutory guidance to the courts but would, of course, be otiose if our proposals were to be implemented statutorily, unless a new discrete offence were to be created. This factor applies to some degree to all "broad-banded" offences (that is, where a number of separate offences are subsumed under one major head, such as theft, and a single maximum penalty affixed), like those created by the Theft Act 1968 and the Criminal Damage Act 1971. There is no reason, however, why the problem should increase in the future since we know from our discussions with the Criminal Law Revision Committee and the Law Commission that broad-banding is essentially a pragmatic policy to both bodies, and not an article of faith.

179. A more difficult problem arises in the converse situation where offences which appear separately on the statute book are lost in much larger statistical groupings, where they are not separately identified. At worst, this is a minor problem which will apply to the less frequent, less important, offences. The only way we have been able to surmount it is by applying the penalty appropriate to the statistical category to all the offences within it that are not separately identifiable, except of course in the case of an offence whose existing maximum is lower than the proposed new value. Where anomalies occur, the solution lies in the future collection of more refined statistics.

180. Other problems we have had to contend with have been of a policy rather than a technical nature. The inchoate crimes—attempting, conspiring or inciting to commit crime—are classified for statistical purposes usually under the heading of the consummated offence. But there are dotted around the statute book a number of inchoate crimes which are separate statutory offences for which there are separate classifications in the *Criminal Statistics*. Incitement to commit murder, for example, is an offence under section 4 of the Offences against the Person Act 1861, carrying a 10-year maximum penalty; attempted rape is also a separate statutory crime and is classified separately from the completed offence, carrying a seven-year maximum. The former is so infrequent a crime that it can be treated under the procedure we have adopted for un-common offences. The offences of rape and attempted rape produce, under the 90% level procedure, proposed new maxima of seven years' and five years' imprisonment respectively. Since, however, attempts under the Criminal Law Act 1967 and virtually all conspiracies under the Criminal Law Act 1977 carry the same maximum penalty as for the consummated offence, we have followed this statutory precept, even though a separate statistical classification might give a different level of penalty on a 90% calculation.

Exceptions to the application of the new maxima

181. There were a few offences which, by their nature, we found to be exceptions to the application of a 90% penalty. Murder, which uniquely carries a mandatory

penalty of life imprisonment, cannot be subjected to our method of calculation, if only because the sentencing practice of the courts is pre-determined by the statutory mandatory element in the sentence. We describe our proposals for dealing with the homicide offences in Chapter 11. For nearly all other crimes for which life imprisonment is the maximum penalty, we are able to calculate a proposed new maximum, either on the basis of the 90% level procedure or by the procedure for uncommon offences referred to in Appendix B. Our view, which we explain in detail in Chapter 11, is that the maximum penalty of life imprisonment for these offences should be abolished, to be replaced by the newly calculated maxima for the ordinary offender, although the life sentence should still remain available for certain offences where the new maxima are exceeded.

182. There is left over the group of offences against the State—treason, treason felony, sedition and incitement to disaffection. Like the Law Commission, which has recently produced a Working Paper[1] on these offences and made effective proposals for modernising the law, we are not confident that we have anything useful to contribute to the debate on what punishment should be available to the courts. Prosecutions, let alone convictions, in peacetime for these offences are comparatively rare. We would, therefore, have nothing to guide us, other than the procedure outlined in Appendix B for dealing with uncommon offences. We are content to leave it to those who will ultimately be responsible for restating and modernising the law in this field to select penalties appropriate to their proposals. The same considerations apply to offences of piracy and mutiny.

183. We have had to consider those few instances where the maxima at present have been the subject of criticism by the judiciary as being too low.[2] We have in mind the penalty of two years' imprisonment for cruelty to or neglect of children,[3] indecent assault on a female aged 13 and over,[4] fraudulent trading,[5] and corrupt transactions.[6] In the case of the latter two offences, it would appear that the courts' practice has been quite exceptionally constrained by the maximum penalty, since we found a very high proportion of sentences bunched together at the point of the maximum. But in the case of cruelty to or neglect of children, the distribution of sentence lengths was fairly even. The number of cases in 1974–76 for that offence was, however, so few—only 24—that we were

---

[1] Working Paper No. 72. Second Programme, Item XVIII. Codification of the Criminal Law—Treason, Sedition and Allied Offences. May 1977.
[2] The classic instance of a judge expostulating at the inadequacy of a statutory maximum was Mr. Justice Wills in 1895 when sentencing Oscar Wilde under section 11 of the Criminal Law Amendment Act 1885:
"It is the worst case I have ever tried . . . I shall, under such circumstances, be expected to pass the severest sentence that the law allows. In my judgment it is totally inadequate for such a case as this. The sentence of the Court is that . . . you be imprisoned and kept to hard labour for two years."
The Trials of Oscar Wilde by H. Montgomery Hyde (Notable British Trials Series) (Hodge, 1948), page 339.
[3] Section 1 of the Children and Young Persons Act 1933.
[4] Section 14 of the Sexual Offences Act 1956.
[5] Section 332(3) of the Companies Act 1948.
[6] Section 1 of the Prevention of Corruption Act 1906 and sections 1 and 2 of the Public Bodies Corrupt Practices Act 1889. Where the corrupt transaction involves contracts with the Government or a public body, the penalty is increased by section 1 of the Prevention of Corruption Act 1916.

prevented from making a 90% level calculation. We concluded that, where the cruelty or neglect was serious, the offender was usually charged with a more serious general offence against the person, not restricted to children.[1] There seems therefore to be no need to alter the two-year maximum.

184. In the same way, although there have been a number of cases in recent years where the judiciary have criticised[2] the low penalty for indecent assault on a female aged 13 and over, where the assault is a serious one there is usually an additional charge for some other offence carrying a higher maximum penalty, such as causing actual bodily harm or grievous bodily harm. If our scheme of penalties is adopted, the really grave cases of this offence may qualify for a sentence exceeding the maximum. We do not feel, therefore, that there is any pressing reason for raising the existing maximum penalty.

185. For the two offences of fraudulent trading and of corruption different considerations apply. The offence of fraudulent trading provided only a handful of cases. Since the offence is very restricted in its application—it can only be committed by a director of a company that at the time of prosecution has gone into liquidation—and offences of fraud will have been committed and be the subject of separate charges, it is not a problem of serious concern. There is, of course, a question whether English law is not defective in failing to provide a general offence of fraudulent trading, but that is strictly outside our terms of reference. We have for our purposes simply left the maximum penalty at its present level, which is two years.

186. The penalty for offences of corruption has attracted a good deal of judicial and public comment in recent years as a result of the series of prosecutions involving the former architect, John Poulson, and the cases brought against some of the former members of the Obscene Publications Squad at Scotland Yard.[3] Again the numbers are too small for the proper calculation of the 90% level. In some of these cases, the sentences were made consecutive so as to produce total sentences in excess of the maximum, although in some cases also the convictions for conspiracy allowed for larger penalties to be passed without a

---

[1] The Court of Appeal has approved the policy of prosecuting in appropriate cases assaults against children under some provision other than section 1 of the 1933 Act, thus avoiding the low maximum penalty: "If the circumstances justify it, there is nothing wrong in the prosecution proceeding not under that Act, but under an Act which enables them to obtain from the court a proper sentence for the particular offence involved"—*R* v *Beanland* (1970) 54 Cr. App. R. 289. See also *R* v *Roe* (1967) 51 Cr. App. R. 10. If no violence is used against the child, but the ill-treatment is by omission rather than commission, the courts appear to think that the two-year maximum is adequate—*R* v *Lowe* [1973] Q.B. 702.

[2] See, for example, *R* v *Giffin* No. 1447/B/74, 8 July 1974, quoted in footnote [1] on page 96 Some concern has also been expressed from time to time, particularly in the media, over the two-year maximum penalty for unlawful sexual intercourse with a girl under 16 (section 6 of the Sexual Offences Act 1956). The Court of Appeal has, however, indicated that the two-year maximum is adequate to deal with the worst type of case: "a man in a supervisory capacity who abuses his position of trust for his sexual gratification, ought to get a sentence somewhere near the maximum allowed by law, which is two years' imprisonment"—*R* v *Taylor, Roberts and Simons* (1977) 64 Cr. App. R. 182 at page 185.

[3] In one of the latter cases, *R* v *Drury*, heard in July 1977 at the Central Criminal Court, Mr. Justice Peter Pain described the maximum penalty of two years as "wholly inadequate" and added: "This might well occupy the minds of those who amend the criminal law from time to time"—see *The Guardian*, 8 July 1977. See also Lord Justice Lawton's remarks in *R* v *Ambler and Hargreaves*, quoted in paragraph 79.

resort to the device of consecutive sentencing.[1] As with the offences of cruelty to or neglect of children, and with fraudulent trading, we have proposed that the maxima under the three corrupt practices statutes should remain as they are.[2] The decisions about these four types of offence conform with the rule we adopted (see paragraph 177) that an existing penalty as low as two years should not be disturbed. Our proposals in the next chapter for exceeding the maxima will mean that the penalty for exceptional cases of all these offences will be unlimited.

The length of prison sentences

187. The new penalties we have now described will provide one arm of a new penalty structure, that which deals with the ordinary offender. Our proposals for the exceptional offender are set out in the next chapter. The idea of a two-tier system of this kind is not new, and we recognise that there will be some who criticise it on the grounds that it cements an ill-defined distinction between offenders, much to the disadvantage of the more serious offender who will suffer the longer sentences on grounds that are not clearly distinguished.[3] We do not share these pessimistic doubts. On the contrary, we believe that as a result of our proposals the problem of "dangerousness" will be further highlighted and greater efforts will be made to provide a suitable conceptual framework[4] which will protect the serious offender from unjust treatment.

188. The other side of the coin is the effect that the new structure may have on the lot of the ordinary offender. In our interim report published in June 1977, *The Length of Prison Sentences*, we stated that in the early stages of our review we had come unanimously to the conclusion that a large number of sentences of imprisonment passed by the courts were longer than they needed to be. Without reference to what we might be proposing about maximum penalties, we urged the courts to restrict their use of imprisonment, not only by continuing to resort to non-custodial penalties, but also by cutting the length of prison sentences (including those that are suspended). Our advocacy of much shorter sentences was prompted by the sound penological doctrine that it is wrong that an offender should lose his liberty for a day longer than is absolutely necessary to satisfy the proper aims of penal policy. We concluded that there was no reason to suppose that longer sentences have a greater impact than shorter ones on the prisoner, and that whatever deterrent value imprisonment might possess, it is not lessened in its impact by a reduction in sentence lengths. Whereas in the years following the Criminal Justice Act 1948 courts had been counselled, and had consequently responded to the plea, to avoid short sentences as being unhelpful in promoting programmes for treating offenders in prison, the general rule should now be the reverse: shorter sentences are much to be preferred.

---

[1] Since the passing of the Criminal Law Act 1977, a conspiracy conviction will carry the same maximum as for the consummated offence (see paragraph 180). See also *R v Tilbrook and Sivalingam* [1978] Crim. L.R. 172.

[2] We are conscious that the Salmon Commission on *Standards of Conduct in Public Life* (Cmnd. 6524, paragraph 64) has recommended a maximum penalty of seven years for all corruption offences involving public bodies. We consider, nonetheless, that the serious cases will be caught by our provisions for exceeding the new maxima.

[3] Such a criticism is implied by Professor Bottoms in his inaugural address to the Centre for Criminological Studies at Sheffield University—see Howard Journal, Vol. XVI, No. 2, October 1977, pages 70–96.

[4] See paragraph 197.

189. A copy of our interim report was sent to all judges and to every bench throughout the country. Press comment on it was largely uncritical; those newspapers that commented did so favourably. The political reaction was also favourable. In a speech opening the international conference to celebrate the bi-centenary of John Howard's *The State of the Prisons in England and Wales*, the Home Secretary endorsed our proposals. In a debate in the House of Lords a fortnight after our report was published, most of their Lordships expressed strong sympathy with our proposals.[1] The general response to our interim report encourages us to think that our proposals for a new system of maximum penalties, that will in part facilitate the passing of shorter sentences, will not put us entirely out of step with public opinion.

190. It is impossible in the short interval since our report was published to assess in detail the reaction to it in the Crown Court; but we were heartened by at least one case in the Court of Appeal (Criminal Division) which prayed our report in aid. In June, a few days after publication, Lord Justice (now Lord) Scarman cited the report when granting leave to appeal to an offender serving a sentence of three years' imprisonment as the result of the accumulation of an odd assortment of suspended and immediate sentences of imprisonment:

> "The Applicant is 26, of no fixed address; he has a number of previous convictions, and it cannot be said that his record contains any features worthy of consideration as a matter of mitigation. Nevertheless, we think this is a sentence which should be reviewed by the full Court, particularly bearing in mind the recent White Paper on the length of prison sentences."[2]

We feel sure that this decision, and others[3] less explicit, will continue to have their influence.

191. We hope that our proposals for reducing the maxima will assist courts in reducing the length of prison sentences, and thus help to reduce the prison population. We are, however, aware that there will be no such reduction if it turns out that a substantial proportion of earlier released prisoners commit further offences shortly after their release from prison, and receive fresh terms of imprisonment. For those prisoners who on release will re-offend, imprisonment is merely a neutralising interlude in their criminal career. Given then that imprisonment for potential recidivists merely postpones crime, the crucial question which arises is: will postponement of re-offending be materially curtailed by an earlier release?

192. Regular information on the length of time between release from prison and the first reconviction is published in the annual volume of prison statistics published by the Home Office. There is also available the recent study of the Home Office Research Unit, *Parole in England and Wales*.[4] Figures from both these sources, which we reproduce in Appendix L, show that reconviction occurs fairly quickly for those persons who are going to be reconvicted in any event,

---

[1] House of Lords Official Report, Vol. 384, No. 83, Cols. 1115–41 and 1147–1211. 29 June 1977.
[2] *R v Faye*, No. 32/B/77, 17 June 1977. When the appeal was heard on 6 October 1977, the total sentence was reduced to allow Faye's immediate release from prison.
[3] *R v Hogan* [1978] Crim. L.R. 101.
[4] Home Office Research Study No. 38 (HMSO), 1977.

and that in all 50%–60% of released prisoners are reconvicted within two years of release. Data from the parole research did not show a consistent relationship between reconviction rate and sentence length, but the prison statistics indicate some decrease in reconviction rate as sentence length increases.[1]

193. We draw some comfort from the conclusion of the parole study which stated that a more liberal policy on the part of the Parole Board in recent years, compared with the policy adopted when parole was introduced in 1968, had not worsened the failure rate of parolees during the period of the licence. As we record in Chapter 3, a policy of reducing sentences has been effected in the past, admittedly in different circumstances from today, without apparently increasing the crime rate. Although the reconviction figures we studied do not give cause for optimism, it is, after all, easy to exaggerate the effect that shorter sentences might have on the totality of offending. We acknowledge that there is likely to be some increase in the commission of offences, but we believe that this is a risk that we must all be prepared to take.[2]

---

[1] This does not, of course, imply a   causal   relationship.

[2] One important piece of recent research in this area tends to indicate that even the mandatory imprisonment of convicted offenders for very long periods does not materially affect the total volume of crime—see *The Incapacitation of the Dangerous Offender: A Statistical Experiment*, by Stephen Van Dine, Simon Dinitz and John Conrad, *Journal of Research in Crime and Delinquency*, January 1977, page 22.

CHAPTER 10

EXCEEDING THE NEW MAXIMA

194. The new maxima we have proposed would form the limits of punishment for the ordinary offender who comes before the Crown Court. We were then faced with the more difficult question of how the exceptional offender would fit into this new sentencing pattern; in particular, what sort of cases would qualify for a sentence higher than the maxima, how the courts would identify them and what form their sentences should take.

The criterion for exceeding the maxima

195. Sentences of exceptional length may be necessary for several reasons. One is the need to protect potential victims from the commission of a similar or more serious offence by the same offender. It is a reason which was recognised in the successive attempts to devise a suitable custodial sentence for persistent offenders, but with the negative results chronicled in Chapter 5. It seems that nowadays mere persistence in offences which are not in themselves regarded as particularly harmful does not give rise to a significant demand for long sentences. Nor do we think that even the reduction of the maximum which we are proposing for such offences will revive the demand. It is not persistence alone which makes courts feel the need for a protective sentence but the prospect of repetition coupled with serious harm. The Butler Committee, when faced with the occasional use of restriction orders under section 65 of the Mental Health Act 1959 to deal with petty offenders who were being committed by criminal courts to mental hospitals, recommended that the section should be amended so as to limit its use to the protection of the public against *serious harm*.[1]

196. Our concern is with prison sentences; but so far as the protection of the public is concerned the approach should be the same. We agree that exceptionally long sentences are justified only where serious harm is involved. What constitutes serious harm is of course debateable. We have no doubt that it includes serious physical injury; serious psychological effects of the kind which impair a person's enjoyment of life or capacity for functioning normally (for example, some sexual offences); exceptional personal hardship (for example, financial loss which markedly affects a person's way of life); and damage to the security of the State (for example, as a result of espionage), or to the general fabric of society. It is arguable that other categories should be added: for example, the theft or destruction of unique works of art or architecture. But about such categories there is unlikely to be any widespread agreement, let alone unanimity; and this being so, we think that serious harm should normally be interpreted as being confined to the four categories we have listed.

197. They constitute our own conception of what is dangerous, in the context of the penalty system we are now proposing. The whole question of dangerousness is, of course, wide and complex, but it is currently being studied by the

---

[1] Report of the Committee on Mentally Abnormal Offenders, Cmnd. 6244, October 1975, paragraph 14.24.

Committee on The Dangerous Offender, to which we referred in paragraph 4. We await the report of that Committee with interest.

198. We are not arguing, of course, that in order to qualify for an exceptional sentence an offender must actually have inflicted serious harm, for it is the potential victim we are particularly concerned with protecting. An offence which is very likely to cause such harm, even though by good fortune it has not done so in the present instance, should be regarded in the same light as an offence which has. So should an attempt, a threat or a conspiracy to do serious harm.

199. On the other hand, not all offenders who have done, risked, attempted, threatened or conspired to do serious harm are likely to repeat their behaviour. There are, for example, a few violent or sexual offenders who repeat their behaviour, but when one looks at the detailed figures, it is clear that they constitute only a small minority of such offenders. It is much rarer for an individual to incur repeated convictions for violent than for dishonest offences; nor can this be attributed to higher clear-up rates for dishonest offences, for the reverse is the case. Most types of sexual offence also have a low reconviction rate; and what is probably the most repetitive of the non-consensual sexual offences—indecent exposure—is on the whole the least harmful.

200. Indeed, it has been argued that any decision to prolong a person's detention solely in order to protect others from violence or sexual molestation is unjustifiable, because out of any group of persons so detained only a minority would in fact repeat their offences, with the result that the majority would be unnecessarily detained. There are statistics to support this argument,[1] although they are for the most part based on rather short follow-up periods. We cannot accept, however, that such arithmetic is decisive. That would be so only if unnecessary detentions and mistaken releases were counted as equivalent; and of course the consequences are very different. The death or injury of a blameless victim cannot be put in the same moral scales as the further detention of a person who has culpably done, risked, attempted or threatened serious harm.

201. At the same time, it must be recognised that even if the offender is accurately classified as likely to repeat his offence, merely to delay his release is likely to achieve merely the postponement of that repetition, and not its prevention. There may be cases in which a short postponement of release does achieve genuine prevention (for example, in the case of a man intent on revenging himself on someone who is about to emigrate), but they are exceptional. Such cases apart, anyone seeking the protection of the public must be prepared to contemplate really long sentences, and not merely a slight stretching of the normal range of sentences.

202. The protection of the public, however, is not the only possible effect of exceptionally long sentences. We also have to consider them as potential deterrents, either of the sentenced offender (individual deterrence) or of others who might follow his example (general deterrence). So far as individual deterrence is concerned, we doubt whether the addition of a few years to a medium-length sentence would tip an offender's mental scales in favour of a law-abiding life. Quite apart from the fact that many offenders commit their offences either

---

[1] The case is argued in Professor Bottom's address cited in footnote [3] on page 86.

impulsively or in a mood of optimism about their chances of detection, it is difficult to picture even a rational and calculating offender who would be prepared to risk, say, a four-year sentence but not an eight-year one. Such research as has been published does not support the notion that the longer the sentence, the lower the reconviction rate.[1]

203. In any case, we do not believe the judges would wish to exceed the new maximum solely in the hope of deterring the offender himself. They are more likely to have in mind the general deterrent effect upon those who might otherwise follow his example. We are sceptical, however, about the assumption that an occasional[2] sentence of exceptional length (sometimes called "an exemplary sentence") is likely to have this effect. It is extremely difficult to find any unquestionable demonstration of this; but although the evidence is not wholly conclusive, a number of examples have contributed to our attitude of scepticism. The example most often cited is in connection with the outbreak of racial violence in Notting Hill in the summer of 1958. Nine youths, who were arrested in the first wave of attacks on coloured people, were sentenced at the Old Bailey to four years' imprisonment (at least double the normal sentence) in spite of the fact that all but one were admitted to be of good character. It was clear from the judge's remarks that the sentences were intended as exemplary deterrents and following their imposition the violent attacks apparently ceased. Investigation has, however, shown that other factors (such as increased police activity) are just as likely to have been responsible.[3]

204. What might be justifiable would be the use of exceptionally long sentences to deal with offenders convicted of extremely lucrative crimes, if there were reason to think that the gains from such crimes were being regarded as sufficient recompense for serving shorter sentences. Such sentences could not be "exemplary"; they would in effect amount to the recognition of an exceptional category of robberies, frauds or similar offences.

205. With such rare exceptions, however, we would wish to see sentences of lengths exceeding the new maxima used for the protection of the public rather than for deterrence. This being so, we would emphasise that a protective sentence is not justified solely by the seriousness of the harm done, risked or intended at the time of the original offence. There must be good reason to believe that on release the offender is substantially more likely than other men or women of similar age and circumstances to do serious harm. For example, there might be evidence that his offence was not an isolated incident resulting from an unusual situation which is unlikely to recur, but is part of a recurring pattern; or that it was intended to achieve a declared objective to which he remains dedicated (such as unaccomplished revenge).

---

[1] See *The Effectiveness of Sentencing*, Home Office Research Study No. 35 (HMSO, 1976), pages 14–16 and page 39, which sums up by saying "It can be concluded that there is no evidence that longer custodial sentences produce better results than shorter sentences."
[2] It is possible that a policy of imposing uniformly long sentences instead of uniformly medium-length ones might have the desired effect; but that is not the question here.
[3] See *Sentencing in a Rational Society* by Nigel Walker (Penguin Books, 1972), page 93. See also the article *Severe sentences: no deterrent to crime?* by R. Baxter and C. Nuttall in *New Society*, 2 January 1975, pages 11–13.

206. Again, the court should be satisfied that no other permissible way of dealing with the offender offers the necessary degree of protection against him. This is especially important where there is any evidence to suggest that he may be mentally disordered. We agree with the Butler Committee[1] that before imposing a special sentence for protective purposes the court should be satisfied that the case is not a suitable one for a hospital order.

207. Examples of the kind of cases for which a protective sentence should be designed are illustrated by those we have set out in paragraph 196. We attempted to embody them in a single formula to govern the conduct of the courts, but after much deliberation abandoned the attempt because we felt that an over-specific formula ran the risk of excluding relevant cases by mischance. We eventually decided upon a broader formulation, wide enough to embrace all examples of the cases we have in mind. Consequently *we recommend that no court should pass a sentence of imprisonment exceeding the new maximum term unless, by reason of the nature of the offence and the character, conduct and antecedents of the offender, the court is of the opinion that a custodial sentence of exceptional length is necessary for the protection of the public against serious harm.*

Sentencing procedure

208. We do not think that an exceptional sentence should be imposed without prior indication that the judge has this in mind, so that the offender can prepare his arguments against such a sentence. We realise that unless he has signified his intention to plead guilty to the relevant offence or offences, this may involve a remand after conviction.[2] A judge could not properly begin to consider a sentence of exceptional length until the offender had been found (or pleaded) guilty; but the offender and his legal advisers will not be unaware of the possibility that the court may impose such a sentence.

209. The likelihood of an appeal against an exceptional sentence raises the question whether the court should be required to state its reasons for deciding that an exceptional sentence is necessary. A statement of reasons is of obvious value both for the appellant and for the appellate court. On the other hand, although magistrates are sometimes required by statute to state reasons (for instance, when passing a prison sentence on an offender who has not yet served one), the Crown Court is not subject to such a requirement, and attempts to introduce them into the law have been resisted. We feel, however, we can rely on the fact that the Crown Court almost invariably gives reasons for unusual sentences without being specifically required to do so, and we have no doubt that if a judge failed to give his reasons, the Court of Appeal (Criminal Divison) would have something to say about it.

---

[1] Cmnd. 6244, paragraph 4.42(c).

[2] The extended sentence procedure whereby notice is given to an offender by the prosecution that it intends, if he is convicted, to prove previous convictions or sentences which render him eligible for an extended sentence—section 29(3) of the Powers of Criminal Courts Act 1973—could not be easily adapted to cover the sort of evidence which we have in mind (see paragraph 205); and in any case, as we said in Chapter 5, it has not worked particularly well.

The form of the protective sentence

210. We gave a great deal of thought to the ways in which the length of exceptional sentences might be limited. At present, there are two kinds of sentence which might be imposed on the offender whom the courts consider to be dangerous. First, there is the long determinate sentence which may be passed within the high statutory maxima whose history we traced in Chapter 3. Second, and more important, there is the life sentence which can be imposed for a considerable number of serious offences, and is commonly regarded as the standard protective sentence available today. The life sentence, as a maximum penalty, operates of course in two ways. Either the full maximum is imposed, and the offender is committed to prison indefinitely; or, more commonly, the court imposes a very long determinate sentence. Thus a maximum penalty of life imprisonment means in effect that there is no statutory limit to the length of the determinate sentence which may be imposed.

211. We were confronted with three basic choices: broadly to maintain the *status quo* and retain dependence upon the life sentence; to fix a new limit to determinate sentences higher than the proposed new maxima; or to abolish limits on sentencing for these offenders altogether. The first of these options involved the perpetuation of two categories of offence, those subject to a maximum of life imprisonment for which there would be no statutory limit to the length of the determinate sentences which could be imposed, and the rest which would be circumscribed by the existing statutory maxima. Under this proposal, it would be possible either to preserve the *status quo*, leaving offences in the categories in which they now are, and leaving unaltered such statutory maxima as are already on the statute book, or to transfer offences from one category to the other, and perhaps to propose new statutory maxima for some or all of the second category. We were discouraged by the complexity of such a proposal. It would involve a three-tier sentencing system, in which for all offences there would be the new maxima proposed in Chapter 9; for some offences there would be higher maxima for the exceptional case; and for some offences there would be the possibility of determinate sentences without limit. The only argument in favour of such a solution is that it represents the minimum of departure from the *status quo*, and could even be achieved without legislation. Ultimately, our one concession to the *status quo* was our decision to retain the life sentence as an additional power in the case of certain offences.

212. Our second option was to provide that all sentences of determinate length exceeding the maxima should be subject to either a uniform limit or one fixed for the offence in question. We considered a large number of possible methods of fixing such a limit. A uniform limit, which would not be unprecedented,[1] of, say, 20 years on determinate exceptional sentences would have the merit of simplicity. The sentence would be subject to review by the parole machinery when one third of it had been served, and would be shortened by the usual remission. It is arguable that it is hard to imagine circumstances in which the protection of the public would point to a *determinate* sentence exceeding 20 years. In the exceedingly rare cases in which the offender seemed likely to remain

---

[1] Sentences of preventive detention were from 1948 until 1967 subject to a limit of 14 years; and extended sentences are subject to limits of 10 years or five years, depending on the statutory maximum for the offence in question.

a grave danger for longer than he could be detained under such a sentence, it would be more logical to impose the indeterminate life sentence. The alternative of fixing a new maximum for the exceptional sentence for each offence has little to recommend it. Since we were at pains to avoid value judgments, we should have had to base such limits on the past practice of the courts—for example, by adopting the longest sentence imposed for the offence in question in the last decade. This would have been open to obvious objections. The longest sentence could well have been imposed in unique circumstances, and for reasons other than the protection of the public. On the whole, however, we found the rigidity of a fixed limit unattractive as a means of dealing with cases which would have widely ranging characteristics.

213. We decided eventually upon the third, more radical option: that where the maximum was to be exceeded, there should be no statutory limit to the length of any determinate sentence. This is already the case with life-carrying offences, and the proposal would simply extend the principle to the infrequent case in which an exceptional sentence seemed necessary for an offence which does not carry life. It is not unthinkable within a British context, for in Scotland the High Court can pass a determinate sentence of any length for the great majority of cases brought before it. We decided upon this solution because of the useful breadth of discretion it would confer upon the courts in dealing with serious cases. As we indicate in the next chapter, we also decided that it would be necessary to retain the power to pass life sentences when exceeding the maximum in the case of those non-homicide offences where the life sentence has been used in recent years. If the power to pass the life sentence for non-homicide offences is further phased out (if, as we hope, its use declines), the long determinate sentence will be available to take its place. Accordingly, *our view is that when a court decides to exceed the new maxima on the grounds set out in paragraph 207 there need be no statutory limit to the length of a determinate sentence it may impose. For certain non-homicide offences[1] where it is currently used, the life sentence should continue to be available as an additional power.*

214. The possibility that a court might impose a sentence of quite inordinate length has to be faced. The fact that the prisoner would become eligible for parole after one third of it is only a partial safeguard, since the judge who wanted to ensure that he was not released for, say, 10 years could do so by passing a 30-year sentence, with only the Court of Appeal (Criminal Division) to restrain or correct him.[2] We consider that this improper incentive might best be removed by increasing the flexibility of the rules governing eligibility for parole. *We therefore recommend that a prisoner receiving a determinate sentence in excess of the new maxima should be eligible for parole after serving one third of it or the maximum ordinary sentence he could have received under our proposals in Chapter 9, whichever is the less.* This would not imply that he should be released at that date; it would merely mean that the sentencing court could not tie the hands of the Parole Board for longer than that period. To take our previous example, a rapist receiving a determinate sentence of 30 years would become

---

[1] See paragraph 233.

[2] The other objection that such a system could be abused for political purposes under an undemocratic regime can be answered by pointing out that under such a regime any statutory protection against it could easily be removed.

eligible for parole after seven years (the new maximum penalty for rape) instead of 10 years as now, and his maximum liability, assuming normal remission, would be 20 years' imprisonment. One feature of this proposal is that it forges a link between the sentencing practice adopted in relation to the ordinary offender and that adopted in relation to the exceptional offender: where the exceptional sentence is more than three times the ordinary maximum, the maximum for the ordinary case becomes the minimum for the exceptional case.

215. Under present practice, paroled prisoners are subject to supervision and recall up to the point when two thirds of their sentence has elapsed when, with normal remission, they would expect to be released. Life-sentence prisoners are, however, subject to supervision and recall for the remainder of their natural lives. We recognise, therefore, that in counselling a reduction in the use of the life sentence for non-homicide offences we should be reducing the effectiveness of this additional safeguard in the case of the more serious offender. We feel that there is some justification, therefore, in the cause of protecting the public, in specifying periods of supervision longer for the exceptional than for the ordinary offender and accordingly *we recommend that a prisoner who receives a determinate sentence in excess of the new maxima should be subject to a licence involving supervision by the probation and after-care service and the possibility of recall to prison until his total nominal sentence has expired.*

216. The imposition of a sentence in excess of the new maxima, under powers that are subject to no statutory limit, is a serious matter. Those who received such a sentence would fall into a special category, and their cases should always be reviewed by the Court of Appeal (Criminal Division), without the procedure of making an initial application to the single judge for leave to appeal. *We therefore recommend that a prisoner subject to a sentence in excess of the new maxima should be entitled to legal aid for an application for leave to appeal.* The effect of this recommendation will be to ensure that his application for leave to appeal can be heard direct by the full court, before whom he will be legally represented.

217. The powers we now propose for exceeding the new maxima are not designed to replace the extended sentence, whose abolition we have recommended in paragraph 115. They are not concerned, as was the extended sentence, with mere persistence in crime; their concern is with the exceptional offender. In this respect, they are designed to fulfil the original intentions of the proponents of extended sentences—that is, the control of the "real menaces" delineated by the 1965 White Paper (see paragraph 106).

Consecutive sentences

218. We were well aware that the distinction we have carefully drawn between the sentencing powers applicable to the ordinary offender and those applicable to the exceptional offender could be eroded by an untrammelled approach to consecutive sentencing. It would, in theory at least, be possible for a sentence in excess of the new maxima to be built up by an accumulation of a number of

consecutive sentences[1] for ordinary offences without any recourse to the criterion we have laid down in paragraph 207. The application to our scheme of the established principles which today govern consecutive sentencing will, however, serve to ensure that such a situation does not arise.

219. There are two fundamental principles that currently guide the courts in their use of consecutive sentences (the case-law upon which they are based is set out in detail in Appendix M).[2] First, consecutive sentences cannot in general apply to offences arising out of the same transaction, or series of transactions. Where a number of offences are involved, this principle may effectively assist courts in deciding whether the case satisfies our criterion for exceeding the maxima. If more than one transaction is involved, the number of offences committed will be a relevant factor in that decision; where there is a single transaction, the number of offences will not be of relevance.

220. The second principle is that where a case qualifies for consecutive sentencing, the total sentence passed should not be excessive. This normally means that a string of offences should not result in a total period in prison longer than would be served for a bad example of a very grave crime, such as murder. Where a number of grave offences are concerned, the case will almost certainly qualify to exceed the new maxima we have proposed. Where the offences do not fall within the category of really grave crime, and are therefore less likely to satisfy our criterion, *we recommend that the second principle, safeguarding against an excessive total sentence, should apply in the shape of the following rules:*

(i) sentences passed on the same occasion for a number of offences should not in total exceed the maximum that could have been imposed for the most serious of the offences, unless the criterion for exceeding the maximum is satisfied;

(ii) one or more sentences passed on an offender already subject to a term of imprisonment should not increase the total term to which he is subject to a length which exceeds the maximum that could have been imposed for the most serious of the offences dealt with by any of the sentences involved, unless on the occasion when he is last dealt with the criterion for exceeding the maximum is satisfied; and

(iii) a suspended sentence should not be ordered to take effect in such a manner as to make the offender subject to imprisonment which in total exceeds the maximum that could have been imposed for the most serious of the offences for which the suspended sentence was passed or which gave rise to the power to activate it, unless in regard to the latter the criterion for exceeding the maximum is satisfied.

---

[1] Although this can be done now in relation to existing maxima, the practice has been disapproved by the Court of Appeal: "We know that the maximum sentences which can be imposed sometimes leave the Court with the feeling that its powers of punishment are inadequate, but feelings of frustration must not, in our judgment, be obviated generally speaking by the imposition of consecutive sentences". *R v Giffin* No. 1447/B/74, 8 July 1974.

[2] For a more detailed account, see *Sentencing the Multiple Offender: Concurrent and Consecutive Sentences* by Michael Newark, Alec Samuels and Stephen White, *Northern Ireland Legal Quarterly*, Vol. 23, No. 2, Summer 1972, page 133.

We are confident that the application of these three ground rules will support the present philosophy of consecutive sentencing and, at the same time, ensure the viability of our new scheme of sentencing, both in the ordinary and the exceptional case.

CHAPTER 11

LIFE IMPRISONMENT

Introduction

221. The sentence of imprisonment for life is the mandatory penalty for murder.[1] It is also the maximum penalty for manslaughter[2] and for a number of non-homicide offences. (We list in Appendix N offences for which life imprisonment is the statutory or common law penalty.) The effect of the life sentence is not merely to mark out the seriousness of the offence but also to transfer from the courts to the Executive, on recommendation by the Parole Board, the determination of the time to be spent by the offender in custody. In our review, we considered the validity of indeterminacy as a principle in sentencing, and the more specific question whether life imprisonment (or another form of indeterminate penalty) should play a part in our proposals for exceeding the new maxima, in addition to the power recommended in the previous chapter for determinate sentencing without limit. We also considered the distinct question of the fixed penalty of life imprisonment for murder. This is a mandatory, and not a maximum, sentence; as such, it does not fall squarely within our terms of reference. Since it need not affect our new scheme of sentencing, we have dealt with it separately in the first chapter of the next section of our report.

The size of the problem

222. Until the mid-1960s, the imposition of sentences of life imprisonment had almost invariably been confined to convictions for murder[3] and, since 1957, for manslaughter on the grounds of diminished responsibility.[4] For other types of manslaughter and other non-homicide offences which carry the penalty of life imprisonment, the courts had rarely imposed (and in respect of many crimes, not at all in recent times) a sentence of life imprisonment. But in the late 1960s, a few life-carrying non-homicide offences attracted a comparatively high proportion of the total number of life sentences imposed by the courts. From 1958 to 1965, the proportion of those sentenced to life imprisonment who had

---

[1] It is also the mandatory penalty for genocide offences involving killing, and the recommendations on the penalty for murder in this report apply equally to such offences.

[2] Manslaughter is categorised for our purposes to include infanticide. In this, we have followed the annual *Criminal Statistics* by classifying as homicide the three offences of murder, manslaughter and infanticide. Child destruction and death by dangerous driving (now death by reckless driving under the terms of the Criminal Law Act 1977) have never been included in the *Criminal Statistics* as homicide offences.

[3] Until 1965, those serving life imprisonment for murder (and, after 1957, capital murder) had had their death sentences commuted under the prerogative power of mercy. After the Homicide Act 1957, all those convicted of non-capital murder were automatically sentenced to life imprisonment.

[4] The reduction of the offence of murder to manslaughter, on the grounds that the killer was suffering from mental incapacity such as to have substantially impaired his mental responsibility, was introduced into English law by section 2 of the Homicide Act 1957.

committed non-homicide offences varied between nought and 6%; whereas from 1966 to 1976, the proportion ranged from 10% to 26% (see Appendix O, Table 1).

223. Since the Homicide Act 1957, the "lifer" population of the prisons has increased tenfold. Since 1965, this growth has reflected, to some extent, increased numbers of persons sentenced for non-homicide offences, and is only in part due to the abolition of the death penalty, which naturally led to some (although small) increase in life sentences for murder. On 31 December 1957, there were 122 persons serving life sentences; on 31 December 1976, there were 1,257[1] (see Appendix O, Table 2). The estimates of the Prison Department are that, at the present rate of increase, the lifer population is likely to reach 1,500 by 1980. Of the present "lifer" population of 1,257, 25% are serving life sentences for offences other than murder, of whom less than half were convicted of manslaughter and the rest of non-homicide offences (see Appendix O, Table 3). The non-homicide offences that most often attracted a life sentence were rape, arson, grievous bodily harm, buggery and armed robbery (see Appendix O, Table 1).

The length of periods in custody

224. One striking disadvantage of the life sentence in our view is the confusion caused by the difference between the description "life" and the period which a prisoner so sentenced actually spends in custody. On the one hand, the imposition of the life sentence for a homicide offence has a powerful symbolic significance, indicating that those who take life should permanently place their own liberty at the disposal of the State. The practical demonstration of this theory is to be found in the fact that all life-sentence prisoners remain on licence for life and are therefore subject to recall to prison at any time until they die. On the other hand, this symbolic effect is diminished by the widely, and erroneously, held view that a life sentence in actuality means only about nine years in prison. In this case, a concentration on the average sentence served tends to obscure the fact that some prisoners spend longer in custody than the average and that nine years of actual incarceration (taking account of remission and parole) represents a much longer nominal sentence.[2]

225. People serving life sentences have died in prison before being given a definite release date, but there is no recorded case in which a positive decision

---

[1] The figure for 1976 includes 29 recalls; that for 1957 does not include recalls. The latest provisional figure for 31 December 1977 is 1,350.

[2] For an official statement (albeit at an earlier period) of the significance of the "average" period served, see the letter of 4 July 1961 from the Home Secretary, Mr. R. A. Butler, to Edward Gardner QC, MP, reproduced in the Appendices to *A Calendar of Murder* by Terence Morris and Louis Blom-Cooper (Michael Joseph, 1964), pages 370–2. The Court of Appeal in a recent case seems to have concluded that a determinate sentence of 15 years is more severe than the normal life sentence: ". . . although technically speaking a sentence of life imprisonment must . . . be construed as a more severe sentence than any fixed term, as a matter of practical reality it may well be that a fixed term as long as fifteen years will turn out to be a more severe penalty than would have been likely to be the case with an indeterminate sentence"—*R* v *Handoll*, No. 4858/B/77, 9 February 1978.

has been taken that a person shall be kept in prison until he dies.[1] It is difficult to draw any inferences about the length of the periods to be served by life-sentence prisoners in the future from the statistics of those sentences served in the past. The great majority of prisoners released from life sentences to date were sentenced before 1965. The abolition in that year of capital punishment for murder has changed the picture, since those who would previously have received the death penalty are now sentenced to life imprisonment. It is rather too early to make any firm predictions as to how long the post-1965 life-sentence prisoner is likely to spend in prison. With this important reservation in mind, it is nevertheless interesting to note that of those released in the last 20 years, four fifths were kept in prison for fewer than 11 years and most of these (69%) were in fact released after serving between eight and 11 years. Many of the remaining fifth have stayed in prison for very long periods; four prisoners released in recent years had to serve longer than 20 years. It has only been possible to make limited comparisons between the length of time served by non-homicide life-sentence prisoners and lifers who had committed murder or manslaughter—nine non-homicide lifers have to date served 10 years or more—but we assume that non-homicide lifers would tend not to serve on average quite as long a time as murderers, the majority of whom were released within eight to 11 years (see Appendix O, Table 4). The confusion about the practical significance of the sentence is one strong argument for its abolition from a logical sentencing system, or at least for a change of name. We have, however, concluded that in this difficult area, where public feelings play a particularly prominent part in determining social policy, a neat, logical solution is not necessarily the right one.

The disadvantages of indeterminate sentences

226. As a Council, while in favour of flexible release powers (such as parole), we are not attracted to wholly indeterminate sentences, notably because of their effects upon the individual prisoner. Long-term prisoners often become introverted and highly institutionalised. The very indeterminacy of his sentence can only increase the insecurity of the life-sentence prisoner whose anxiety, as recent research shows, appears to increase considerably after the "normal" release point is passed.[2] Even a prisoner convicted of a domestic murder with many mitigating features, who is ultimately released after five years, can never be absolutely certain until he receives his release date that he will not be incarcerated for a much longer period. A realistic determinate sentence, where it is

---

[1] The case which has perhaps come closest to that position is that of *R* v *Skingle* at Oxford Assizes on 15 October 1971 when Mr. Justice Chapman, in making a recommendation of a minimum period to be served for the crime of murder, stated: "The law only allows me to pass sentence of imprisonment for life. My recommendation to the Home Secretary will be that those dreadful words I have just used should have their awful, dreadful meaning. In other words life should mean life". This was probably not a legal recommendation, but since there is no right of appeal against a recommendation the matter was never tested. In any event, a minimum recommendation, which in many cases is mistakenly regarded by the public and the media as equivalent to a determinate sentence, does not bind either the Parole Board or the Home Secretary in deciding the date of the prisoner's release. A number of other judges in passing sentence have made informal remarks to the effect that in the particular case "life should mean life".

[2] Our views expressed here are supported by some interesting research carried out by the Home Office Research Unit on *Life-Sentence Prisoners: Psychological Changes During Sentence*. We are indebted to the author, Mr. R. J. Sapsford, for allowing us a sight of his report prior to its publication.

feasible for the court to impose it, would put an end to this needless uncertainty As we have indicated in paragraph 152, the life-sentence prisoner, with his typical alternation between optimism and pessimism as hopes of release wax and wane, becomes emotionally dependent on senior prison staff, and as the numbers increase this places a correspondingly severe managerial burden upon the prison service.

227. The mystique of the life sentence has led to the creation of a complex administrative structure which, while necessary when life sentences *have* to be passed, is hardly justified by many of the cases to which it applies. Unlike the parole procedure for prisoners serving determinate sentences, there is no fixed time at which the cases of life-sentence prisoners are referred to the Parole Board. The timing of the first formal review, which starts with the reference of the case to the local review committee at the prison, is decided by a joint committee consisting of the Chairman of the Parole Board, the Vice-Chairman (who is a High Court judge) and a psychiatrist member of the Board, together with two Home Office officials. The joint committee looks at the cases of all life-sentence prisoners when they have served about three to four years, and either fixes a date when the case should be referred to the local review committee and, subsequently, to the Parole Board or, if it is clear that the prisoner cannot be released for several years or it is not immediately clear how soon he might be released, asks for the case to be brought before it again after a specified interval. The Home Secretary can release a life-sentence prisoner only if he is recommended to do so by the Parole Board (though he is not bound to accept their recommendation) and he has also a statutory obligation to consult the Lord Chief Justice and the trial judge, if he is available, before doing so. In considering all life-sentence cases, the panel of the Board, which must include a High Court judge and a psychiatrist, has before it all relevant information, and may either recommend that the prisoner should be given a provisional date for his release or ask for the case to be reviewed again after a specified period. In considering the release of a life-sentence prisoner, the Home Secretary's principal concern is the safety of the public. He would not accept a recommendation from the Parole Board unless he were as satisfied as it is reasonably possible to be that the prisoner's release was unlikely to constitute a risk to the public. If the Home Secretary accepts the recommendation of the Parole Board that a life-sentence prisoner should be released, a provisional date for this is fixed some time ahead—usually a year, though it may be longer or shorter depending on the particular circumstances—and release is normally made conditional on the prisoner's good behaviour, often on his satisfactorily completing a period—usually six months—on the pre-release employment scheme and on his having suitable resettlement arrangements. The prisoner is released on a licence under the terms of which he may be recalled to prison at any time during the remainder of his life, should his conduct again give cause for concern. The licence is subject to conditions (which have to be agreed with the Parole Board, either generally or specifically) and will always require him to be supervised by a probation officer who submits reports periodically to the Home Office on the licensee's progress, drawing attention to any particular problems that might lead to consideration of the revocation of the licence (which would be an action needing the endorsement of the Parole Board). These administrative safeguards,

which are necessary and desirable to minimise injustice in the case of life sentences, would be largely unnecessary if determinate sentences were to be passed. They are made necessary by the assumption that all life-sentence cases have more complications than determinate sentence cases, whereas some life-sentence cases, those involving domestic murder, for example, tend to be more straightforward. All else apart, a reduction in the number of life sentences imposed (as we would advocate) would reduce this volume of work, with profit to all concerned.

228. In spite of our reluctance to retain any wholly indeterminate sentence within our new scheme of sentencing, we nevertheless felt bound to review the most commonly advocated indeterminate alternative to the life sentence. We considered the indeterminate reviewable sentence as recommended by the Butler Committee[1] for mentally abnormal offenders and by the Scottish Council on Crime[2] for all offenders, but in spite of its initial attraction, we feel there are arguments for not introducing into the penological dictionary yet another form of sentence, with a new label, unless there are very positive advantages to be gained which its precursors did not have. Although the indeterminate reviewable sentence would provide for more regular review of cases and has the advantage of shifting the onus of proof in a release situation, in practice it would be unlikely to operate very differently from the present life sentence. Its main attraction is a more acceptable and realistic name. Other indeterminate sentences which we considered, such as the renewable sentence,[3] have little more to offer and are open to positive objections. In any event, we have made provision for early review of sentence in our recommendation for changes in parole eligibility (see paragraph 214).

Homicide offences

229. Given that we dislike indeterminate sentences, we nevertheless recognise that life imprisonment is wholly appropriate as a maximum penalty for homicide offences, both because of its symbolic significance referred to above and because it marks out homicide as the most serious of the offences. The availability of the life sentence also obviates the need for the court, in the truly dangerous cases, to make instant judgments as to when the offender might safely be released. *We therefore propose that life imprisonment should be the penalty for murder[4] and manslaughter.* Nonetheless, we believe that there are many homicide cases where determinate sentences can be imposed without danger to the public, and if courts were to adopt the policy of determinate sentencing wherever possible, the numbers of life-sentence prisoners would be greatly reduced. It is partly for this reason that we advocate in the next chapter the abolition of the mandatory element in the penalty for murder.

---

[1] Cmnd. 6244, paragraph 4.39–4.45.

[2] In its report *Crime and the Prevention of Crime* (HMSO, 1975), Chapter 4: section 2: Appendix 5.

[3] This would involve the identification of dangerous prisoners in prison and the power to extend their period of detention on completion of a determinate sentence. It was also considered and rejected by the Butler Committee in paragraph 4.37 of its report.

[4] The question whether it should be the mandatory or maximum penalty for murder is discussed in Chapter 12.

Non-homicide offences

230. We referred in paragraphs 222 and 223 to the growth in the life-sentence population as a result of the increased use of that sentence in respect of those non-homicide offences for which life imprisonment is the maximum penalty. And we noted how infrequently the sentence had been used for non-homicide cases until 1967. We found this puzzling, because there had been no legislative change that could have directly affected the courts' sentencing policy towards the use of life imprisonment. Before we made any recommendations, therefore, we thought it sensible to explore the reasons for this change in judicial practice.[1]

231. We ultimately concluded that there must have been a shift in judicial policy towards the use of the life sentence that had the consequence of putting the total numbers up so sharply.[2] Accordingly we looked at the decisions of the Court of Appeal over the last 30 years to discern the policy of the courts over that period, and discover whether there has been some policy change in the last 10 years. The results of this study are set out in detail in Appendix P. Our conclusion is that there has indeed been a distinct shift in policy as declared by some divisions of the Court of Appeal. Until the late 1960s, the principle was that if the criminal events that gave rise to the conviction of a life-carrying offence were not in the first rank of seriousness then a life sentence was always inappropriate, even though the offender disclosed to the court a propensity to dangerousness. The relaxation of an essential criterion, that the offence must be of the grave kind, has undoubtedly led the courts to resort to life imprisonment where in earlier days they would not have countenanced it. There has also been a tendency to broaden the other criterion for using the life sentence. Until recent years, the courts have said that it was necessary to show that the offender was suffering from a mental disorder that indicated he should not be released before successful psychiatric treatment had been undertaken; and that this required decisions from the doctors which would be assisted by the indeterminacy of the life sentence. That criterion has been extended to cover not only the offender who may be suffering from some recognisable, treatable mental condition but also the offender whose unstable character indicates a likely repetition of his offence.

232. Since, as we have already said, we do not favour wholly indeterminate sentences, we should, in any neatly logical sentencing system, have wished to see the complete disappearance of the power to impose life imprisonment for all non-homicide offences. This would have helped to reinforce the feeling that many people share that homicide should be treated as a crime apart. A life sentence is not in most cases appropriate to the gravity of the non-homicide offence—a view we share with many life-sentence prisoners convicted of non-homicide offences, who feel themselves harshly treated on the ground that such an extreme penalty should properly be reserved for those who kill unlawfully. But, in the event, the most we have felt able to propose is the abolition of life imprisonment *as a maximum penalty* for all the non-homicide offences to

---

[1] It is not, we think, wholly a reaction to the failure of mental hospitals to cater satisfactorily for the mentally abnormal offender. Our researches showed that only a small fraction of non-homicide lifers had previously received a disposal under the Mental Health Act 1959.

[2] We noted with interest that an internal study by the Home Office Research Unit had reached the same tentative conclusion.

which it at present applies, and the substitution of the new maxima in Appendix A, which we have calculated on the basis of our 90% rule.

233. The power to impose determinate sentences of any length when exceeding the new maxima will apply to these offences as to the others in our scheme. We recognise, however, that there will be a few cases—for instance, the psychopath convicted of a number of offences of rape—where the gravity of the offence and the mental instability of the offender raise acute problems. In such cases it is often extremely difficult for the Executive, after some years' observation of the offender in prison, to decide when it will be safe to release him; even more difficult is it for a court to predict a suitable release date on the basis of the information provided at the trial. We therefore accept that where life imprisonment is currently used by the courts in non-homicide cases it should continue to be available in future, as the alternative to a determinate sentence when exceeding the maxima. The test of whether it should be retained would be whether courts have found a need to impose it over a recent finite period of time—the last 10 years. *We recommend that the power to impose a sentence of life imprisonment should be abolished for all non-homicide offences, except those for which a sentence of life imprisonment has been imposed in the 10 years preceding the implementation of this recommendation, or those newly enacted within the same period of 10 years.* Thus, if our recommendations in this report were to be implemented tomorrow, life imprisonment would be retained as the maximum penalty for murder and manslaughter and as an alternative penalty when exceeding the new maxima in the case of the following offences:

Offences in respect of which life sentences have been imposed in the last 10 years	*Offences newly enacted within the last 10 years*
Serious wounding	Possessing firearms with intent to endanger life
Buggery	
Rape	Using firearms with intent to resist arrest
Incest	
Unlawful sexual intercourse with a girl under 13	Hijacking an aircraft in flight
Aggravated burglary	Destroying, damaging or endangering aircraft
Robbery	Biological weapons offences.
Arson	
Criminal damage endangering life	
Kidnapping	

For all other offences at present carrying life imprisonment, courts would have power, as recommended in paragraph 213, to impose a determinate sentence of any length where the new maxima were exceeded. For the non-homicide offences listed above, *we recommend that when a sentence of life imprisonment has not been imposed for a particular offence in the course of 10 years, the power to impose a sentence of life imprisonment for that offence should lapse.*

234. Although we thus propose to retain life imprisonment for those offences for which it is currently imposed, we should welcome a reconsideration of the recent sentencing practice of the courts. We do not support the concept of the "merciful" life sentence. Our own experience tells us that the natural conservatism of any

system of executive release is likely, taken overall, to result in longer periods in custody than the court might have intended to impose. If a court is undecided whether to impose a determinate sentence or a life sentence, the more "merciful" course will, in our view, generally be the imposition of the determinate sentence. Since the life sentence must be retained for some non-homicide cases, we consider that its use should be more restricted than it has been in recent years. In our view, this would mean that life imprisonment should be imposed only in very serious cases (in the non-homicide cases, the criterion for exceeding the maxima would, of course, first have to be satisfied); it should never be imposed "in mercy"; and, where questions of the mental disability of the offender arise, it should be imposed only in cases involving a serious psychological or personality disorder or a dangerous instability of character. This would indicate that we prefer the case-law evolved by the courts in the 1950s and 60s. That earlier jurisprudence accords with our view of the proper use of life imprisonment. Accordingly, we propose that the courts should consider uniform adherence to that jurisprudence.

CHAPTER 12

THE PENALTY FOR MURDER

235. We recommended in the previous chapter that life imprisonment should remain the penalty for murder and manslaughter, and that it should continue to be available to the courts when exceeding the new maxima for a number of non-homicide offences. There remains the specific question whether life imprisonment should continue to be the *mandatory* penalty for murder, or whether it should become the *maximum* penalty, thus permitting the imposition of determinate sentences of any length for the offence. This question is not crucial to our general consideration of maximum penalties and the extent to which they provide a valid guide to sentencing practice. Our main proposals could be implemented without any change in the mandatory penalty for murder and, since any such change might well be regarded as controversial and not demand early consideration, we would not wish the recommendations made in this chapter to prejudice the substantive proposals made elsewhere in this report. Nevertheless, we considered the distinction between a mandatory and a maximum sentence to be too germane to our terms of reference to enable us to ignore it and this chapter therefore examines the arguments both for and against the retention of the mandatory element. We were aware that the Criminal Law Revision Committee is currently considering the penalty for murder as part of its review of offences against the person and we have been kept informed of its thinking, but we saw no reason why this should deter us from expressing our own views.

The case for the mandatory penalty

236. The mandatory penalty of life imprisonment was substituted for the death penalty by the Murder (Abolition of Death Penalty) Act 1965. The Government at that time supported the new penalty essentially on two grounds: that murder was a unique offence and should be marked by a unique penalty; and that to permit determinate sentencing for the offence could be risky, since there might be cases in which the Home Secretary would have to release a prisoner who had served a determinate sentence, less remission, even though he might feel that it was unsafe to do so.

237. One of the arguments of those who believe that murder merits a unique penalty is that the mandatory life sentence reflects the retributive view that anyone who murders another must place his life at the disposal of the State to the extent that both his release and his liberty to remain at large will always be subject to executive decision. This view is usually associated with the argument that to sentence murderers in the same way as other offenders would be to devalue murder as an offence and to reduce the deterrent effect of the existing penalty.

238. Another argument in favour of the mandatory element is that acts of murder can arouse a good deal of public passion and indignation which would attract more than usual interest to apparent discrepancies in sentencing decisions and tend to bring the administration of justice into undesirable public controversy. This, it is argued, would be likely to cause particular difficulty in what are considered the less culpable types of homicide, where a judge might think it appropriate to pass a shorter sentence than in a bad case of, for instance, robbery, but would immediately become susceptible to the accusation that the courts care more for property than for lives.

239. It is also argued that the absence of the mandatory element in the penalty for murder might actually lead (as the result of public attitudes to the crime of murder) to a situation in which the least dangerous of murderers might remain in custody longer as a result of relative determinate sentencing than they would have done if sentenced to life imprisonment. A related objection to the abolition of the mandatory sentence is that it would lead to over-long sentences in very serious cases. The Criminal Law Revision Committee recognised the strength of these arguments in its Twelfth Report on the *Penalty for Murder*,[1] where it proposed the retention of the mandatory penalty essentially because the flexibility of the sentence at the release stage both safeguarded the public against the unavoidable release of a prisoner who was still considered dangerous and enabled the release of prisoners convicted of less culpable crimes after only a relatively short period in prison.

240. We acknowledge that this is a difficult and complex issue upon which opinions are bound to vary and we respect the views of those who reach a different conclusion from ourselves. Nevertheless, we do not find the arguments cited above convincing. We are extremely doubtful whether the retention of the mandatory element is of much practical effect in marking out murder as a crime apart. The *Criminal Statistics* for 1976 show that while 102 people were sentenced to life imprisonment for murder and attempted murder in that year, 21 offenders received the same sentence for manslaughter and 23 for various non-homicide offences. In terms of the effective sentence imposed, the uniqueness of the penalty for murder is not therefore immediately apparent, and we question whether public awareness of the mandatory element is great enough either to make the penalty appear unique or to give it any special deterrent effect. If our proposals in Chapter 11 were accepted and new maximum penalties were introduced for all non-homicide offences now carrying life imprisonment, with the life sentence to be used only in the limited circumstances described in that chapter, we believe that murder could be sufficiently marked out by the fact that it would be the only offence, except for manslaughter, for which the new maximum penalty would be the life sentence without any requirement to justify exceeding a determinate maximum. We recognise that this solution does not meet the objections of those who believe in the uniform application of the retributive principle of a life for a life; this reflects a fundamental difference of opinion to which we do not believe there can be any solution.

241. The fear that if judges had sentencing discretion in murder cases they would become embroiled in public controversy about disparities in sentencing

---

[1] Cmnd. 5184. January 1973.

for murder is speculative and, we think, exaggerated. Any great inconsistency in sentencing murderers would be subject to the overriding control of the Court of Appeal (Criminal Division) (to the extent that it might regard some sentences as excessive) and in the longer term it would be affected by judicial practice, sentencing conferences and other forms of judicial consultation. We can see no reason why sentences for murder should raise any greater controversy than sentences for manslaughter where the issues involved often differ very little from those in murder cases and yet judges make use of the whole range of sentences.

242. The argument that dangerous offenders could be released too soon under a determinate sentencing system does not seem to us to be persuasive since the life sentence will still be available whenever it is considered appropriate and there is no reason to believe that judges would not continue to use it in potentially dangerous cases. The reverse argument, that discretionary sentencing could lead to longer periods in custody in the less culpable cases or, indeed, inordinately long determinate sentences in the most serious cases, is one on which no-one can be dogmatic. We think it probable that a system of executive release will always err on the side of caution and that, certainly in the less culpable cases, an indeterminate sentence is likely to produce a longer period in custody than a determinate one. But the danger of an over-long determinate sentence in any case is alleviated by the existence of the Parole Board with its power to consider release after only one third of a sentence has been served, and in the case of very long determinate sentences we would assume that the Court of Appeal would exercise its influence to discourage the imposition of sentences longer than, say, 25-30 years. A further safeguard, which we recommend in paragraph 254, would be the establishment of parole eligibility in homicide cases at one third of the sentence or 10 years, whichever is the shorter. This would also act as a disincentive to the courts to impose sentences of a very great length. The possible effects on sentencing practice of the abolition of the mandatory element in the penalty for murder are discussed at greater length in paragraphs 251-5.

The case for change

243. In addition to the negative arguments already cited, we see a number of positive arguments to justify the abolition of the mandatory element in the penalty for murder. The Criminal Law Revision Committee rightly recognised that the main advantage to be derived from the mandatory life sentence is its flexibility in providing the releasing authorities with the freedom to gauge the public interest and the needs of the offender throughout the period of his imprisonment and after release. The prison service and the Parole Board can take account of continuing observation of the prisoner's development in prison and the Board can monitor his behaviour while on licence and, if necessary, recall him without recourse to the courts. These are powerful considerations in favour of the indeterminacy implicit in the life sentence. We do not, however, consider that they necessarily imply that the life sentence must be imposed indiscriminately on every person convicted of murder. Where the nature of the offence connotes dangerousness and there is evidence of a likely continued threat that it will be repeated, the life sentence may be the appropriate, indeed the only wise, sentence to pass. But for some murderers we think that there

are strong reasons for giving courts the power to pass fixed terms of imprisonment.

244. Although murder has been traditionally and distinctively considered the most serious crime, it is not a homogeneous offence but a crime of considerable variety. It ranges from deliberate cold-blooded killing in pursuit of purely selfish ends to what is commonly referred to as "mercy killing". Instead of automatically applying a single sentence to such an offence, we believe that sentences for murder should reflect this variety with correspondingly variable terms of imprisonment or, in the exceptional case, even with a non-custodial penalty. This is primarily because we do not think that anyone should, without the most specific justification, be subjected to the disadvantages which we see in indeterminate sentencing (see paragraph 226). It is also because we cannot believe that the problems of predicting future behaviour at the time of conviction are inherently more difficult in a murder case than in any other case where there is a measure of instability, or that judges are any less able to make predictions or to assess degrees of culpability in murder cases than in any others. But it is also because efforts to alleviate the harshness of the mandatory penalty have led to complications in legal proceedings for which we believe there can be no proper justification.

245. The efforts at alleviation to which we refer are, first of all, the two special defences of provocation and diminished responsibility which, if successful, reduce the conviction to manslaughter. Although a conviction for manslaughter may be considered less of a stigma than a conviction for murder, to the offender the important difference often is that the lesser conviction avoids the mandatory penalty. The jurisprudence that has developed out of this defence demonstrates the conceptual difficulties of seeking to mitigate a penal consequence via the substantive law. Provocation may be a factor in any crime; it can and does properly affect the sentence passed on the offender, but only in this one case does it reduce the finding of guilt to a lesser offence. Similarly, the legal concept which enables the defence of diminished responsibility, under section 2 of the Homicide Act 1957, to reduce the crime of murder to manslaughter, creates difficulties. If the mental incapacity is not sufficient to negative the requisite mental element for murder, there are problems in describing the offence as any other crime. If judges had discretion in sentencing, the issues of provocation and diminished responsibility could be considered in their proper place, as mitigating factors in the sentencing process.

246. Another similar effort at alleviation was the tentative proposal by the Criminal Law Revision Committee[1] to create a new crime of "mercy killing" with a maximum penalty of two years' imprisonment. While we wholly sympathise with the motives of the Criminal Law Revision Committee in making this proposal, because we share the view that someone who kills out of compassion should not be treated in the same way as other murderers, we also appreciate the reasons why the suggestion was widely criticised, particularly by legal and ecclesiastical commentators. We are convinced that the way to accommodate cases of this kind is not to create a new offence, but to abolish the mandatory

---

[1] In its *Working Paper on Offences against the Person*, paragraphs 79–87.

element in the murder penalty so that the latter may take full account of all mitigating circumstances.

247. The natural impulse to relieve people convicted of murder of the severe penal consequences where their offence has in it major mitigating circumstances and a lessening in the full rigour of criminal responsibility is considered apt, is, in our view, the strongest argument for removing the mandatory element from the penalty of life imprisonment. If the mandatory element were to be removed, we would hope that mitigating factors in cases of mental incapacity, provocation, self-defence, or mercy killing could all be accommodated within the range of non-custodial disposals and custodial disposals of varying lengths.

248. In case it should be thought that the idea of abolishing the mandatory element is peculiar to this Council and almost as revolutionary as the abolition of the death penalty which preceded it, it may be useful to set this proposal in its proper perspective by pointing out that our advocacy of it is by no means new.

249. During the protracted debates on the Murder (Abolition of Death Penalty) Bill throughout 1965 there was expressed, both in and out of Parliament, a strong body of opinion calling for an unfettered discretion in the sentencing of persons convicted of murder. Indeed, the inclusion in the 1965 Act of the power to make minimum recommendations represented a compromise between the fixed penalty and the unfettered discretion. At the Committee Stage of the Bill in the House of Lords, the Lord Chief Justice, Lord Parker, moved an amendment whereby life imprisonment would have become the maximum penalty for murder. In the course of his speech he said:

> "I dislike a fixed sentence, and now that it is proposed to abolish the fixed sentence of the death penalty I do not wish to see another fixed sentence in its place. In a fixed sentence there is no room for any matters of mitigation. . . I do not think that any Home Secretary would claim to have a monopoly of the quality of mercy. Certainly I think that judges have this quality, and wish to exercise it."

Lord Parker went on to claim that his proposal would also

> "enable the judge to pass a sentence which marks the seriousness of the crime and signifies the public feeling of revulsion."[1]

His amendment was accepted by 80 votes to 78. All the peers who held high judicial office and voted were in favour of the amendment,[2] except the Lord Chancellor, Lord Gardiner, who voted against it in accordance with Government policy. And it was opposition from the Government which paved the way for the later abandonment of this vote in favour of discretionary sentencing.

---

[1] House of Lords Official Report, Vol. 268, Cols. 1213–14. 27 July 1965. We understand that Lord Parker later intimated to the Criminal Law Revision Committee that he had revised his opinion, but, nevertheless, the force of the arguments he enunciated at the time remains.

[2] They were Lord Denning, the Master of the Rolls, Lord Guest, Lord Hodson, Lord Morris of Borth-y-Gest, Lord Pearson, Lord Reid and Lord Wilberforce. Viscount Dilhorne, a former Conservative Lord Chancellor, and subsequently made a Law Lord, also voted for the amendment. The support for Lord Parker's amendment was irrespective of whether the judicial peers were abolitionists or retentionists.

250. More recently, the Butler Committee in its report on Mentally Abnormal Offenders,[1] while acknowledging that the question of the mandatory life sentence for murder was for the Criminal Law Revision Committee and not for it to consider, thought it necessary to comment on the mandatory sentence because of its implications for the legal provisions on diminished responsibility and infanticide. The Butler Committee expressed the view that

> "many in the legal profession and other professions associated with the law believe in the abolition of the mandatory life sentence and in giving the courts the widest possible discretionary powers in sentencing. Our impression is that such a change is seldom advocated publicly because of the fear that it will be unlikely to commend itself to public opinion."[2]

The report goes on to list a number of arguments against the mandatory life sentence, with all of which we agree.[3]

Effects on sentencing practice

251. The theoretical arguments so far advanced seem to us to weigh heavily in favour of the abolition of the mandatory element in the life sentence for murder, but even so we would hesitate to recommend it if we believed that it would have an adverse effect on the average length of prison sentences which, as we have previously made clear, we are anxious to reduce. When the original decision to make the life sentence mandatory for murder was reached in 1965, there were very few life-sentence prisoners other than those convicted of homicide offences, and the number of life-sentence prisoners then was one third of what it is today. There was also at that time no possibility of parole. If the pressure on the prison system then had been as it is today and if the parole scheme had existed, the decision might have been different; we now have to consider that decision in the light of the changed circumstances.

252. The first question to be asked is whether the abolition of the mandatory element would lead to a wholesale switch to determinate sentencing or whether the courts would continue to pass a life sentence in most cases of murder. We see no reason why judges should be particularly reluctant to impose determinate sentences for murder. They would have available to them the offender's social and medical history just as they do in any other case of serious crime and we are confident that they could make appropriate assessments as to sentence. The best guide to what might happen is perhaps the sentences passed in cases of manslaughter where, as we have already pointed out in paragraph 241, the issues involved often differ very little from those in murder cases and yet judges have full sentencing discretion. In 1976, 102 people were sentenced to life imprisonment for murder and attempted murder. Of the 92 people convicted of manslaughter under section 2 of the Homicide Act 1957 (diminished responsibility) only 20 received life sentences and of the 194 people convicted of other manslaughters only one was sentenced to life imprisonment. The comparatively rare use of life imprisonment indicates that judges readily exercise their

---

[1] Cmnd. 6244, paragraphs 19.8–19.16.
[2] *Ibid.*, paragraph 19.11.
[3] We were also interested by the New Zealand Criminal Law Reform Committee's recent *Report on Culpable Homicide* which likewise advocates abolition of the mandatory penalty. For a useful summary of the report, see [1978] Crim. L.R. 1–4.

discretionary powers while, nevertheless, feeling free to decide to leave the power of release to the Executive in those cases where indeterminacy is considered appropriate. It is not, however, possible to conclude from these figures that a similar pattern of life sentencing would emerge in respect of murder. It may be that the absence in murder cases of those factors which led to the reduced charge of manslaughter would mean that a larger proportion of murderers would be sentenced to life imprisonment or it may be that determinate sentences would be used in many borderline cases where, if the relevant factors could have been urged in mitigation instead of argued in defence, they would have led to a reduced penalty. There is no way of judging in advance which of these situations would be most likely.

253. On the assumption that abolition of the mandatory sentence would lead to some determinate sentencing, the second question is what effect this would have on the prison population. Again, on the analogy of the 1976 manslaughter figures, over half of the diminished responsibility cases were dealt with non-custodially (for example, by hospital orders, suspended sentences or probation) and of those convicted of other manslaughters more than a quarter were dealt with otherwise than by immediate terms of imprisonment. Of the 160 people sentenced to immediate imprisonment for manslaughter in 1976 (excluding the 21 life sentences) only 18 received sentences of more than seven years and 98 were sentenced to not more than four years' imprisonment. This suggests to us that some of those currently sentenced to life imprisonment for murder might be treated non-custodially, or receive short or medium-term prison sentences.

254. The likely length of determinate sentences for murder is entirely a matter for speculation. One hypothesis would be that sentences for murder would follow broadly the same range as sentences for manslaughter but with a greater preponderance of sentences over seven years. This would bring many of the less culpable murderers back into the community after fairly short periods, especially if they were granted parole, and would be unlikely to lead to much longer periods in custody for the most serious offenders than at present. Another possibility which cannot be ruled out is that courts, possibly influenced by the belief that under the present system nine years is the "average" length of time spent in custody, would pass sentences in the majority of cases which would ensure that an offender was not released before that time even with early parole, that is, in the 25–30 year bracket or even longer.[1] This could have the effect of increasing the average length of time spent in custody. As we have said in paragraph 242 above, we believe that the Court of Appeal (Criminal Division) and the Parole Board would between them reduce the possibility of an adverse effect of this kind. In order to guard against exceptionally long determinate sentences which might be passed primarily for their deterrent and retributive effect, we would suggest that every prisoner should become

---

[1] One proposal for avoiding very long determinate sentences was that any sentence of over, say, 20 years should be life. This could be applied not only to homicide offences where it would answer one of the arguments against the abolition of the mandatory sentence, that is, the possibility of very long sentences; it could also be extended to non-homicide offences for which life imprisonment is the maximum or even to all offences when the new maxima are exceeded. We concluded, however, that the relaxation of the restrictions on parole eligibility and the likely attitude of the Court of Appeal would act as sufficient safeguard against inordinately long sentences.

eligible for parole after 10 years in prison, even if he has not served one third of his sentence. Since 10 years is the level our 90% rule would produce for manslaughter cases (see footnote 2 on page 81), this proposal would be in accordance with our general recommendations for parole when the normal maximum sentence is exceeded (see paragraph 214).

255. Finally, we must ask when the life sentence would be likely to be imposed if it were no longer mandatory. We would hope that the courts would take account of the views expressed in paragraph 234 of this report and that life imprisonment would be reserved for those cases where both the gravity of the offence and the instability of the offender suggested that an indeterminate sentence was necessary for the protection of the public. The effect of this would probably be a presumption that any murderer given a life sentence should remain in custody longer than most of those given fixed sentences; the Parole Board and the Home Secretary would be bound to take account of the length of determinate sentences when deciding on release from life imprisonment and this, because life imprisonment would be restricted to the worst cases, would mean that the period served would be substantially longer than the average period at present. This, in our opinion, would increase, rather than diminish, public confidence in the life sentence.

256. It is clear from what is said above that the effect on sentencing practice of the abolition of the mandatory element in the penalty for murder cannot be predicted with any degree of certainty. This would, of course, be true of any change in sentencing policy and is, in our view, no reason for doing nothing. We believe that the arguments in paragraphs 243–50 are strong enough to justify abolishing the mandatory penalty in spite of this uncertainty; that the widespread discussion and consultation necessary before Parliament would take such action would leave the courts in little doubt as to the effects on sentencing practice that the change in policy would be expected to achieve; and that the judges could be relied upon to exercise their new discretion in such a way that no-one would be kept in custody any longer than was absolutely necessary for the protection of the public. We would therefore like to see life imprisonment become the *maximum* instead of the *mandatory* penalty for murder, with the safeguard that every prisoner receiving a determinate sentence for murder or manslaughter should be eligible for parole after serving 10 years, or one third of his sentence, whichever is the less. Our proposal has far-reaching consequences which, although we consider them desirable, we do not see as essential to our scheme for the revision of maximum penalties. Since the latter does not raise the same highly emotive issues as the mandatory penalty, we have thought it better to treat the two subjects separately and to stress that we would not wish our firm belief that the mandatory penalty should be abolished to interfere in any way with the general consideration of our scheme for maximum penalties.

Recommendations under section 1(2) of the 1965 Act

257. In considering the mandatory penalty, it was inevitable that we should examine the use made of section 1(2) of the Murder (Abolition of Death Penalty) Act 1965, which provides that on sentencing a person convicted of murder to life imprisonment, the court may at the same time declare the period which it recommends to the Secretary of State as the minimum period which should

elapse before the offender is released on licence. If it had been widely used, this power might have provided a useful indication of the length of determinate sentences likely to be passed in lieu of a life sentence. In fact, we discovered that it had been used in only 8 % of the total number of convictions for murder and that the minimum recommendations, ranging from 10 to 35 years, were inevitably regarded as marking out long periods of custody as an expression of public revulsion at the more serious cases.[1]

258. The introduction of this provision in the 1965 Act was at the time an acknowledgment that judges should have some effective say in the length of time that convicted murderers should spend in prison, and it is clear from the reports of the parliamentary proceedings[2] that the intention of Ministers was that courts would be able to recommend anything from a very short to a very long sentence. Indeed, the then Home Secretary, Sir Frank Soskice (now Lord Stow-Hill) expressly said that he did not believe that the power to recommend should be limited to cases where a long period of imprisonment was considered necessary.[3] It is clear that the use now made of the provision is not in accordance with the original intentions of Ministers and in view of this, as well as for the reasons given below, we consider that it should now be repealed.

259. The Criminal Law Revision Committee in its Twelfth Report expressed the view that the value of the power to make minimum recommendations depended on the fact that they are made exceptionally and not as a matter of routine.[4] If, as suggested in Scotland by the Committee under the chairmanship of Lord Emslie in 1972, a minimum period were recommended in every case,[5] such a recommendation would no longer be an indication of either strong mitigating or strong aggravating circumstances sufficient to warrant a public indication of the time the judge considered should be spent in custody, and it would be a very short step to conferring the power to pass a determinate sentence in those cases where indeterminacy was considered inappropriate. If, on the other hand, recommendations by the judiciary continue to be conceived as an appropriate method of expressing particular public revulsion, it is difficult to see why the use of the recommendation power is so apparently inconsistent. No recommendations were made, for instance, in such notorious cases as the Moors murders, the M62 coach bomb, the Hosein brothers, or the Birmingham IRA bombers, while in the Guildford public house bombings in 1975 formal recommendations were made in the case of two offenders, but in the case of the acknowledged leader there was only an informal indication that "life should mean life".

260. We believe that this inconsistency means that recommendations can be of little use to either the Home Secretary or the Parole Board in determining the appropriate date of release of a life-sentence prisoner. It has long been the practice of some trial judges, at the time of conviction, to communicate their views informally to the Home Secretary and the Home Secretary is required

---

[1] The Court of Appeal has indicated that no minimum period recommended should be for less than 12 years—*R* v *Flemming* (1973) 57 Cr. App. R. 524.
[2] House of Lords Official Report, Vol. 269, Col. 421. 5 August 1965.
[3] House of Commons Official Report, Vol. 718, Cols. 378–9. 28 October 1965.
[4] Cmnd. 5184, paragraphs 31–3.
[5] *The Penalties for Homicide*, Cmnd. 5137, November 1972, paragraph 92.

by section 2 of the 1965 Act to consult both the Lord Chief Justice and the trial judge (if available) before authorising release on licence. Three of our members who served on the Parole Board were emphatically of the view that the trial judge's informal comments at the time of conviction and the later-expressed views of the trial judge and the Lord Chief Justice are of much greater value to the Parole Board when considering a prisoner's release than any public recommendation. When the 1965 Act was passed, the Parole Board did not exist and Parliament's desire for judges to be able to indicate the need for an early review was an important factor in the discussions leading to the recommendation provision. Since the provision is not used to indicate when a short period of custody is considered appropriate and the Parole Board considers all cases at an early stage, we think that the other methods of assisting those who have to decide on the release of life-sentence prisoners are adequate and that the power to make a public recommendation is not only superfluous but, because of the inconsistency of its use, also undesirable. Whether or not the mandatory penalty for murder is abolished, *we therefore recommend that section 1(2) of the Murder (Abolition of Death Penalty) Act 1965 should be repealed.* The consultation at the time of release is at present statutory and we think it should remain so. Usually, it is at the time of release that the judge's views are most relevant; comment at the time of conviction is really needed only where the judge feels that the case should be considered even earlier than under the normal review procedure. In all other cases, we feel that judges should be free to express their views privately to the Home Secretary if they wish to, but that they should not be required to do so.

CHAPTER 13

SUSPENDED SENTENCES

261. We were asked to consider, as part of our terms of reference, the law governing the suspension of imprisonment and whether any changes needed to be made. We looked in particular at the possibility of suspending a part of a sentence. This idea generally reflects the latter part of our terms of reference which concerned the combination of other penalties with sentences of imprisonment with the aim of reducing sentence lengths. We looked therefore at suspended sentences not merely as a penalty in their own right, but also in conjunction with other forms of penalty.

262. The suspended sentence—the suspension of the *execution* of the whole or part of a sentence of imprisonment—is essentially a characteristic of foreign penal systems. Until the limited introduction of the penalty in the Criminal Justice Act 1967, the English penal system during the 20th century had preferred to develop sanctions designed to suspend the *imposition* of a sentence of imprisonment, primarily by the use of probation and conditional discharge. The suspended sentence began its career at the end of the last century in Belgium and France, and was introduced to weaken the rigid link between crime and punishment entrenched in the classical codes of penal law. One country after another adopted the Continental model, only latterly picking up the English solution of using supervision in the community as an alternative to imprisonment. Most countries now permit their courts to use one or more devices derived from probation as an alternative, or in addition, to the suspended sentence. Very commonly a regime of supervision or rehabilitation can accompany suspension. But the origins of such combination of penal orders are rooted in the simplicity of suspending execution of imprisonment so long as the offender does not re-offend during the period of suspension.

263. The suspended sentence had been the subject of limited discussion in England for some time before its introduction. It was rejected by the Advisory Council on the Treatment of Offenders in 1952 and again in 1957. The 1952 report did not mince its words: "The suspended sentence is wrong in principle and to a large extent impracticable. It should not be adopted, either in conjunction with probation or otherwise."[1] The issue was revived in the memoranda submitted by various bodies to the Royal Commission on the Penal System during 1965, in the context of a dramatic rise in the prison population. Thus it was adopted by the legislature in 1967 as part of a wider search for ways of reducing the numbers in prison. The acceptance of suspended sentences in the Criminal Justice Act 1967 was made against the background of no detailed examination of the use and development of the suspended sentence in the countries where it had originated, and in the context of competition with

---

[1] *Alternatives to Short Terms of Imprisonment*, Report of the Advisory Council on the Treatment of Offenders (HMSO, 1957), Appendix D, paragraph 23(b).

existing substitute for imprisonment, such as probation. The literature on the subject in the English language is meagre, to the point of demonstrating English penological isolation from non-Anglo-Saxon influences. Since 1971 there has appeared Marc Ancel's work *Suspended Sentence*,[1] but little else.[2]

264. The present law, contained in section 22 of the Powers of Criminal Courts Act 1973, provides that a court passing a sentence of imprisonment of not more than two years may order that the sentence shall not take effect unless, during a period specified in the order that must not be less than one year nor more than two years from the date of the order ("the operational period"), the offender commits another imprisonable offence. On convicting the offender of such an offence, the court is required by section 23 to order the full term of the suspended sentence to take effect, unless of the opinion that to do so would be unjust in view of all the circumstances that have arisen since the sentence was passed, including those of the fresh offence. The differences between the provisions now in force and those of the 1967 Act are that the maximum operational period was originally three years (not two) and suspension was mandatory in the case of most sentences of six months or less. Mandatory suspension was highly unpopular with the courts and was repealed by the Criminal Justice Act 1972, which also reduced the maximum operational period to two years.

265. We set out in Appendix Q a detailed statistical account of the operation of the suspended sentence since 1967. The accumulated evidence is not very encouraging. If the main object of the suspended sentence was to reduce the prison population, there are considerable doubts as to whether it has achieved this effect. It may even have *increased* the size of the prison population. One reason for this disappointing result is that courts, initially at least, misused the sanction by passing it on offenders who would not, but for the existence of the suspended sentence, have been given a custodial sentence.[3] Experience suggests that courts have passed suspended sentences greater in length than the sentences of immediate imprisonment they might otherwise have given, and when these have been activated in full the result has been a longer stay in custody for the offender.

266. This is not, of course, the whole story. The number of cases in which the suspended sentence enables courts to avoid the actual imprisonment of an offender who will never incur another prison sentence, while indicating at the same time that his offence *merits* imprisonment, is often overlooked by those who regard the suspended sentence as a failure. It has been pointed out[4] that if something like one third of suspended sentences are subsequently "breached", but only about three quarters of the breaches lead to immediate imprisonment, then roughly three quarters of offenders given suspended sentences are not imprisoned for the offences for which the suspended sentences were given.

---

[1] Heinemann, 1971.

[2] There are two valuable articles on the operation of the sanctions under the 1967 and 1972 Acts: *The Use of Suspended Sentences* by R. F. Sparks [1971] Crim. L.R. 384–401 and *Suspended Imprisonment* by Stephen White [1973] Crim. L.R. 7–11. There is also a review of the Israeli experience in *Suspended Sentences in Israel* by S. Shoham and M. Sandberg, *Crime and Delinquency*, Vol. 10, No. 1, January 1964, pages 74–83.

[3] Section 22(2) of the Powers of Criminal Courts Act 1973 prohibits a court from passing a suspended sentence unless the case appears to be one in which a sentence of imprisonment would otherwise have been imposed.

[4] See *Criminal Statistics, England and Wales* 1975, Cmnd. 6566, paragraph 4.32.

267. We have considered in detail the provisions governing suspended sentences in operation today, including the question of the length of the operational period, but have no major changes to propose. One small, but nonetheless useful, change we do propose concerns the use of suspended sentences in combination with certain financial penalties. We were reminded of a problem here by an appeal case[1] heard early in 1977 concerning an offender who had been given a two-year suspended sentence in conjunction with a compensation order for over £800 following conviction of theft from an hotel. He had subsequently re-offended and the suspended sentence was activated, leaving a problem in respect of the compensation order. The court decided, in line with the general view that no financial penalty should be imposed which will place an onerous obligation on the offender on his release from custody, to reduce the order to the amount (£15) already paid. We discuss in the next chapter the principles governing the imposition of a financial penalty in combination with a sentence of imprisonment. This particular case shows the difficulty of applying the principles to a suspended sentence; a financial order which may be realistic and properly made on the assumption that the offender will not serve the sentence may become unrealistic if the sentence is subsequently activated. The difficulty arises because the court activating the sentence has no power to vary the terms of the order. *We therefore recommend that a court activating a suspended sentence should be given power to review and vary any incidental orders requiring the payment of fines, compensation or costs passed at the time that the suspended sentence was imposed.*

Partial suspension

268. The provisions in the 1973 Act dealing with suspended sentences confer no power to suspend only a part of a sentence. During the course of our review, the Criminal Law Act 1977 has added such a power to the statute book. We thought that it would be useful to investigate the idea of partial suspension as a new sanction in the cause of reducing prison sentences. A number of the countries[2] whose systems of penalties we reviewed—notably France, Belgium, the Netherlands, Israel and the United States—have given power to their courts to suspend part only of a sentence, and the provision is widely used. The main penological arguments in favour of it are that it enables the court of trial to pronounce a sentence of imprisonment that in itself appears adequate and yet does not need to be fully executed. It has the merit over the wholly suspended sentence that it avoids the all-or-nothing situation. It also provides the court with a double deterrent effect—the deterrent element in actual custody and a postponed deterrence during the suspension period. Any deterrent effect in the suspended part of the sentence is enhanced by the immediately preceding experience of custody, which may well be more effective if the period of actual custody is sufficiently short, at least for the first offender to avoid acclimatisation to the prison ethos. In practical terms, partial suspension encourages the court to impose a shorter period of actual custody than it otherwise might, if it knows that on release from prison there will automatically be a further known period of contingent liability to imprisonment. At present, often the only way of offsetting the excessive mitigation inherent in suspending

---

[1] *R* v *Whenman* [1977] Crim. L.R. 430.
[2] It is interesting to note that Scotland has no power to suspend a sentence, either wholly or partially, but tends to rely upon deferment of sentence to fulfil a similar function.

the whole of the appropriate prison sentence is to add a substantial monetary penalty. The partially suspended sentence would allow the court, in cases where the offender cannot prospectively pay any substantial sum of money, to achieve an equitable result as between comparable offenders by suspending a portion (even a major portion) of the prison sentence.

269. Taking note of these positive arguments, at an early stage of our review we determined to recommend a new power to suspend part of a prison sentence. In addition to its purely penological merits, we thought that it might help to reduce the prison population. When the Criminal Law Bill was first presented in 1976, we even considered whether there might be advantage in issuing an interim report on the subject with a view to catching this early legislative opportunity; in the event, we decided that the only argument for producing an early report would be if the new power were likely to make a significant reduction in the prison population and, since we concluded that this was far from certain, we decided to leave the recommendation until our final report. This decision was overtaken by events when the Opposition tabled a new clause at the Commons Committee Stage of the Criminal Law Bill providing for partial suspension. The Government then undertook to bring forward its own provision, and we were asked for our views on what form it might take. Thus section 47 of the Criminal Law Act 1977, which now provides a power of partial suspension but is not yet in force, closely resembles the recommendation we should otherwise have made.

270. The new power differs from that governing wholly suspended sentences in a number of respects. It applies to sentences of six months to two years, thus imposing a lower limit to prevent the fragmentation of very short sentences. The amount of the sentence that a court can suspend is also circumscribed in two ways. First, a court must suspend a minimum of at least one quarter of the sentence, to ensure that the new power does not overlap with the power to grant parole, which effectively applies only to sentences of 18 months and over. We considered at length the complex problem of the interaction of a partially suspended sentence with parole, and concluded that no overlap between the two provisions could be countenanced, primarily because it would involve the coexistence of two separate liabilities to recall to prison; the suspension of a quarter of the maximum two-year sentence will ensure[1] that no such overlap takes place. Second, the maximum period a court may suspend is limited to three quarters of the sentence; this is designed to avoid a requirement to serve very short sentences of imprisonment with the consequent disruptive effects that a large number of such sentences would have on the prison administration. The operational period, during which the commission of an offence may lead to the activation of the suspended part of the sentence, is not one to two years as for full suspension, but the whole period of the original sentence.

271. When formulating our own proposals for the new sentence, we gave much thought to what period of imprisonment a person should be liable to serve on reconviction during the suspended period and what discretion the court should be given in activating a sentence. For a time, we seriously considered the

---

[1] Assuming that the prisoner serving two years is not paroled after having previously lost some remission, an almost inconceivable situation.

proposition that an offender's liability to imprisonment might diminish in length as the period of suspension progresses; that is, the liability to return to prison should be "used up" as the offender works his way through the suspended portion without committing further offences, as an incentive to continuing good behaviour. We ultimately decided, however, that there was something to be said for maintaining the full deterrent threat of activation uniformly throughout the period of suspension, and that the offender should be liable to serve (subject to remission) the whole of the suspended portion. The Criminal Law Act so provides.

272. The question of the court's discretion in activating a suspended sentence is a difficult one. The provision for activation of a wholly suspended sentence (see paragraph 264) represents a limited discretion; and if the court considers total activation would be unjust, the court can decide to activate part of the sentence, or extend the operational period, or do nothing. Under section 47 of the Criminal Law Act 1977, the court has again been given a limited discretion, but of a slightly different nature: if the court considers it would be unjust to activate the whole of the suspended portion, it must either activate a part or do nothing. For the partially suspended sentence, the discretion is wider. On the whole, we would have favoured conferring on the court a simple and complete discretion in the length of sentence it chose to activate (if it chose to activate at all), bearing particularly in mind that the offender has already served a period in custody for the original offence and, therefore, more flexibility is required in activation than would be the case for a sentence wholly suspended. The power in section 47 does, however, in practice provide a discretion almost as wide as that we would have proposed, and we would not therefore wish to see the legislation amended on that account.

273. The power in section 47 differs from the wholly suspended sentence in that it does not apply to offenders under 21 years of age. This was inevitable in view of the fact that the power applies to sentences from six months to two years and imprisonment, under the terms of section 3 of the Criminal Justice Act 1961, cannot be imposed on young adults (those aged 17 and under 21) for periods between six months and three years, except in certain special circumstances. This means that in broad terms only a six-month sentence could have attracted partial suspension for this age group, and to have made such a narrow provision would have been quite anomalous. A new situation will arise if the restrictions imposed by section 3 are lifted. We understand that the Government will shortly bring forward proposals for replacing the current system for young adults with a new sentence, based upon the custody and control order recommended by the Council in 1974,[1] but without its resource implications. This will provide an opportunity for this issue to be considered.

274. Partial suspension, as it has now been enacted, also differs from full suspension in not providing for the possibility of supervision by the probation and after-care service during the suspended portion, on the lines of the suspended sentence supervision order in section 26 of the Powers of Criminal Courts Act 1973. We considered whether the suspended portion might be subject to supervision on a discretionary basis, but concluded that the sanction of recall is what

---

[1] In its report on *Young Adult Offenders* (HMSO, 1974).

matters most in this context, and that the help of the probation and after-care service will be available in any case to those who wish to seek it on a voluntary basis. We also considered the idea of mandatory partial suspension of a fixed part of a sentence, particularly in the context of the first custodial sentence, but the experience of mandatory suspension between 1967 and 1972 was sufficient warning to us not to make such a recommendation in this instance.

275. Our initial enthusiasm for partial suspension was eroded not a little by some of the statements made about it in the debates on the Criminal Law Bill. We had always recognised that the new power might have the effect of encouraging sentencers to impose short periods of custody in cases where currently they would either not impose imprisonment, or would suspend the whole of a prison sentence. It is important to emphasize that we saw the role of the partially suspended sentence as an alternative to a full sentence of imprisonment and not to a wholly suspended sentence. The depiction of the sentence in the debates on the Criminal Law Bill as a "short, sharp shock" provision made us fear that it would be widely represented as an alternative to non-custodial penalties, with obvious and undesirable repercussions on the prison population. We were, to some extent, reassured by the firm statements from Home Office Ministers, both before and after the passing of the Act, that it should only be used as an alternative to imprisonment. This message, however, cannot be repeated too often or too loudly.

276. One of the criticisms of the introduction of suspended sentences in 1967, which we have intimated in paragraph 263, was that it was made without any deep discussion of the penological merits of the provision and without giving any guidance to the courts as to the kind of cases in which it might most effectively be used. We have therefore devoted the remainder of this chapter of our report to how we see the new provision operating in practice, following the principles established by the courts in the use of wholly suspended sentences.

277. The question affects magistrates' courts as much as the Crown Court. Most of our recommendations for new and reduced maximum penalties are likely to have only a very limited effect on the work of magistrates' courts[1] for which, of course, the relevant maximum sentence (normally six months) is determined by the limits of their jurisdiction. In the success or failure of partially suspended sentences, however, the way in which magistrates' courts exercise their new powers will undoubtedly play a significant part. Although partial suspension can apply only to sentences of at least six months, for this purpose two or more consecutive sentences passed on the same occasion are treated as a single term, so that two three-month or three two-month consecutive sentences would attract the power. As a result, magistrates' courts would not have to impose anything approaching the maximum for any individual offence before they could partially suspend; in the case of two or more indictable offences tried summarily (offences "triable either way" under the 1977 Act), they could do so although the total of the sentences they passed was only one half of the statutory maximum of 12 months available to them.

---

[1] See Appendix G.

278. Since 1967, courts have established certain principles which apply to suspended sentences. The basic principle is that they do not represent a "soft option"; before considering a suspended sentence the court must have eliminated the other possible courses, and reached the decision that the case is one for imprisonment.[1] Further, the Court of Appeal has made it plain that no question of a suspended sentence can arise for consideration at all until it has been decided not only that a sentence of imprisonment is necessary but also that its length, related to the offence, antecedents and all other relevant considerations, should be within the statutory limit for suspension; otherwise, the record of the sentence might give a quite misleading impression.[2] It follows that the mere fact that a sentence of imprisonment is suspended cannot justify its use when some alternative is appropriate, nor can it justify passing a sentence longer than it would have been if not suspended. Since a sentence of imprisonment only partially suspended is even more clearly a sentence of imprisonment than one wholly suspended, those principles and their consequences must apply to the exercise of the new power.

279. Accordingly, they would prevent its use instead of, for example, a fine or a probation order, with the sole object of giving the offender the lesson of spending a short period in prison (part of a sentence of at least six months) when otherwise the non-custodial course would have been taken. Similarly, they would make it wrong, in a case where a quite short term of imprisonment—of less than six months—would otherwise have been imposed, to pass a longer sentence of at least six months, so as to suspend the excess beyond what was really merited, to be held over the offender's head as a deterrent. These two statements, although negative in form, are in our view crucial, since failure to observe them in practice could make the scheme of partially suspended sentences self-defeating.

280. On the other hand, we think it important also to show in what circumstances the new sentence can effectively be used. When the court is convinced that the nature of an offence, its gravity, and the public interest makes imprisonment unavoidable, that decision may have to be taken notwithstanding that it may be positively undesirable in the interests of improving the offender as a member of the community, or may cause very great hardship to him or his family. In such cases, these latter considerations may just turn the scales in favour of suspension, although so great a mitigation of the penalty may need to be offset by, for example, adding a fine.[3] It may well be that a court in future will feel able to suspend a part—maybe a substantial proportion—of a sentence in a comparable case where considerations of public duty and public interest would have rendered total suspension unacceptable, even though offset by a fine. Both the court and the public may well regard such a course as by no means a "let-off" for the offender—a view sometimes understandably taken where total suspension is used in a case clearly meriting immediate imprisonment.

281. Even more important is its application to first offenders, or those receiving their first prison sentence. An offender may well have reached a stage in a

---

[1] *R* v *O'Keefe* [1969] 2 Q.B. 29. The principle is now enshrined in section 22(2) of the Powers of Criminal Courts Act 1973 (see footnote [3] on page 117).

[2] *R* v *Trowbridge* [1975] Crim. L.R. 295.

[3] *R* v *Leigh* (1970) 54 Cr. App. R. 169; *R* v *King* [1970] 1 W.L.R. 1016.

pattern of offending that the court decides calls, in all the circumstances, for a term of imprisonment. Although in such a case the sentence would be kept, we hope, to a minimum, if the term has to be at least six months the court may well conclude that serving even a short part of it, when coupled with the probability of having to serve the remainder if a new offence is committed in the near future, may prove the most effective deterrent. The early days of a first sentence of imprisonment should, if anything ever does, bring home most effectively to an offender what imprisonment involves, whereas a longer period (although well merited), in which he acclimatizes himself to it, in some degree reduces the deterrent effect of the threat or the fear of future imprisonment. On this view, where six months is the right sentence, its effect may prove more lasting if three quarters of it is suspended than if the full two thirds, remaining after remission, is served.

Conclusion

282. To sum up, we view the partially suspended sentence as a legitimate means of exploiting one of the few reliable pieces of criminological knowledge— that many offenders sent to prison for the first time do not subsequently re-offend. We see it not as a means of administering a "short, sharp shock", nor as a substitute for a wholly suspended sentence, but as especially applicable to serious first offenders or first-time prisoners who are bound to have to serve some time in prison, but who may well be effectively deterred by eventually serving only a small part of even the minimum sentence appropriate to the offence. This, in our view, must be its principal role.

123

CHAPTER 14

COMBINED SENTENCES

283. In addition to our consideration of maximum penalties and suspended sentences, we were asked to consider a more esoteric aspect of the penalty system, namely the scope for combining imprisonment with non-custodial penalties or disabilities. The issue is highly pertinent to the aims of our report. We propose that the existing maximum penalties should be greatly reduced and we ask courts to endeavour to shorten prison sentences imposed on the ordinary offender. In theory, a useful way of assisting courts in this endeavour would be a range of suitable non-custodial penalties which, used in conjunction with imprisonment, would effectively offset the reduction in sentence lengths. We envisaged that we should be able to recommend particular penalties as most suited to particular offences: for example, requirements to report to the police, or restrictions on employment or place of residence as suitable to less serious offences of violence or the more serious sexual offences; criminal bankruptcy orders as suitable to fraud cases; and compensation, forfeiture or restoration orders as fitting the great bulk of crime, that is, offences against property. Initially, we saw the combined sentence as playing a vital part in our proposals, but, on looking more deeply into the practical possibilities, we came to realise that the scope for its application is much narrower than we had imagined. We see no justification in the proliferation of minor penalties for their own sake; each must demonstrate a practical utility. The theme of our whole report is, after all, that the penalty system should be both simple, practical and intelligible. Against this background, we have concluded that it is the financial penalties, imposed in cases of fraud and property offences, which offer the optimum opportunity for combination with sentences of imprisonment, and it is with these that this chapter is primarily concerned. The most complex of the existing financial orders and, in some respects, the most potentially fruitful—the criminal bankruptcy order—has been assigned a chapter of its own.

284. In Appendix R, we have set out a list of disposals and penalties which could in theory be combined with a sentence of imprisonment. Many of these disposals the Council discussed in its report on *Non-Custodial and Semi-Custodial Penalties*,[1] and it would not be appropriate to rehearse them in detail here. We considered the possibility of combining a prison sentence with a community service order to be served on release, but concluded that a penalty paid in leisure time following a prison sentence could appear vindictive, particularly since the offender might regard the later penalty as fresh punishment. The problem with most of the other penalties and disabilities is the converse of the problem with community service: they are in most cases too slight in their penal effect sufficiently to offset a reduction in the length of the prison sentence. The consequences of forfeiture can, for example, soon be made good

---

[1] HMSO, 1970.

124

by new acquisition and many of the powers of disqualification are difficult to enforce against the determined or feckless offender, who will continue the activity regardless of the disqualification.

285. Although our terms of reference limited us to consideration of the combination of *existing* forms of penalty with imprisonment, we found the field so sparse that we decided to consider also penalties that are not a present part of English law. One example will suffice. We formulated a proposal for what we called a residential limitation order, modelled on the French *interdiction de séjour*, designed to prohibit a person convicted of an indictable offence from residing in or visiting a specified geographical area when this would assist in the prevention of further such offences. Informal soundings told us, however, that the power would not be attractive either to the judiciary or to the police, who envisaged enforcement problems; furthermore, the experience of the probation service when such conditions have in the past been included in probation orders was not encouraging. The order would, in any case, have been suitable to only a small number of offences, such as extortion offences or those connected with protection rackets. We dropped the idea.

The fine

286. The combination of imprisonment with a fine is not one to which the courts are likely to have much recourse. In the following table we show the extent to which the Crown Court in 1976 used this combination of penalties for particular offences; in total, the fine was combined with a prison sentence in only 0·2% of all cases of immediate imprisonment.

Persons sentenced* for indictable offences at the Crown Court in 1976: use of the fine in combination with immediate imprisonment and with suspended sentences

Offence group	Total sentenced	Total immediate imprisonment	Immediate imprisonment and fine	Total suspended sentence	Suspended sentence and fine
Violence against the person	8,505	2,897	3	1,655	338
Sexual offences ...	2,355	1,026	—	441	70
Burglary	19,370	6,575	2	2,904	331
Robbery	2,792	1,614	—	178	25
Theft and handling stolen goods ...	22,473	6,574	18	4,321	710
Fraud and forgery	4,179	1,619	9	1,269	188
Criminal damage ...	2,612	649	—	313	39
Other offences ...	6,159	1,514	17	913	179
Total indictable offences	68,445	22,468	49	11,994	1,880

*Trials and committals for sentence.

287. We do not foresee a case for much wider use of this combination. In the first place, we regard it as wrong in principle to impose a fine and thereby place a heavy burden on offenders on their release from prison, at a time when they have lost their jobs and are struggling to rehabilitate themselves. Many of those sentenced to immediate imprisonment would not in any case

125

have sufficient means to qualify for the imposition of a fine. There is also the insuperable difficulty that some offenders who are already subject to a prison sentence would opt to extinguish the fine by serving a short additional period of imprisonment in default of payment, thus defeating the object of a fine. As we see it, probably the best opportunity for imposing a fine jointly with imprisonment is in the case of lucrative offences where the proceeds of crime have been retained, and where a criminal bankruptcy order, for example, cannot be imposed. The additional financial penalty will ensure that on release from prison the ill-gotten goods are not freely enjoyed. But for the reasons we have indicated, we would not encourage the wide use of such a sanction in other circumstances.

288. The use of the fine in combination with a wholly suspended sentence is, however, another matter. On the assumption that the sentence is not activated, the offender will remain in the community and the burden of payment will be no greater than if he had received only a fine. Furthermore, the fine would be particularly useful in reinforcing the offender's recognition of the continuing possibility of activation. As the table in paragraph 286 shows, this combination is much more popular with the courts than that of immediate imprisonment with the fine; it was used in 16% of cases of suspended imprisonment in the Crown Court in 1976. We should like to see it even more widely used. Where the suspended sentence is activated, this combination of penalties can raise problems which we have discussed in paragraph 267. Our recommendation to give additional powers to the activating court will increase in urgency as the combination becomes more popular.

289. Considering how high a proportion of convicted offenders is sentenced by way of a monetary penalty, we find it remarkable how little attention has been paid to the question of fines in the penal system. The Council itself, in its report on *Non-Custodial and Semi-Custodial Penalties* in 1970, devoted only one chapter to the subject and made only one minor recommendation. Since the Home Office Research Unit is soon to publish a report of research findings on fines and methods of enforcing payment, we think that the time is ripe for a thorough review of this very important, but least spectacular, part of the penal system. *We recommend a review of the system of fines and their enforcement.*

Compensation orders

290. The Criminal Justice Act 1972 greatly extended the powers of the courts to make compensation to the victim of an offence, and the provision for making compensation orders, now contained in section 35 of the Powers of Criminal Courts Act 1973, is increasingly used. Many of the difficulties we have described in relation to the fine apply to the combination of compensation with imprisonment. In particular, the offender can still serve the alternative of an additional period of imprisonment, although in the case of the compensation order the debt is not extinguished since civil liability remains. Research has shown that the combination of compensation orders with custodial sentences is not, however, frequently used. In a sample of offenders in 1973 it was found that roughly 12% of those given custodial sentences were ordered to pay compensation, compared with 44% of those given non-custodial sentences (or who received

126

a suspended sentence).[1] Twenty-five per cent of the compensation orders in the sample were, however, made in combination with a custodial sentence. Further research by the Home Office Research Unit has shown that when compensation orders are combined with imprisonment there is some risk that such orders will result in an additional term of imprisonment in default and that such orders will generally be difficult to enforce.[2] We adhere to the view previously expressed by this Council in its report on *Reparation by the Offender*[3] that compensation orders should not generally be used in combination with a custodial sentence. Where circumstances (such as the knowledge that the offender has salted away the proceeds of his crime) make it appropriate, however, we would wish the power of compensation to be used more widely than at present in conjunction with imprisonment. Where a court is undecided whether to make a compensation order or impose a fine, we consider that, in the interests of the victim, the compensation order should always take precedence.

Costs

291. Finally, we considered the imposition of costs when a sentence of imprisonment is passed. This power is not much used at the present time. We see no reason, however, why it should not serve as an additional sanction where a trial has been needlessly prolonged and public money wasted by a patently spurious defence. Provided that the imposition of costs is related strictly to the actual costs incurred, and is not used as a covert fine, we see it as a useful deterrent measure. One advantage is that, unlike the fine, it cannot be disposed of by a period served in default of payment. We do not consider that our advocacy of this measure will in any way put pressure on the ordinary defendant to plead guilty. Rather, it will prevent the unwarranted extension of the length of the sentence of imprisonment, which courts have been known to exact as the price of a spurious defence.

---

[1] *Compensation Orders in the Crown Court* by Roger Tarling and Paul Softley [1976] Crim. L.R. 422–8.
[2] *Compensation Orders and Custodial Sentences* by Paul Softley and Roger Tarling [1977] Crim. L.R. 720–2. See also *Compensation Orders in Magistrates' Courts* by Paul Softley, Home Office Research Study No. 43 (HMSO, 1978).
[3] (HMSO, 1970), paragraph 137.

CHAPTER 15

CRIMINAL BANKRUPTCY

Introduction

292. There has been a common complaint about the English penal system that until very recently it was too concerned with the treatment of the offender and shamefully neglected the needs of the victim. There has been for quite a long time, it is true, limited provision in our law for restitution and compensation by offenders, but the powers were unsystematic and unnecessarily restricted, so that little use was made of them. Hence, reparation to the victim did not appear as a distinctive feature of the penal code.

293. This Council, in its report *Reparation by the Offender*, published in 1970, surveyed this rather technical area of the law and recommended a tidying up and strengthening of the statutory provisions. The ensuing Criminal Justice Act 1972 greatly extended and rationalised the courts' powers of compensation and restitution. The Council recognised that effective reparation by the offender requires, however, not only adequate powers for the courts to order reparation, and the necessary machinery for enforcing payment, but also the existence of resources available to the offender out of which payment to the victim can reasonably be made. There remains the fundamental obstacle that in many cases the profit from crime is dissipated before offenders are brought to trial, and they do not have the wherewithal to make reparation. Where, of course, the offender can appropriately be dealt with by the imposition of a short custodial sentence or a non-custodial penalty, there is the enhanced prospect of future earnings to provide, in the absence of other resources, the means to make reparation. It was against this background of severely practical considerations that the Council in 1970—stimulated by written evidence submitted by the Law Society to the Royal Commission on the Penal System—proposed an adaptation of the bankruptcy procedures so as to make it possible, in strictly selected cases, to take control of an offender's assets and income, and distribute a proportion by way of compensation to the victim. Out of this proposal came the provisions in the 1972 Act, on an experimental basis, of criminal bankruptcy.

294. Criminal bankruptcy was the one non-custodial measure that instantly attracted us as a potentially useful addition to a wholly or partially suspended sentence of imprisonment. We had in mind the use that criminal bankruptcy might be to the courts in dealing with the fraudulent offender whose crime ordinarily attracts an immediate sentence of imprisonment of either a short or medium term. We see less advantage in the use of criminal bankruptcy in addition to long sentences of imprisonment, although the possibility of it even for offenders who qualified for a sentence exceeding the maxima should not be ruled out. It was clear to us, however, that it would be rash to alter radically the scheme experimentally introduced only five years ago unless it clearly indicated possibilities of useful expansion. Although five years of experimentation is insufficient to form any firm conclusions, our study of the

workings of the scheme has convinced us that while the experiment has exposed serious shortcomings in the scheme, there remains potential for its development, given a reshaping of the aim and scope of criminal bankruptcy. In line with the Council's 1970 report, criminal bankruptcy has so far been confined mostly to cases involving medium and long terms of imprisonment (see Appendix S). Much less frequently has an order of criminal bankruptcy been used in addition to a suspended sentence, or even to a non-custodial penalty. But while criminal bankruptcy in this experimental stage was seen as having as its primary purpose the uncovering of assets of those engaged in large-scale fraud, it was also acknowledged that it could have potential application in securing a proportion of offenders' future earnings for the benefit of victims.[1] Such a development would certainly involve the use of criminal bankruptcy in conjunction with shorter sentences of imprisonment or even with non-custodial penalties. We think that the experiment has indicated that, in the current climate of opinion about the limited utility of imprisonment, the courts and the public would accept criminal bankruptcy (accompanied by the partially or wholly suspended sentence) as a credible alternative to imprisonment, at least for non-violent offenders. In this chapter, we describe the outcome of the experiment and indicate the ways in which we would like to see the scheme adapted to give effect to the new role we now envisage for criminal bankruptcy.

The scheme of criminal bankruptcy

295. Under section 39 of the Powers of Criminal Courts Act 1973, the Crown Court may make a criminal bankruptcy order where it appears that, as a result of offences of which a person has been convicted, loss or damage exceeding in the aggregate £15,000 has been suffered by one or more persons known to the court. The effect of the order is to make available the machinery of civil bankruptcy administration for the recovery of the money. A criminal bankruptcy order is an additional sanction and may be combined with any other disposal, except a compensation order. The order is unique in bankruptcy law in that it involves proceedings independently of any state of insolvency of the debtor. The limit of £15,000 may be altered by statutory instrument, but no such alteration has yet been made. Where an order is made it is the duty of the Official Petitioner (whose functions are exclusively vested in the Director of Public Prosecutions) to consider whether it is in the public interest that he should present a bankruptcy petition. If the Official Petitioner presents a petition, a receiving order may be made[2] and the normal bankruptcy proceedings follow. Although any creditor can also petition, the Director of Public Prosecutions is almost invariably the petitioner. In 23 cases to date, no petition has been presented. Where the Director decides not to petition, he writes to each of the creditors explaining his decision, and creditors have usually been influenced by the decision in relinquishing further action. In four cases, however, petitions for receiving orders have been presented privately.

---

[1] *Reparation by the Offender*, paragraph 107.

[2] On only three occasions so far has a petition for a receiving order been dismissed. Although the legislation does not envisage the petition being defended, if the convicted person pays off, or reaches an agreement with all the injured parties, he can defeat the petition. The criminal bankruptcy order will have had the effect of ensuring compensation to known creditors, although there may be other creditors unknown who will not have benefited.

296. In deciding whether to present a petition the Director applies two criteria: first, whether the offender has sufficient assets to make bankruptcy proceedings worthwhile; and second, whether it is in the public interest to take proceedings in respect of those assets (so far as they can be ascertained at that stage) because, for example, such action might cause severe hardship to the criminal bankrupt's family. We question whether the second criterion need be applied in cases where the offender suffers nothing harsher than a suspended sentence. Since the loss of the family home is a common occurrence in ordinary bankruptcies, we see no reason to treat the criminal bankrupt more favourably in this regard.[1] Where, however, the consequence is to create a one-parent family for a long time, there is good reason for maintaining the criterion. Once the decision has been taken to present a petition, the majority of the work after the receiving order has been made devolves upon the Official Receiver, although the Director's Office is kept fully informed and continues to finance the proceedings. We were assured that the Director's role in the operation of the scheme was straightforward and he has experienced no administrative difficulties. The additional work involved has been absorbed by the Department, which has been overstretched for some time, without undue burden. The real burden of criminal bankruptcy has fallen on the Insolvency Service.

297. Under the present law a criminal court can make a bankruptcy order only if it specifies the amount of the loss resulting from the offence, names the persons appearing to have suffered that loss, and states the amount of that loss which it appears to the court that each of the persons has suffered. The prosecution's inability to identify the particular loss and to relate it to a known victim reduces the scope or even applicability of criminal bankruptcy. While we would not want to change the rule that there should be a minimum aggregate amount of loss below which a criminal bankruptcy order could not be made, we see great merit in a criminal bankruptcy order being made without the court having to fix a finite sum or to identify all the creditors. We are aware of major frauds where it was impossible to prove the size of the fraud in concrete financial terms or to identify all the victims before a thorough investigation (which might take months or years) could be undertaken. Criminal bankruptcy should be viewed in the same light as proceedings against delinquent directors of companies: as long as it is established that loss has been suffered equal to or greater than the minimum limit, then all the victims should be treated as creditors in the criminal bankruptcy whether or not they are immediately identifiable and whether the amount in excess of the statutory minimum can be specifically ascertained. *We recommend that section 39 of the Powers of Criminal Courts Act 1973 should be amended accordingly.*

298. A criminal bankruptcy order does not constitute a penalty; this is clear from the provision that disallows any right of appeal against the making of the order. The power of the Court of Appeal either to rescind or amend a criminal bankruptcy order is limited to those cases where the order is dependent upon a conviction which the Court has quashed or varied or where the order was a nullity.[2] If our recommendation in paragraph 297 (that amounts in excess of the

---

[1] The Bankruptcy Court has displayed an increasing lack of tenderness towards the bankrupt's wife or mistress in respect of their legal or equitable rights in the matrimonial home— *In re Bailey (A Bankrupt) (No. 25 of 1975)* [1977] 1 W.L.R. 278.
[2] See the judgment in *R v Anderson* No. 5536/A/76, 15 November 1977, reproduced in Appendix T.

statutory minimum are to be rendered more indefinite) is accepted, *we would think it right to give the offender a right of appeal against the making of the order.*

299. Up to the end of February 1978, 124[1] criminal bankruptcy orders have been made in England and Wales[2] in respect of which receiving orders have been obtained. We publish in Appendix S a list of all 124. The list bears out what we said in paragraph 294 that the scheme has been limited in the scope of its application to the most serious cases, largely because considerations of cost and manpower have led the courts to select only those cases where the recovery of substantial ill-gotten gains might assuage public anxiety, leaving it to the victim to seek recovery of the smaller amounts of money. In the wide discrepancy between the amount specified in the order and the known assets of the offender, the list reveals the inherent defect of applying criminal bankruptcy to large-scale fraud offenders on whom long-term imprisonment has been imposed. The key to the successful operation of criminal bankruptcy is the co-operation of the offender; where the offender is imprisoned for any length of time, co-operation has been so far almost totally lacking.[3] Thus in the short term the Insolvency Service have achieved few returns for victims, while there has been a significant addition to the existing workload of an overworked service. The lack of effective co-operation clearly has been a severe drawback, and we have considered how this might be overcome. We would point out, however, that in the long term there may be some real benefits from criminal bankruptcy that are not yet discernible. A criminal bankruptcy order acts as a kind of "permanent flypaper"; it continues to apply after the offender has served his prison sentence, irrespective of his unco-operativeness during incarceration. Anything the discharged prisoner may purchase belongs to his trustee in bankruptcy.[4] And, under criminal bankruptcy (unlike civil bankruptcy), any gifts or under-valued sales made on or after the earliest date on which the criminal offence has been committed can, on application to the Bankruptcy Court by the Official Receiver, be ordered to be transferred by any person acquiring the whole or part of the

---

[1] The total number of criminal bankruptcy orders made to date is, of course, higher than this. In addition to the 124, 23 orders have been made in respect of which no petition was presented (see paragraph 295) and a further three where the receiving order was dismissed (see footnote [2] on page 129). Finally, there are a few further orders which are still in process of investigation by the Director of Public Prosecutions.

[2] Scotland has not introduced the measure, and the Dunpark Committee on *Reparation by the Offender to the Victim in Scotland* (Cmnd. 6802, Chapter 15) reported in 1977 that it felt unconvinced of the need or desire to confer upon the criminal courts the power to make criminal bankruptcy orders. The absence of a state bankruptcy service in Scotland is a powerful disincentive to any replication of the English provisions.

[3] A newspaper report of a recent case provides a typical example:
"Mailbag thief Ted May had just two words to say when asked where he had stashed £189,000. He nodded, smiled, then told Assistant Official Receiver Mr Trevor White: 'No comment'. Again Mr White, who is in charge of the criminal bankruptcy proceedings taken against May, said sternly: 'I want to know what you have done with this money'. May, dressed in an old cardigan and grey trousers, just smiled. Three times Mr White asked the question. And three times the answer remained the same. Up to that point 40-year-old May had been the model of helpfulness. He admitted stealing at least £225,000 from mailbags on British Rail trains—for which he is serving a ten-year sentence. And he willingly agreed at London Bankruptcy Court yesterday that he still had £189,000 hidden away. Mr Registrar Parbury said that with at least six years and eight months to run on May's sentence, any jail threat would have little meaning. He adjourned the hearing and told the Assistant Official Receiver to bring the case before him again just before May was due for release."

[4] *In re Pascoe* [1944] Ch. 219.

property given or sold at an under-value.[1] Furthermore, if powers were to be taken to deny the discharged prisoner the privilege of holding a passport, assets secreted abroad might become available to creditors. We point to these factors to indicate our view that there is a place for criminal bankruptcy in respect of serious offences, but it should not form the primary purpose of the sanction.

300. The investigation of the criminal bankrupt's affairs depends exclusively on information provided by the bankrupt himself. The Insolvency Service has found that it has frequently proved slow, difficult and expensive to extract the necessary information. Visits to distant prisons have not made the task any the easier. Unless there is the prospect of co-operation, the financial results will not justify the undue proportion of time the Service is having to devote to criminal bankruptcy, and co-operation is unlikely from a prisoner serving a long term of imprisonment.[2] Normally, where a civil bankrupt fails to co-operate, the Official Receiver seeks an order of committal to prison, but this sanction is ineffective against the long-term prisoner. If committal proceedings were taken, the Bankruptcy Court could only make an order that ran concurrently with the prison sentence and it would in most cases be impractical to defer the institution of committal proceedings until the prisoner was released.

301. We considered whether eligibility for parole might be used as an influence in improving co-operation. The Parole Board should certainly be made aware (if it is not already) not only of the existence of a criminal bankruptcy order but also of the progress of the bankruptcy, whenever it is considering releasing a prisoner on parole. *We recommend that the Official Receiver should invariably be asked to indicate to the Parole Board at the moment of eligibility for parole (and at intervals thereafter) what state a prisoner's bankruptcy has reached.* Such information is as likely to operate in the prisoner's favour as not. It would give the prisoner, moreover, a substantial opportunity to influence his own future by contributing to the successful execution of the order. We recognise, of course, that parole can have only a limited effect in resolving this problem since co-operation with the Insolvency Service cannot be made an overriding criterion in the grant of parole. There will be cases where a prisoner co-operates but cannot be granted parole for other reasons. Nevertheless, there will be other cases where good co-operation will help to tip the scales in favour of an earlier release.

302. The criminal bankrupt could be charged with a bankruptcy offence if he failed to provide certain information. Section 154(1)(1) of the Bankruptcy Act 1914 already contains a provision making it a criminal offence punishable by imprisonment for up to two years if a bankrupt fails to disclose all his property

---

[1] Paragraph 10 of Schedule 2 to the Powers of Criminal Courts Act 1973. Surprisingly, no use appears to have been made of this provision to date.
[2] The Bankruptcy Court does not rely exclusively on the bankrupt for information regarding his estate. The bankrupt's wife, mistress, business associates or professional advisers can, under the bankruptcy laws, be privately examined.

132

and details about the disposal of any part of his property.[1] The burden of proving that there was no intent to defraud is on the bankrupt. This offence does not, however, cover the failure to give information about his assets either by refusing to answer questions or by giving false information. Although any such failure is dealt with under the existing law as a ground for committing the bankrupt to prison, *we feel that consideration might be given to broadening the scope of section 154, at least in the case of a person made criminally bankrupt who fails to co-operate with the Official Receiver.* There are, we think, good reasons for treating non-compliance with bankruptcy orders by a criminal bankrupt more strictly than that by his civil counterpart. If, in any case, a bankruptcy court were to make an order of committal for a fixed period in respect of non-compliance with its orders, such sentence would presumably be made to take effect consecutive to the current prison sentence, rather like a consecutive sentence of imprisonment in default of payment of a fine for another offence.

Reduction of the financial limit

303. The number of orders made in the first years of the scheme has been less than was first envisaged when the statutory limit of £15,000 was fixed. On that account alone we think it would be feasible to reduce the limit without over-burdening the Insolvency Service. At the present time, banks and public companies constitute a large proportion of those specified in criminal bankruptcy orders as persons suffering loss, and most of the orders have been for amounts far in excess of the statutory limit. Any reduction in the limit is likely to bring a greater proportion of private individuals who have suffered loss within the ambit of the procedure. Far from disapproving such a development, we would welcome it, since we regard the device of criminal bankruptcy as designed to provide reparation to the victims who have suffered small losses as much as to those who have been defrauded of large amounts. The lower the amount of the bankruptcy, moreover, the greater, we think, is the likelihood of the recovery of assets. But the overriding consideration for us is that shorter terms of imprisonment (or even non-custodial sentences) could be more readily imposed if provision could additionally be made for the recovery of money that had been misappropriated. If the financial limit were reduced so that the provisions impinged upon people (the lesser white-collar criminal, for example) against whom they could be effectively enforced, the deterrent effect of the sanction might be enhanced. Although the figure of £15,000 which was set in 1972 has fallen in real terms to about £10,000, and thus effected a significant reduction in the limit already, we should like to see the process carried further in the interests of extending the use of the provision. *We therefore recommend that the Secretary of State should use his statutory power to reduce the level of the financial limit to £10,000.*

---

[1] Any person who has been adjudged bankrupt or in respect of whose estate a receiving order has been made shall . . . be guilty of a misdemeanour:—

    (1) If he does not to the best of his knowledge and belief fully and truly discover to the trustee all his property, real and personal, and how and to whom and for what consideration and when he disposed of any part thereof, except such part as has been disposed of in the ordinary way of his trade (if any) or laid out in the ordinary expense of his family, unless he proves that he had no intent to defraud.

304. We are very conscious that the reduction in the financial limit is likely to encourage courts to make greater use of criminal bankruptcy orders; indeed, we ourselves seek to encourage this development in order to reduce the amount of unnecessary imprisonment. The consequences might be a larger number of criminal bankruptcy orders than the Insolvency Service could cope with. If that were to be the effect, we would hesitate before proposing any such extension. It would be disastrous if, furthermore, the results did not differ markedly from those achieved so far in the cases where criminal bankruptcy orders have been made under the present limit. But we are satisfied that the volume and flow of criminal bankruptcies can be safely controlled. First, we would anticipate that the criminal courts would tend to make orders only where there are prospects of assets being recovered. And second, the Director of Public Prosecutions in applying his criteria will not proceed to petition in every case. The right to petition would still be open to the private creditor, but at present that still entails the Official Receiver being the trustee.[1] It might be healthy if a larger number of criminal bankruptcies led to private bankruptcy proceedings, for victims should be encouraged to use the legal machinery to recover their losses. In order, however, to prevent the Insolvency Service from being overloaded, *we recommend that where the Director of Public Prosecutions declines to petition, the Official Receiver should not automatically be appointed trustee, but that a person appointed under section 19 of the Bankruptcy Act 1914 could perform this function.*

Earnings

305. Although we have considered a number of aspects of criminal bankruptcy that seem to us to require attention, we have not felt it our task to go beyond the penological implications of the order. We have had informal talks with some members of the Insolvency Law Review Committee,[2] chaired by Mr. Kenneth Cork, which is currently sitting to consider reform of the insolvency laws, and they appreciate the thinking behind our recommendations. We are more than content to leave it to that body to consider technical matters of bankruptcy law, such as the relationship of criminal bankruptcy to civil bankruptcy, and the problems caused by the long period of relation back in criminal bankruptcy. There is one matter, however, to which we have felt it necessary to devote some attention. If, as we envisage, criminal bankruptcy should have a useful potential application in securing a proportion of offenders' future earnings for the benefit of their victims, the existing power in the bankruptcy law to achieve that should be exercised more often. Section 51(2) of the Bankruptcy Act 1914 provides that a trustee in bankruptcy can apply to the court for the payment to him of a bankrupt's earnings, but the courts are not keen on the power, and trustees apply infrequently. The courts take a generous

---

[1] Paragraph 8 of Schedule 2 to the Powers of Criminal Courts Act 1973.

[2] Its terms of reference are:—
  (i) to review the law and practice relating to insolvency, bankruptcy, liquidation and receiverships in England and Wales and to consider what reforms are necessary or desirable;
  (ii) to examine the possibility of formulating a comprehensive insolvency system and the extent to which existing procedures might, with advantage, be harmonised and integrated;
  (iii) to suggest possible less formal procedures as alternatives to bankruptcy and company winding-up proceedings in appropriate circumstances; and
  (iv) to make recommendations.

view of the income a person requires for his livelihood, and any amounts of earned income above that needed for everyday life have been squeezed by inflation in recent years. It is only in the case of a person whose income is considerable where future earnings could reasonably be attached. We think that there are a number of white-collar criminals who do come into that category, and that rather than pass an immediate sentence of imprisonment, *courts should instead use criminal bankruptcy orders with a view to an application in due course by the Official Receiver (or other trustee if our recommendation in paragraph 304 is adopted) under section 51(2)*. For the rest of offenders subjected to criminal bankruptcy, we would like to see a greater use of the section by the courts, but recognise that it would not be appropriate to those on low incomes.

Extended use of criminal bankruptcy

306. As we have stated, our assessment of the effectiveness of criminal bankruptcy as revealed during the experimental period has led us to the conclusion that this novel sanction should be deployed more widely, to include the less serious offences—namely those fraud offences (albeit of quite large amounts of money) that do not involve any violence. We see criminal bankruptcy as a penalty that can be made to claw back misappropriations by offenders such that courts are led to impose much shorter sentences of imprisonment or even forbear to sentence the offender to an immediate term of imprisonment, and impose a suspended sentence or a non-custodial penalty. We proceed to consider the ways in which this combination of orders could work.

307. Initially, we thought that the best means of obtaining the offender's co-operation would be to use the deferred sentence under section 1 of the Powers of Criminal Courts Act 1973. The idea would be that the court would defer sentence for six months during which time the Director of Public Prosecutions would decide whether to present a petition and, if a receiving order were subsequently made, sentence could be deferred for a further six months for the co-operation of the offender to be assessed. But for two main reasons we have not thought it right to recommend this form of combined sentence. First, we think that deferment of sentence is designed mainly for the lower courts in respect of minor offences (in any event magistrates' courts have no power to make criminal bankruptcy orders) and is not entirely apt to deal with fraud offences involving sums in excess of £10,000. Second, the law would have to be amended to allow for a second deferment of six months, and even then we are not at all sure that the extended period of 12 months from the date of the court order of criminal bankruptcy would provide enough time for the court, on the return day, to be provided with material indicating the defender's co-operativeness or lack of it. Some cases take many months of investigation before the Director can even decide whether to petition.

308. We see no obstacle to the court of trial combining a criminal bankruptcy order with a suspended sentence, either wholly under section 22 of the Powers of Criminal Courts Act 1973 or partially under section 47 of the Criminal Law Act 1977. The problem is to fit a breach of the criminal bankruptcy order into the cases which give rise to the activation of the suspended sentence. The power to order a suspended sentence, or the suspended portion of the sentence,

135

to take effect (or to extend its operational period) arises when the offender is convicted of an offence punishable with imprisonment and committed during the operational period of the sentence. Since bankruptcy offences under the Bankruptcy Act 1914 are punishable with imprisonment, a conviction for such offences would activate any subsisting suspended sentence. There are two situations that require specific consideration. There is the case where the bankruptcy offence relates to an occurrence before the suspended sentence was passed; for example, the bankrupt might have failed to keep proper books of accounts. This, and other offences committed before the making of the criminal bankruptcy order, could not justifiably constitute a failure to co-operate in the investigation or administration of the bankrupt's estate. It would be quite inappropriate to extend the power of enforcement of a suspended sentence to include a conviction for any of them. Only imprisonable bankruptcy offences relating to acts committed during the operational period of the suspended sentence would qualify.

309. The second situation is where the criminal bankrupt's failure to co-operate with the Official Receiver or trustee falls short of a criminal offence. *Where there is a failure to co-operate in the investigation or administration of the bankruptcy, it would be necessary to provide that the suspended sentence should be capable of enforcement on the additional, alternative ground that the criminal bankrupt has been committed to prison by order of the Bankruptcy Court for failure to comply with any requirement of the Bankruptcy Act or Rules.* Under the existing law a suspended sentence must be implemented unless circumstances that have arisen since it was passed (including those of the fresh offence) would render it unjust to do so. We think that in the case of the criminal bankrupt, the activation of a suspended sentence ought not to be so rigorously invoked but ought to be a matter for discretion; this will, of course, be the case in respect of a partially suspended sentence. The question is: which court? We have no doubt that the court that imposed the suspended sentence should alone have the power to order that the sentence should, or should not, be activated. It will be necessary to provide therefore that the Bankruptcy Court making a committal order on a criminal bankrupt should bring the matter to the notice of the relevant criminal court. The simplest method would be to send the Crown Court a copy of the order of committal.

310. We have alluded to the fact that investigation into the financial affairs of the bankrupt often takes a long time, and that administration may be prolonged over many years. The question arises, therefore, whether the limit of two years on the operational period of a suspended sentence is enough to cater for the case of the criminal bankrupt. It could be argued that a sentence of imprisonment should be suspended until the criminal bankrupt obtains his discharge from bankruptcy. But that might be for the rest of his natural life, and we do not think it would be right that potential activation of a suspended sentence should subsist that long. After all, the criminal bankrupt will still be liable to be committed to prison for non-compliance with the bankruptcy order at the instance of the Bankruptcy Court long after the suspended sentence has spent itself. We have, accordingly, concluded that the two-year limit on the operational period of the suspended sentence should remain, but we would strongly urge any court which decides to impose a criminal bankruptcy order

in combination with a suspended sentence to fix the maximum operational period of two years in order to ensure that the combination is given full effect.

Conclusion

311. Criminal bankruptcy in its short experimental phase has not worked well. We hope that the extension of the provision along the lines we have recommended in this chapter will prove more fruitful as a viable penal sanction.

EPILOGUE

"If he were
To be made honest by an act of parliament,
I should not alter in my faith of him."

Ben Jonson, *The Devil is an Ass* (1616)

CHAPTER 16

IMPLEMENTING OUR PROPOSALS

312. There are very few of our proposals—and they are minor ones—which could not to some extent be put into practice without legislation. The abolition of the extended sentence by statute would do little more than set the seal on what is happening in the courts. Our recommendations in paragraph 267 in relation to suspended sentences and in the previous chapter in relation to criminal bankruptcy orders are desirable, but peripheral to our terms of reference. All of our other proposals are, however, closely linked with our main remit to review the maximum penalties of imprisonment and to assess how far they represent a valid guide to sentencing practice. Their implementation therefore depends largely on the extent to which our main recommendations are accepted and the way in which they can best be put into practice. Before considering this, it may be helpful if we summarise our most significant suggestions.

313. Our main thesis is that the existing maximum penalties do not represent a valid guide to sentencing practice because the maxima are fixed with regard to the "worst possible" case and accordingly bear little or no relation to the great majority of cases dealt with by the courts. We therefore suggest a change of principle in the way in which maximum penalties are fixed, so that instead of allowing for the "worst possible" case, the maximum would indicate the highest penalty likely to be appropriate for the majority of cases, leaving the exceptional cases to be dealt with in an exceptional manner. We suggest that this change would have at least three consequences of considerable importance. In the first place, maximum penalties fixed on the new basis would provide the courts with a relevant guide to sentencing in all cases. Secondly, the lowering of the maxima would, we believe, have a beneficial effect on the length of prison sentences. Our views on the length of prison sentences were given in some detail in our interim report of June 1977 where we expressed the opinion that for many ordinary offenders a shorter sentence than the one imposed would be just as effective as the longer one and that a reduction in sentence lengths would have considerable advantages to the prison system as a whole. We believe that many prison sentences are longer than they need to be because their length is decided in the context of maxima which, as we hope this report shows, have little or no relevance to the reality of the situation. If the maxima were lowered, we hope that one natural consequence would be for the average length of sentences to be reduced, even if only slightly, to create a new and more realistic relativity.

314. The third consequence of our proposals is that the courts, while having an apparently[1] reduced discretion in the majority of cases, would have a much wider discretion in those cases which at present cause the greatest difficulty in

---

[1] The limitation is apparent rather than real because our proposals for fixing the new maxima depend on the existing sentencing practice of the courts.

sentencing. The suggestions we make in Chapter 10 for exceeding the new maxima provide the courts with the greatest possible flexibility in dealing with offenders against whom it is felt that society should be protected; the rights of the individual are recognised by our proposals for a modification of the parole system.

315. Ultimately, if the principles underlying our proposals are accepted, legislation will be necessary to remove the existing maximum penalties and to establish the new maxima, to give the courts new powers in exceptional cases, and to make the necessary consequential changes to parole. Clearly, the main difficulty in such legislation will be fixing the level of the new maxima. In this report, we have suggested that if the new maxima are to be a reliable guide to sentencing practice, they must be related to the current sentencing practice of the courts. We have proposed that they should, therefore, be fixed for each offence at a level which would cover 90% of Crown Court trials which result in the imposition of a prison sentence, on the assumption that the remaining 10% can reasonably be considered to be exceptional cases. We recognise that this is to some extent an arbitrary distinction but we think that it serves to provide a good working guide to what the new maxima should be.

316. Immediate legislation to implement our proposals, even if the parliamentary timetable would allow for it, would have a number of disadvantages. The history of imprisonment and sentencing which we have traced in this report suggests that legislation used to introduce an innovation often misfires; the unsuccessful attempts to provide for persistent offenders and the need to amend the provisions relating to suspended sentences soon after they had been brought into effect illustrate this. The legislative innovations which have survived with the least alteration have been those which were adopted unofficially and only later embodied in statute; an example is probation. On a more immediately practical level, in spite of our emphasis on the fact that the new maxima we propose are based on the actual sentencing practice of the courts, there will undoubtedly be argument about the maximum for individual offences, and a failure to understand the principles on which our proposals are based could lead to compromises on specific points which could damage important parts of a complicated measure. There is also likely to be controversy about the criterion for exceeding the maxima since the guiding formula we have suggested in paragraph 207 may not be considered sufficiently precise to become statute law.

317. For these reasons, we hope that the Government will feel able, in the light of the initial reaction to this report, to accept the principle of what we suggest and to seek the co-operation of the courts in finding the best way of putting our proposals into effect. While, within the bounds laid down by Parliament, the courts have an absolute discretion to decide the most appropriate sentence in every individual case, sentencing policy is determined largely, if not exclusively, by the decisions of the Court of Appeal. If what we propose finds acceptance with the judiciary, it would be perfectly possible for the courts, under the direction of the Court of Appeal (Criminal Division), to work for an experimental period to new maxima calculated as we have suggested. During this period it would be possible to assess whether the 90% cut-off did cover the majority of ordinary cases, what criteria the judges were applying to exceed the new maxima, and whether reference to the new maxima was having the effect we would expect of reducing the average length of prison sentences. An approach

of this kind would enable legislation to be framed on the basis of practical experience instead of hypothesis. This should ensure both that our proposals are properly understood and that those most clearly concerned have had a full opportunity to assess their merits.

318. If this method of implementation is followed, the reference to research made in paragraph 35 will be of crucial importance. It will obviously be essential for the Home Office to provide the judiciary each year with an analysis of sentencing which shows the 90% level, for each of the most common offences, decided during the preceding year. This will provide the notional maximum for the following year. But this alone will not be sufficient. If properly informed decisions are ultimately to be made on the need for legislation and the new maxima which should be created, it will be necessary to examine with some care the changes in sentencing practice in relation to a selection of major offences from year to year and in particular to compare the scatter of penalties below the 90% level. The overall effect of the new system on the length of prison sentences will need to be monitored and a detailed record will be necessary of the circumstances of every case in which the notional maximum is exceeded. All this information will need to be fully recorded and made publicly available so that there will be the optimum amount of discussion and understanding before any decisions are reached.

319. We believe that the work required to provide a comprehensive analysis of the kind described will be amply justified. If the Government is convinced that our proposals offer a viable system of maximum penalties as a valid guide to sentencing practice, an appropriate research programme could be devised to supply answers to most of the questions which actively concern both the public and Parliamentarians. The Government would need to decide the term of an experimental period for testing our proposals—say, three to five years— followed by legislation. An early commitment by the Government to this phased approach to a new system of maximum penalties should attract the wholehearted co-operation of the courts, so essential to the success of our proposals.

SEROTA (*Chairman*)
ARTHUR ARMITAGE
ALAN BAINTON
LOUIS BLOM-COOPER
STEPHEN BROWN
DEREK GLADWIN
ALAN GOODSON
M. HARGREAVES
GERALD HINES
RICHARD LOWRY
TERESA ROTHSCHILD
HUGH SANDERS
W. R. STIRLING
NIGEL WALKER
GEORGE S. WALLER
WOOTTON OF ABINGER

C. L. SCOBLE (*Secretary*)
28 February 1978

LIST OF PRINCIPAL RECOMMENDATIONS

The scheme

1. For the ordinary offender, new maximum penalties should be fixed at the level below which 90% of sentences of immediate imprisonment passed by the Crown Court for the particular offence have fallen in recent years (paragraph 170).

2. For the exceptional offender who qualifies to receive a sentence in excess of the new maxima, a court may impose a determinate sentence of any length (paragraph 213).

The new maxima

3. The major exceptions to the application of the new maxima would be the offences of murder and manslaughter, where the penalty should be life imprisonment (paragraph 229).

4. Existing maxima should not be reduced below two years (paragraph 177).

5. The maximum penalty for new offences enacted in the future should be determined by reference to the maximum penalty for existing analogous offences (paragraph 175).

6. The new maxima should be reviewed from time to time by the Home Secretary in consultation with some standing advisory body (paragraph 175).

Exceeding the new maxima

7. The new maxima may not be exceeded unless by reason of the nature of the offence and the character, conduct and antecedents of the offender the court is of the opinion that a custodial sentence of exceptional length is necessary for the protection of the public against serious harm (paragraph 207).

8. In the case of those non-homicide offences which currently carry a maximum penalty of life imprisonment and for which that maximum penalty has been imposed in the 10 years preceding the implementation of this recommendation (or in the case of any offence with a maximum penalty of life imprisonment enacted within the same period of 10 years), a court when exceeding the maxima for these offences may impose a sentence of life imprisonment as an alternative to a determinate sentence of any length (paragraph 233).

9. A prisoner receiving a determinate sentence in excess of the new maxima should be eligible for parole after serving one third of it or the maximum ordinary sentence he could have received under the system of new maxima, whichever is the less (paragraph 214).

144

10. On release, he should be subject to a licence until his total nominal sentence has expired (paragraph 215).

11. A prisoner subject to a sentence in excess of the new maxima should be entitled to legal aid for an application for leave to appeal (paragraph 216).

12. The current principles governing the use of consecutive sentences should be strictly applied to ensure that a sentence in excess of the new maxima cannot be imposed unless the criterion for exceeding the maxima is met (paragraph 220).

Extended sentences

13. Extended sentences should be abolished (paragraph 115).

Research

14. A detailed research programme should be undertaken to monitor the new scheme of penalties (paragraph 35).

Life imprisonment

15. Section 1(2) of the Murder (Abolition of Death Penalty) Act 1965, which empowers a court to recommend the minimum period of a life sentence which an offender should serve in custody, should be repealed (paragraph 260).

16. When no sentence of life imprisonment has been imposed for a non-homicide offence for a period of 10 years, the power to impose life imprisonment for that offence should lapse (paragraph 233).

Criminal bankruptcy

17. The statutory limit on the amount of loss or damage from offences which qualifies the offender for the imposition of a criminal bankruptcy order should be reduced from £15,000 to £10,000 (paragraph 303).

18. A suspended sentence imposed in combination with a criminal bankruptcy order should be capable of activation on the additional ground that the criminal bankrupt has been committed to prison by order of the Bankruptcy Court for failure to comply with the requirements of the Bankruptcy Act or Rules (paragraph 309).

19. For certain classes of offender, courts should make greater use of the power to impose a criminal bankruptcy order, with the view to a future attachment of the bankrupt's earnings under section 51(2) of the Bankruptcy Act 1914 (paragraph 305).

20. The Official Receiver should be asked to indicate to the Parole Board at the moment of eligibility for parole (and at intervals thereafter) the extent of the prisoner's co-operation in the execution of the criminal bankruptcy order (paragraph 301).

21. Section 39 of the Powers of Criminal Courts Act 1973 should be amended to obviate the need to fix a finite sum above the statutory minimum aggregate amount of loss or damage or to identify all the creditors in the case (paragraph 297).

22. If recommendation 21 is accepted, there should be a right of appeal against the making of a criminal bankruptcy order (paragraph 298).

23. Consideration should be given to broadening the scope of section 154 of the Bankruptcy Act 1914 to include an offence, in the case of the criminal bankrupt, of failing to give information about his assets, either by refusing to answer questions or by giving false information (paragraph 302).

24. Paragraph 8 of Schedule 2 of the Powers of Criminal Courts Act 1973 should be amended to permit a person appointed under section 19 of the Bankruptcy Act 1914 to be the trustee in a criminal bankruptcy case, as an alternative to the Official Receiver (paragraph 304).

Suspended sentences

25. A court activating a suspended sentence should have power to review and vary any incidental orders requiring the payment of fines, compensation or costs passed at the time that the suspended sentence was imposed (paragraph 267).

Fines

26. There should be a review of the system of fines and their enforcement (paragraph 289).

THE NEW MAXIMA

TABLE 1

New maximum penalties derived from 90% levels (based upon offenders convicted at the Crown Court in 1974–76 and sentenced to immediate imprisonment)[1]

Key: † Not applicable to exceptional cases—see Chapter 10.
* Offence grouped with other offences for the purpose of determining the new maximum penalty.

Offence	Statutory provision	Existing maximum penalty	New maximum penalty†
Murder	Common law and Murder (Abolition of Death Penalty) Act 1965, section 1	Life imprisonment	Life imprisonment
Manslaughter	Common law and Offences against the Person Act 1861, section 5	Life imprisonment	Life imprisonment
	Homicide Act 1957, section 2	Life imprisonment	Life imprisonment
Wounding with intent to do grievous bodily harm	Offences against the Person Act 1861, section 18	Life imprisonment	5 years
Inflicting grievous bodily harm unlawfully	*Ibid.*, section 20	5 years	3 years
Assault with intent to resist arrest	*Ibid.*, section 38	2 years	2 years*
Assault occasioning actual bodily harm	Common law and Offences against the Person Act 1861, section 47	5 years	2 years
Common assault	Common law and Offences against the Person Act 1861, section 47	12 months	12 months
Possessing in a public place an offensive weapon	Prevention of Crime Act 1953, section 1	2 years	2 years
Possessing a firearm with intent to commit an indictable offence	Firearms Act 1968, section 18(1) and Schedule 6	14 years	5 years
Rape	Sexual Offences Act 1956, section 1 and 2nd Schedule	Life imprisonment	7 years
Sexual intercourse with a girl under 13 years	*Ibid.*, section 5 and 2nd Schedule	Life imprisonment	5 years

[1] This table (and Table 2 which follows) does not include offences newly created or where the law has been radically altered since 1974; for example, offences under the Road Traffic Act 1974 and offences under section 3 of the Explosive Substances Act 1883 as amended by section 33 of the Criminal Law Act 1977.

TABLE 1—*continued*

Offence	Statutory provision	Existing maximum penalty	New maximum penalty†
Sexual intercourse with a girl under 16 years	*Ibid.*, section 6 and 2nd Schedule	2 years	2 years
Incest by a man	*Ibid.*, section 10 and 2nd Schedule	7 years. If girl under 13 years, life imprisonment	5 years*
Incest by a woman	*Ibid.*, section 11 and 2nd Schedule	7 years	5 years*
Buggery with a boy under 16 years, a woman or an animal	*Ibid.*, section 12 and 2nd Schedule	Life imprisonment	7 years
Indecent assault on a woman	*Ibid.*, section 14 and 2nd Schedule as amended by the Indecency with Children Act 1960, section 2	2 years. If under 13 years, 5 years	2 years 3 years
Indecent assault on a man	Sexual Offences Act 1956, section 15 and 2nd Schedule	10 years	5 years
Man living on earnings of prostitution	*Ibid.*, section 30	7 years	4 years*
Woman exercising control over a prostitute	*Ibid.*, section 31	7 years	4 years*
Theft	Theft Act 1968, section 1	10 years	3 years
Robbery and assault with intent to rob	*Ibid.*, section 8	Life imprisonment	6 years
Burglary	*Ibid.*, section 9	14 years	3 years
Aggravated burglary	*Ibid.*, section 10	Life imprisonment	6 years
Taking motor vehicle or other conveyance without authority	*Ibid.*, section 12	3 years	2 years
Obtaining property by deception	*Ibid.*, section 15	10 years	3 years
Obtaining pecuniary advantage by deception	*Ibid.*, section 16	5 years	3 years
False accounting	*Ibid.*, section 17	7 years	2 years
Blackmail	*Ibid.*, section 21	14 years	5 years
Handling stolen goods	*Ibid.*, section 22	14 years	3 years
Going equipped for stealing	*Ibid.*, section 25	3 years	2 years
Conspiracy to defraud	Common law	At large	4 years

TABLE 1—*continued*

Offence	Statutory provision	Existing maximum penalty	New maximum penalty†
Destroying or damaging property	Criminal Damage Act 1971, sections 1(1) and 4(2)	10 years	2 years*
Destroying or damaging property with intent to endanger life	*Ibid.*, sections 1(2) and 4(1)	Life imprisonment	2 years*
Arson	*Ibid.*, sections 1(3) and 4(1)	Life imprisonment	5 years
Causing explosion likely to endanger life or property	Explosive Substances Act 1883, section 2	Life imprisonment	2 years*
Placing explosives against a Post Office or a post box	Post Office Act 1953, section 60	12 months	12 months
Forgery Act offences	Forgery Act 1913	Life imprisonment	3 years
Affray	Common law	At large	3 years
Perjury Act offences	Perjury Act 1911	7 years	2 years*
False statement to secure a passport	Criminal Justice Act 1925, section 36	2 years	2 years*
Indecency with or towards a child under 14 years	Indecency with Children Act 1960, section 1	2 years	2 years
Supplying or offering to supply a controlled drug	Misuse of Drugs Act 1971, section 4(3) and Schedule 4	Classes A and B, 14 years Class C, 5 years	} 5 years
Possession of a controlled drug	*Ibid.*, section 5(2) and Schedule 4	Class A, 7 years Class B, 5 years Class C, 2 years	} 3 years 2 years
Possession of a controlled drug with intent to supply	*Ibid.*, section 5(3) and Schedule 4	Classes A and B, 14 years Class C, 5 years	} 4 years
Unlawful importation of a drug controlled under the Misuse of Drugs Act 1971	Customs and Excise Act 1952, sections 45(1) and 304	Classes A and B, 14 years Class C, 5 years	} 5 years
Assisting illegal entry	Immigration Act 1971, section 25(1)	7 years	4 years
Fabrication of false evidence, causing a person to be wrongly convicted, interference with witnesses	Common law	At large	3 years

TABLE 2

Other new maximum penalties (applying in general to offences giving rise to less than 50 cases in 1974–76)

Key: † Not applicable to exceptional cases—see Chapter 10.
* Maximum penalty as for the completed offence.

Offence	Statutory provision	Existing maximum penalty	New maximum penalty†
Attempted murder	Common law	Life imprisonment	Life imprisonment*
Infanticide	Infanticide Act 1938, section 1	Life imprisonment	Life imprisonment
Soliciting, encouraging, persuading or proposing to another to commit murder	Offences against the Person Act 1861, section 4	10 years	5 years
Threatening to murder	*Ibid.*, section 16	10 years	5 years
Attempting to choke or strangle in order to commit an indictable offence	*Ibid.*, section 21	Life imprisonment	7 years
Administering a drug with intent to commit an indictable offence	*Ibid.*, section 22	Life imprisonment	7 years
Administering poison with intent to endanger life or inflict grievous bodily harm	*Ibid.*, section 23	10 years	5 years
Administering poison with intent to injure or annoy	*Ibid.*, section 24	5 years	3 years
Causing bodily injury by explosions	*Ibid.*, section 28	Life imprisonment	7 years
Causing grievous bodily harm by explosives or corrosives	*Ibid.*, section 29	Life imprisonment	7 years
Placing explosives near a building	*Ibid.*, section 30	14 years	6 years
Placing anything on a railway with intent to endanger passengers	*Ibid.*, section 32	Life imprisonment	7 years
Endangering railway passengers by throwing anything at railway carriages	*Ibid.*, section 33	Life imprisonment	7 years
Doing or omitting anything so as to endanger railway passengers	*Ibid.*, section 34	2 years	2 years
Causing bodily harm by furious driving	*Ibid.*, section 35	2 years	2 years
Abduction of a child under 14 years	*Ibid.*, section 56	7 years	4 years
Bigamy	*Ibid.*, section 57	7 years	4 years

150

TABLE 2—*continued*

Offence	Statutory provision	Existing maximum penalty	New maximum penalty†
Procuring a miscarriage	*Ibid.*, section 58	Life imprisonment	7 years
Supplying poison or instruments with intent to procure a miscarriage	*Ibid.*, section 59	5 years	3 years
Concealment of birth	*Ibid.*, section 60	2 years	2 years
Child destruction	Infant Life (Preservation) Act 1929, section 1	Life imprisonment	7 years
Cruelty to or neglect of children under 16 years	Children and Young Persons Act 1933, section 1(1)	2 years	2 years
Cruelty to or neglect of children under 16 years by persons with a financial interest	*Ibid.*, section 1(5)	5 years	3 years
Making or possessing explosives under suspicious circumstances	Explosive Substances Act 1883, section 4	14 years	6 years
Threats to destroy or damage property	Criminal Damage Act 1971, sections 2 and 4(2)	10 years	5 years
Possessing anything with intent to commit criminal damage	*Ibid.*, sections 3 and 4(2)	10 years	5 years
Possessing a firearm or ammunition without a firearms certificate	Firearms Act 1968, section 1(1) and Schedule 6	3 years. If aggravated, 5 years	2 years 3 years
Possessing firearms with intent to endanger life	*Ibid.*, section 16 and Schedule 6	Life imprisonment	7 years
Using firearms with intent to resist arrest	*Ibid.*, section 17(1) and Schedule 6	Life imprisonment	7 years
Possessing a firearm while committing an offence	*Ibid.*, section 17(2) and Schedule 6	14 years	6 years
Sending an unseaworthy ship to sea	Merchant Shipping Act 1894, section 457	2 years	2 years
Endangering life on board ship by breach of duty	Pilotage Act 1913, section 46	2 years	2 years
Misconduct of master or member of crew	Merchant Shipping Act 1970, section 27	2 years	2 years
Attempted rape	Sexual Offences Act 1956, section 1 and 2nd Schedule	7 years	7 years*
Procurement of a woman by threats	*Ibid.*, section 2 and 2nd Schedule	2 years	2 years
Procurement of a woman by false pretences	*Ibid.*, section 3 and 2nd Schedule	2 years	2 years

151

TABLE 2—*continued*

Offence	Statutory provision	Existing maximum penalty	New maximum penalty†
Administering drugs to obtain intercourse	*Ibid.*, section 4 and 2nd Schedule	2 years	2 years
Attempted sexual intercourse with a girl under 13 years	*Ibid.*, section 5 and 2nd Schedule as amended by the Indecency with Children Act 1960, section 2	7 years	5 years*
Attempted sexual intercourse with a girl under 16 years	Sexual Offences Act 1956, section 6 and 2nd Schedule	2 years	2 years*
Male having unlawful sexual intercourse with female defective	*Ibid.*, section 7 and 2nd Schedule as amended by the Mental Health Act 1959, section 127	2 years	2 years
Procurement of female defective	Sexual Offences Act 1956, section 9 and 2nd Schedule	2 years	2 years
Attempted incest by a man	*Ibid.*, section 10 and 2nd Schedule as amended by the Indecency with Children Act 1960, section 2	2 years. If under 13 years, life imprisonment	5 years*
Attempted incest by a woman	Sexual Offences Act 1956, section 11 and 2nd Schedule	2 years	5 years*
Buggery with a man of or over 16 years without his consent	*Ibid.*, section 12 and Sexual Offences Act 1967, section 3(1)(*a*)	10 years	5 years
Buggery by a man of 21 years or over with another under 21 years with consent	Sexual Offences Act 1956, section 12 and Sexual Offences Act 1967, section 3(1)(*b*)	5 years	3 years
Buggery with a man other than the above and other than with a boy under 16 years	Sexual Offences Act 1956, section 12 and Sexual Offences Act 1967, section 3(1)(*b*)	2 years	2 years
Attempt to commit buggery with a boy under 16 years, a woman or an animal	Sexual Offences Act 1956, section 12 and 2nd Schedule	10 years	7 years*
Indecency between males	*Ibid.*, section 13 and 2nd Schedule as amended by the Sexual Offences Act 1967, section 3(2)	2 years. If by a man of or over 21 years with a man under that age, 5 years	2 years 3 years
Assault with intent to commit buggery	Sexual Offences Act 1956, section 16 and 2nd Schedule	10 years	5 years
Abduction of a woman by force	*Ibid.*, section 17 and 2nd Schedule	14 years	6 years

TABLE 2—*continued*

Offence	Statutory provision	Existing maximum penalty	New maximum penalty†
Abduction of unmarried girl under 18 years	*Ibid.*, section 19 and 2nd Schedule	2 years	2 years
Abduction of unmarried girl under 16 years	*Ibid.*, section 20 and 2nd Schedule	2 years	2 years
Abduction of female defective	*Ibid.*, section 21 and 2nd Schedule	2 years	2 years
Causing prostitution of a woman	*Ibid.*, section 22 and 2nd Schedule	2 years	2 years
Procuration of a girl under 21 years	*Ibid.*, section 23 and 2nd Schedule	2 years	2 years
Detention of a woman in a brothel	*Ibid.*, section 24 and 2nd Schedule	2 years	2 years
Permitting girl under 13 years to use premises for intercourse	*Ibid.*, section 25 and 2nd Schedule	Life imprisonment	7 years
Permitting girl between 13 and 16 years to use premises for intercourse	*Ibid.*, section 26 and 2nd Schedule	2 years	2 years
Permitting female defective to use premises for intercourse	*Ibid.*, section 27 and 2nd Schedule	2 years	2 years
Person responsible for girl under 16 years causing or encouraging her prostitution	*Ibid.*, section 28 and 2nd Schedule	2 years	2 years
Causing or encouraging prostitution of female defective	*Ibid.*, section 29 and 2nd Schedule	2 years	2 years
Solicitation by a man	*Ibid.*, section 32 and 2nd Schedule	2 years	2 years
Male hospital staff having unlawful sexual intercourse with patient	Mental Health Act 1959, section 128	2 years	2 years
Man procuring an act of buggery between two men which by reason of section 1(1) of the Sexual Offences Act 1967 is not an offence	Sexual Offences Act 1967, section 4	2 years	2 years
Man or woman living wholly or in part on the earnings of male prostitution	*Ibid.*, section 5	7 years	4 years
Removal of articles from places open to the public	Theft Act 1968, section 11	5 years	3 years
Abstracting electricity	*Ibid.*, section 13	5 years	3 years

TABLE 2—*continued*

Offence	Statutory provision	Existing maximum penalty	New maximum penalty†
False statement by directors	*Ibid.*, section 19	7 years	4 years
Suppression of documents	*Ibid.*, section 20(1)	7 years	4 years
Procuring execution of a valuable security	*Ibid.*, section 20(2)	7 years	4 years
Bankruptcy offences where no specific penalty is provided	Bankruptcy Act 1914, sections 154(1), 155, 157, 158, 159 and 164	2 years	2 years
Frauds by bankrupts	*Ibid.*, sections 156 and 164	12 months	12 months
Obtaining property or disposing of property	*Ibid.*, sections 154(1)(15) and 154(2)	5 years	3 years
Accepting property from a bankrupt	*Ibid.*, section 154(3)	7 years	4 years
Undischarged bankrupt acting as a director	Companies Act 1948, section 187	2 years	2 years
Fraudulent trading	*Ibid.*, section 332(3)	2 years	2 years
Inducing investment by false statement	Prevention of Fraud (Investments) Act 1958, section 13	7 years	4 years
Buying or selling counterfeit coins	Coinage Offences Act 1936, section 6	Life imprisonment	7 years
Impairing gold or silver coins	*Ibid.*, section 3	14 years	6 years
Uttering counterfeit coins	*Ibid.*, section 5(1)	12 months	12 months
Uttering counterfeit coins resembling gold or silver coin	*Ibid.*, section 5(2)	2 years	2 years
Defacing current coins	*Ibid.*, section 4	12 months	12 months
Making counterfeit coins	*Ibid.*, section 8	12 months	12 months
Making coining implements	*Ibid.*, section 9	Life imprisonment	7 years
Making or uttering counterfeit dies or marks	Hallmarking Act 1973, section 6	10 years	5 years
Aiding and abetting suicide	Suicide Act 1961, section 2	14 years	6 years
Production of a controlled drug	Misuse of Drugs Act 1971, section 4(2) and Schedule 4	Classes A and B, 14 years Class C, 5 years	6 years 3 years
Cultivation of cannabis plant	*Ibid.*, section 6(2) and Schedule 4	14 years	6 years
Occupier of premises permitting certain activities there	*Ibid.*, section 8 and Schedule 4	Classes A and B, 14 years Class C, 5 years	6 years 3 years

TABLE 2—*continued*

Offence	Statutory provision	Existing maximum penalty	New maximum penalty†
Offences relating to opium	*Ibid.*, section 9 and Schedule 4	14 years	6 years
Assisting in or inducing commission outside the United Kingdom of an offence punishable under a corresponding law	*Ibid.*, section 20 and Schedule 4	14 years	6 years
Obstructing exercise of powers of search or concealing books or drugs	*Ibid.*, section 23(4) and Schedule 4	2 years	2 years
Unlawful exportation of a drug controlled under the Misuse of Drugs Act 1971	Customs and Excise Act 1952, sections 56(2) and 304	Classes A and B, 14 years Class C, 5 years	6 years 3 years
Contravention of regulations	Misuse of Drugs Act 1971, section 18(1) and Schedule 4	2 years	2 years
Riot	Common law	At large	7 years
Unlawful assembly	Common law	At large	7 years
Offensive behaviour in public conducive to a breach of the peace	Public Order Act 1936, section 5 and Public Order Act 1963, section 1(1)	12 months	12 months
Publishing a defamatory libel knowing its falsity	Libel Act 1843, section 4	2 years	2 years
Publishing a defamatory libel	*Ibid.*, section 5	12 months	12 months
Keeping a disorderly house	Disorderly Houses Act 1751, section 8	2 years	2 years
Corrupt practices at elections	Representation of the People Act 1949, section 47	2 years	2 years
Personation acknowledging bail	Forgery Act 1861, section 34	7 years	4 years
Smuggling	Customs and Excise Act 1952, section 304	2 years	2 years
Kidnapping	Common law	Life imprisonment	7 years
Hijacking	Hijacking Act 1971, section 1	Life imprisonment	7 years
Corrupt transactions with agents	Prevention of Corruption Act 1906, section 1	2 years	2 years
Assisting prisoners to escape	Prison Act 1952, section 39 and Criminal Justice Act 1961, section 22(1)	5 years	3 years

TABLE 2—*continued*

Offence	Statutory provision	Existing maximum penalty	New maximum penalty†
Harbouring escaped prisoners	Criminal Justice Act 1961, section 22	2 years	2 years
Indecent exposure	Common law	At large	7 years
Genocide	Genocide Act 1969, section 1	Life imprisonment	Life imprisonment
Biological weapons offences	Biological Weapons Act 1974, section 1	Life imprisonment	7 years
Concealment of an offence	Criminal Law Act 1967, section 5	2 years	2 years
Contempt	Common law	At large	7 years
Corruption where H.M. Government or a public body is concerned	Prevention of Corruption Act 1916, section 1	7 years	4 years
Causing a public nuisance	Common law	At large	7 years
Slave trading	Slave Trade Act 1824, section 9 and Punishment of Offences Act 1837, section 1	Life imprisonment	7 years
Unlawful drilling:— being trained training men	Unlawful Drilling Act 1819, section 1	2 years 7 years	2 years 4 years
Assisting offenders	Criminal Law Act 1967, section 4	Varies with the principal offence	In a case of murder, 7 years. Otherwise half that of the principal offence[1]
Incitement to commit crime	Common law	At large	As for substantive offence

[1] This decision attempts broadly to reflect the position under the existing penalty structure.

APPENDIX B (Chapter 9)

CALCULATION OF THE NEW MAXIMA

1. We decided that the new maximum penalty for offences involving the ordinary offender should be determined by reference to the sentence length below which 90% of all sentences of immediate imprisonment imposed upon offenders convicted in the Crown Court currently fell.

2. The calculation of the 90% levels was based upon sentencing practice in Crown Court trials in the years 1974 to 1976. The calculation might have been based upon the most recent single year for which figures were available—1976—or upon a longer period—say, 10 years. A single year, however, would not have provided sufficient cases for many offences, and the longer period would have been unsatisfactory if there were trends in the data. We therefore compromised by using the three most recent years for which figures were available.

3. In order to obtain data on sentence lengths for individual offences, more refined details of offence classifications and sentence lengths were needed than those published in the annual *Criminal Statistics*. The published tables give figures for whole classifications only, whereas reference to the appendix to the *Criminal Statistics* shows that most offence classifications are broken down into sub-classifications. For example, under classification 5 (wounding, or other acts endangering life) there is subsumed a host of offences, ranging from the most serious wounding under section 18 of the Offences against the Person Act 1861 to offences involving the use of explosives and the variegated offences under the Firearms Act 1968. Most of the serious offences are categorised separately so that information relating to individual offences can be obtained. Some sub-classifications cover more than one offence and in these cases information relating to an individual offence cannot readily be obtained (this sometimes occurs where a classification which is not sub-divided covers more than one offence). In such cases the 90% level was calculated on the basis of the combined information relating to more than one offence. Appendix A indicates the offences in respect of which this procedure was adopted.

4. The 90% level method of calculating the new maximum penalties was applied to offences of which at least 50 offenders[1] were convicted and sentenced to immediate imprisonment between 1974 and 1976. These offences (listed in Table 1 of Appendix A) accounted for 95% of Crown Court trials in which immediate imprisonment was imposed in that period. We considered 50 to be the minimum number of cases that would permit a reasonably reliable estimate to be made of the 90% level, but in practice the calculation was based upon more than 100 cases for most offences. For about three quarters of the offences in Table 1 the 90% level was estimated on the basis that the sentence lengths followed a standard "skew" distribution, with the peak towards the end of the distribution which contains the shorter sentence lengths (four examples are given in Charts A–D). Where the distribution of sentence lengths was atypical, cases were simply counted and the sentence length band in which the 90% level fell was noted.

5. The calculation of the 90% level produced, in most cases, answers in fractions of years. Although courts do pass sentences in fractions of a year up to three years, beyond that point we have assumed that sentences imposed for individual offences, as distinct from consecutive sentences, were integers. For example, if the 90% level fell in the sentence band over four years up to and including five years, it was most

---

[1] Some offenders may have been counted more than once in the three-year period.

unlikely that any value other than five years had been recorded in that band, and accordingly five years constituted the 90% level. This assumption was consistent with the decision that we should not recommend any new maxima involving half-years (see paragraph 177 of the report) and meant that for most offences the new maximum penalty encompassed more than 90% of the recorded sentences. (In no case did the new maximum penalty encompass less than 90% of the recorded sentences.)

6. For many offences (listed in Table 2 of Appendix A) the number of cases recorded over the period 1974-76 was less than 50, and this we considered too small a sample to use the procedure described above. New maximum penalties were obtained for these offences by scaling down their statutory maxima according to the reductions already proposed for the statutory maxima for offences of which 50 or more cases had been recorded. For each offence in Table 1, the maximum sentence imposed by the Crown Court over the period 1974-76 was compared with the new maximum penalty (the 90% level). We found that the higher the recorded maximum sentence, the greater was the reduction represented by the new maximum penalty. For example, maximum recorded sentences of 3, 7 and 14 years were, on average, associated with new maximum penalties of 2, 4 and 6 years respectively. Because, however, the numbers of cases were small, the maxima imposed in the chosen period were not necessarily reliable guides to the maximum sentences that might occur in the long run. Therefore the statutory maxima were used in place of the recorded maxima when the new maximum penalties were derived. The result was that the new maximum penalties tended to be higher than they would have been had the calculation been based upon the recorded maxima.

7. Three further rules were superimposed on the procedures described above:

   (i) inchoate offences (for example, attempts) were assigned the same new maximum penalties as the completed offences, regardless of the information available about sentence lengths for these offences;

  (ii) no existing statutory maxima were reduced below two years; and

 (iii) existing statutory maxima of two years or less remained unaltered.

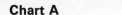

Chart A   Burglary (Theft Act 1968 s.9)

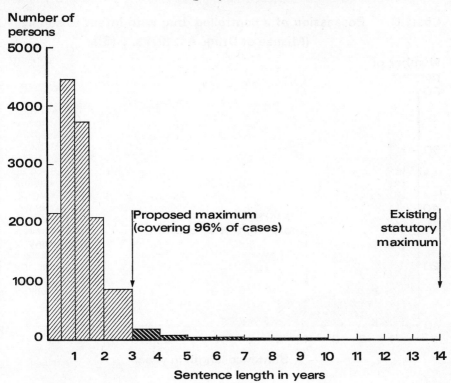

Chart B   Obtaining property by deception (Theft Act 1968 s. 15)

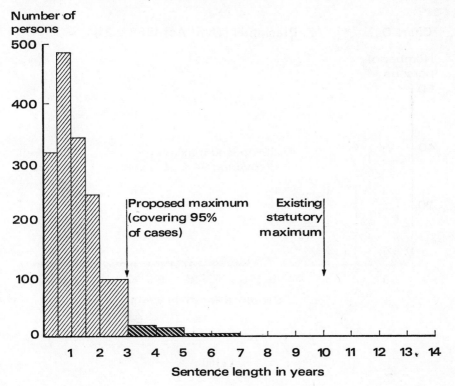

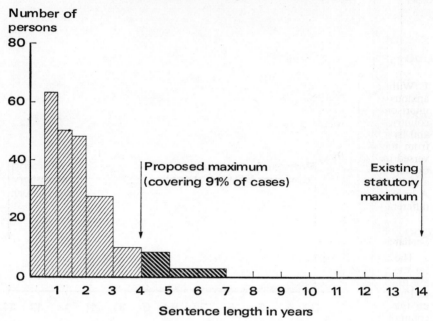

**Chart C   Possession of a controlled drug with intent to supply
(Misuse of Drugs Act 1971 s. 5 (3))**

Number of persons

Proposed maximum (covering 91% of cases)

Existing statutory maximum

Sentence length in years

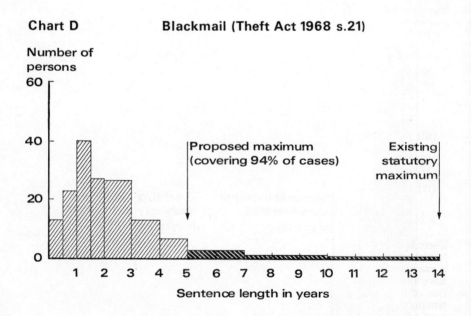

Chart D   Blackmail (Theft Act 1968 s.21)

Number of persons

Proposed maximum (covering 94% of cases)

Existing statutory maximum

Sentence length in years

APPENDIX C (Chapter 2)

MAXIMUM PENALTIES IN OTHER COUNTRIES

1. Without indulging in a major comparative study of modern penal codes, we were anxious to discover how other comparable countries legislated for the penalty of imprisonment. Accordingly, we looked at the system in Scotland, in a selection of countries of Western Europe and of the old Commonwealth, and in the United States and Israel. We did not visit any of these countries but rather sought written evidence from their governments or received oral evidence from academic authorities well versed in their sentencing practice. Our chief interest was to discover their structure of maximum penalties, how it relates to the sentences actually passed by the courts, and its results in terms of the length of the prison sentences to which it gives rise. A brief survey of this kind inevitably overlooks many important features peculiar to different jurisdictions.

Scotland

2. The most striking feature of the criminal law in Scotland to English eyes is that for the great majority of the more serious crimes (homicide, assault, theft etc.) there are no maximum prison terms. This is because they remain crimes at common law and have not been reduced to statute as in England. Consequently there are no limits on the power of the High Court of Justiciary to impose imprisonment for these common law offences and so, in theory at least, the discretion of Scottish sentencers is even wider than that of their English counterparts.

3. In reality, however, sentencing practice is controlled to a great degree in Scotland by the limitations placed upon the sentencing powers of the different types of court. The four types of criminal court in Scotland are:

(i) *the district (summary) court* presided over by justices: it can impose prison sentences only up to a maximum of 60 days in common law cases, and normally the statutory offences it can try carry penalties not exceeding this limit;

(ii) *the sheriff summary court*, with the sheriff sitting alone: it is limited to three months' imprisonment (six months' in the case of a second or subsequent conviction of dishonesty or violence) in common law cases. For statutory offences, it can impose penalties up to the maxima prescribed in the statute, but these do not normally exceed three or four months;

(iii) *the sheriff and jury court*, with the jury reaching the verdict on not guilty pleas, and the sheriff sentencing alone (but with a power to remit for sentence to the High Court): its powers are limited to two years' imprisonment in all cases, whether common law or statutory;

(iv) *the High Court of Justiciary*, with the jury reaching the verdict on not guilty pleas, and the single judge sentencing alone: it has unlimited powers to impose imprisonment subject only, in statutory cases, to the maxima imposed by the statute.

There is no general power as in England and Wales for summary courts to remit cases to higher courts for sentence (the power of the sheriff and jury court to remit for sentence is exercised in less than 2% of the cases that come before it), and this is significant since a large proportion of offences in Scotland are dealt with summarily. The proportion of trials on indictment to summary prosecutions in Scotland since the War has remained at about half that of England and Wales. In 1974, for example, 3,157 cases were tried on indictment in Scotland as against 237,989 dealt with summarily; the equivalent figures for England and Wales were 56,403 as against 2,051,680. The wide discretion of the High Court of Justiciary in sentencing is only of practical relevance to a small minority of cases, since less than 15% of cases tried on indictment (that is, roughly 2% of all Scottish cases) are disposed of in that Court. From this, it will be readily apparent that in Scotland the broad discretion lies not with the judges but with the prosecuting authorities—the Lord Advocate and his officers—who in deciding which court the case should be tried in are in effect determining the sentence band that will apply on conviction.

4. In the absence of a statutory system of penalties for the major offences, it is interesting to speculate how Scottish sentencers are guided in their practice, and why no widespread discrepancy in sentencing has resulted. Pronouncements by judges of the High Court of Justiciary have contradicted any suggestion that the court has a "sentencing policy", that is, any normal range of sentences or consultation on how various crimes are to be dealt with. For a country the size of Scotland, however, the question may be largely academic, since trial judges are much less numerous, are largely concentrated in Edinburgh, will be aware of the decisions of their colleagues and will no doubt be directly influenced by them. Given the restrictions upon the powers of all courts but the High Court of Justiciary, it is scarcely surprising that sentences are on average shorter in Scotland than in England and Wales, as the table below demonstrates.

Length of prison sentences in all courts for all crimes and offences in 1974[1]

	Total sentences excluding mandatory life	Up to and including 3 months	Over 3 months up to and including 1 year	Over 1 year up to and including 4 years	Over 4 years	Life	Mandatory life
Scotland	9,396	5,911	2,722	645	118	—	30
%	100	63	29	7	1·3	—	—
England and Wales	28,122	3,925	12,620	10,572	968	37	128
%	100	14	45	38	3·4	0·1	—

A comparison of this kind between two entirely different systems cannot be strictly fair; it does not, of course, take account of the different use of non-custodial penalties in the two jurisdictions and of the varying proportions of types of crime and criminals, nor of suspended sentences, which are not available in Scotland. Despite these reservations, however, what is striking is the proportionately high use of short sentences in Scotland and conversely the apparently greater use made by the courts in England and Wales of sentences between one year and four.

The remainder of Western Europe

5. Broadly speaking, the other countries of Western Europe operate a system which specifies a minimum and maximum penalty for each offence, within which the judges are permitted a fairly wide discretion, although often the prosecution exercises a strong influence upon the sentencing decision. As in England and Wales, the sentences passed by the courts rarely approach the maximum, even where the maximum is relatively low, and in some countries the average length of prison sentences is notably lower than those imposed in England. We looked in particular at the practice in France, Belgium, the Netherlands and Sweden.

[1] *Sources:* Report on the work of the Prison Department, Statistical Tables, 1974. Cmnd. 6152.
Criminal Statistics, Scotland, 1974. Cmnd. 6081.

6. In France, there are five separate sentencing bands available to the courts. They are:

life imprisonment (e.g. for murder, robbery with aggravation)

5 years to 20 years (e.g. for rape, robbery with violence)

5 years to 10 years (e.g. for assault, indecent assault)

2 months to 5 years (e.g. for less serious assaults, minor theft)

1 day to 2 months (e.g. for minor assaults and woundings).

Within the minimum and maximum sentences thus defined, the judge has a wide element of discretion. Indeed, his discretion is wide enough to enable him to pass sentences below the legal minimum and above the maximum. A sentence less than the minimum can be imposed, for example, where there is provocation, where the offender is a minor, and (most commonly of all) where there are generally mitigating circumstances. The effect is to reduce the penalty to the sentence band falling immediately below it and thus to cushion the impact of what to English eyes are high minimum sentences. As a means of combatting recidivism, the judge is given power to exceed the maximum penalty, often by up to twice its length, on the repetition of an offence. Although the principle involved is more like that governing the extended sentence in England, the mechanism provides an interesting parallel to the recommendation in this report for exceeding the maximum (see Chapter 10).

7. In Belgium, minimum and maximum penalties are prescribed in the Criminal Code, and the judge is free to decide each case according to the circumstances surrounding it. The penalty for ordinary theft, for example, is a sentence ranging from one month to five years; for damage to property the range is from eight days to three years. In general, the maximum sentence prescribed by the law is rarely imposed.

8. Sweden follows a similar system of maximum and minimum sentences for each offence. The lowest minimum is one month's imprisonment and the highest maximum is 10 years. The sentence bands are generally lower than in England for similar offences, but, even so, sentences tend to fall a good deal short of the maxima. This is reflected in Swedish prison sentences, which show that only 10% of offenders against the Penal Code[1] go to prison and only 10% of those receive sentences of more than one year. Two thirds of all receptions into prison are for four months or less.

9. In the Netherlands, the acceptance of the short prison sentence is even more marked—less than three months tends to be the norm. We were particularly interested in the Dutch system, since the Netherlands is a country whose enlightened penal policy is often held up as an example to the world.[2] In the period since the Second World War the Dutch have pursued a deliberate policy of reducing the role of imprisonment in the penal system and have done so without any of the dire consequences often predicted for such a policy. In 1950, the average prison sentence there was 5·6 months; by 1972, it was three months. In any comparison of Dutch figures with those of England and Wales, it has, of course, to be recalled that the population of the Netherlands is only 13 million.

10. The minimum sentence in the Netherlands is one day's imprisonment; the maximum varies according to the crime. The Dutch have two grades of offences, the serious and the minor. For minor offences, the maximum penalty never exceeds one year, and the form of imprisonment is less rigorous than for serious offences. In the case of the latter, the highest determinate maximum is 15 years, the penalty for manslaughter. The maxima provide a general indication of the gravity with which an offence is regarded and are lower than in England: for example, rape carries a maximum penalty

---

[1] Excluding drunk and disorderly behaviour and special legislation, for example, dealing with narcotics or driving offences.
[2] See, for example, House of Commons Official Report, Vol. 929, No. 81, Cols. 567–8. 31 March 1977.

of 12 years; that for serious theft is six years. As in France, the discretion of the judiciary is extended by a power to go beyond the maxima in certain circumstances. Thus the maximum for consecutive sentences is in general one third more than the normal maximum for the offence. The highest maximum of 15 years can therefore be increased to 20 where consecutive sentences are imposed, where the court has power to impose a life sentence or where the offender is a government employee who has misused his position. Life imprisonment is available only for an offence which threatens the continued existence of the State and for serious homicide or attempted homicide. In general, attempts to commit a crime or for being an accessory to a crime carry a penalty one third less than the maximum for the full offence. In certain cases, a court is empowered to order a fine in place of a custodial sentence where it would normally only be able to order the latter.

11. Sentences in the Netherlands rarely approach the maximum penalty, and normally fall well below it. The following table shows the sentences passed for a selection of offences in 1972, and illustrates the extent to which the lower end of the sentencing scale is used.

Sentences passed in the Netherlands in 1972 for a selection of offences

Offence	Total convicted	Total imprisoned	Full suspension	Partial suspension	up to 6 months	over 6 months up to 1 year	over 1 year up to 3 years	over 3 years and under 5 years	5 years and over	Maximum penalty
					— Length of sentence of immediate imprisonment					
Threat	334	158	27	69	50	11	1	—	—	4 years
Manslaughter	68	67	3	24	3	11	11	7	8	15 years
Murder	7	7	—	—	—	1	2	—	4	Life
Rape	85	73	5	34	13	17	3	—	1	12 years
Indecent assault	111	53	10	21	16	6	—	—	—	8 years
Forgery	655	324	127	89	95	7	5	1	—	5 years
Simple theft	6,402	1,506	290	396	770	46	4	—	—	4 years
Theft with combined efforts	4,269	1,252	194	501	445	87	25	—	—	6 years
Theft with breaking and entering	3,737	1,970	191	984	502	209	77	7	—	6 years
Breaking and entering	1,203	791	98	329	266	88	10	—	—	6 years
Embezzlement	705	195	70	52	65	7	1	—	—	3 years
Aggravated embezzlement[1]	340	153	58	64	22	4	5	—	—	4 years
Fraud	556	252	133	49	55	13	2	—	—	3 years

[1] Embezzlement by someone in personal service or in the course of exercising their profession.

Israel

12. We looked at a number of countries whose legal systems have been moulded on the English model. Israel is a good example. As in England, the maximum penalty laid down for each offence, the highest of which is 20 years, is normally far higher than the longest sentence ever imposed. Tax evasion in Israel, for example, carries a maximum penalty of four years' imprisonment; the usual sentence imposed is around three months suspended. As in England, high maxima are regarded as a measure of the worst possible case, and the judges follow a normal range of sentences by keeping abreast of the levels of sentences imposed in each others' courts.

Australia and New Zealand

13. Understandably, the old Commonwealth countries tend to follow the English system of high maxima divorced from the actual sentencing practice of the present day. The judiciary as a result enjoys the same wide discretion as in England. In Australia, the New South Wales Crimes Act 1900 is often held up as an example of a major criminal statute which fails to provide adequate standards to guide the exercise of the judges' discretion; the maximum penalties in this Act are largely the product of 19th and even 18th century statutes. Cattle stealing is punishable by a maximum of 10 years' penal servitude, theft of a motor car by five years' imprisonment. Sentencing practice does, of course, vary from State to State. In Victoria, for example, a system of minimum sentences has developed; judges are obliged to fix a minimum term to any sentence of two years or more, which has to be served before the offender can become eligible for parole. In New Zealand, the system of high maxima is very similar to that of England, and many of the old 19th century penalties (such as the traditional penalty of 14 years) still remain.

Canada

14. In Canada, minimum sentences exist for a few offences, but otherwise the picture is much the same. The combination of high maxima and wide judicial discretion has led, however, to longer sentences being passed than in England and to a higher incidence of imprisonment, a position which has been the cause of growing concern in recent years. In 1975, in its report entitled *Imprisonment and Release*, the Law Reform Commission of Canada voiced many of the same concerns that we express in this report:

> "One of the most striking aspects of prison terms under the present Code is the very wide discretion given judges in selecting a term. Various offences under the Criminal Code are punishable by life imprisonment, fourteen years, ten years, five years, two years or six months imprisonment. Breaking and entering a dwelling house, for example, is punishable by any term up to life imprisonment. So is rape. Theft over $200·00 is punishable by up to ten years and theft under $200·00 by up to two years. Common assault prosecuted as a summary conviction offence can be punished by six months' imprisonment while manslaughter carries a sentence of life imprisonment.
>
> These high maximum sentences place an unreasonable burden on judges in requiring them to exercise an unnecessarily wide discretion. In fact these maximum terms appear to be disproportionately high, even anachronistic, when compared with the range of actual sentences pronounced by the courts. About one to four percent of admissions to penitentiaries in a given year carry terms in excess of fifteen years. It is unusual for a sentence for breaking and entering to exceed three years. The average prison sentence for this offence over the years has varied from fourteen to sixteen months, yet it is punishable by life or fourteen years depending upon whether the premises broken into was a dwelling house or a place of business.
>
> Over the years the very wide discretion given judges in selecting prison sentences appears to have settled around an established average, but wide deviations in particular cases raise a risk of unequal treatment and are a source of unrest in prisons. Moreover, in principle discretion should be no greater than necessary and be subject to reasonable guidelines. The Commission is of the view that the maximum prison terms presently provided by law could be reduced without unduly limiting the discretionary power of the court."[1]

---

[1] Law Reform Commission of Canada, Working Paper 11 (Information Canada, 1975), pages 21–2. The extract is reproduced by permission of the Minister of Supply and Services Canada.

15. In its final report[1] to the Minister of Justice in January 1976 the Commission recommended three upper limits of sentence, strictly related to the purpose of the imprisonment. Life imprisonment would be abolished. For offences demanding the separation of the offender for the purpose of protecting society (offences involving serious violence to persons) the upper limit proposed is 20 years. For offences (such as a flagrant breach of trust or a serious violence offence not representing a continuing risk to other persons) where denunciation is the primary purpose of imprisonment, the maximum term would be three years. For the third category, where imprisonment is used to deal with offenders (such as fine defaulters) wilfully in default of obligations imposed under other sentences, the maximum would be six months.

The United States

16. Over the border in the United States, the traditional penalty structure is at the present time equally under fire. Any attempt to describe the legal system in the United States is of necessity an excursion into comparative law, and it is only possible to provide a broad picture of the dominant systems to which most States adhere. Traditionally, the penalty structure has involved a very high degree of indeterminacy, with no appellate process until very recent times, with time actually served in prison governed largely by the parole system. In many States a huge range lies between the maxima and minima prescribed by law, in some cases a range of penalty from nothing to life imprisonment. In other States where sentences are notionally of a fixed length, the actual date of release is nevertheless decided by the mechanism of parole, and great variation can result.

17. Of the model sentencing codes, the Model Penal Code developed by the American Law Institute in the 1950s has won the most support and has been adopted by about half the State legislatures. The Model Penal Code favours fewer offences and the general lowering of maxima. Instead of the traditional structure of an individual penalty assigned to each offence, the Code reduced the sentencing categories to five, with a distinctive set of minimum and maximum limits; for example, a second degree felony carries a minimum of one to three years and a maximum of 10. Legislation prescribes into which of the categories each offence should fall.

18. The Model Penal Code, with its wide sentencing bands within which release is ultimately determined, depends heavily upon a belief in the individualisation of sentence, and the effective potential of prison. As these concepts have lost ground in recent years, the sentencing structure of the Code has come increasingly under fire from a strong body of opinion favouring sentencing based upon "commensurate desert", the introduction of fixed mandatory sentences with no remission and the abolition of executive release. In 1976 the State of Maine adopted a new criminal code which abolished parole and introduced a system of wholly determinate sentences. Broadly, the number of years selected by the judge within the legislatively authorised maximum became the amount of time which would actually be served. The Uniform Determinate Sentencing Act of 1976, brought into force in California in July 1977, is a further development of this philosophy. Here, sentences are fixed in sets of three time periods; for example, two, three or four years for burglary; five, six or seven years for second degree murder. The new law not only abolishes discretionary release, but also goes a long way towards destroying the discretion of the judiciary. The judge is bound to pick the middle number of these three time periods, unless there are mitigating circumstances, when he must pick the lower number, or aggravating circumstances when he must choose the higher one.

19. This philosophy of fixed determinate sentencing is gathering momentum at the present time as the pressure grows to abandon indeterminacy, with its perceived vices. We were interested, however, by the evidence we received of a third approach, which is also steadily gaining ground and which represents a judicious compromise between the evils of the completely indeterminate and the completely determinate systems.

---

[1] *Guidelines—A Report on Dispositions and Sentences in the Criminal Process* (Information Canada, 1976).

This is the system of sentencing guidelines, developed by the Criminal Justice Research Centre in Albany, New York, which attempts to provide a structure to control judicial discretion, but not to fetter it. The guideline sentence, which is given to the judge when trying a particular case, represents an average of all the sentences given for that particular kind of case by all the judges in that jurisdiction in the recent past. The guideline is calculated statistically, taking account of a wide range of variable factors relating to the offender and the offence based both on a detailed analysis of past cases and intensive discussion with the judges as to sentencing practice in their jurisdiction. Judges are not forced in any way to adhere to the guidelines, but if they depart from them they are required to give their reasons in writing. A more detailed description of the system is provided by the article annexed to this Appendix. The attractions of such a system are highlighted in judicial eyes by the spread of determinate sentencing which allows for little or no discretion. The system has been adopted by a number of local jurisdictions and is likely soon to be adopted by individual States; during our deliberations a Bill was before Congress which would extend the principle to the Federal jurisdiction.

20. The guidelines approach is of particular interest to us because it has roughly the same objective as our own recommendations, namely to give formal recognition to what the courts are already practising. Sentencing guidelines would have, of course, a more direct impact upon sentencing than our own proposals, and we doubt whether such a sophisticated formalisation of the "tariff" would be acceptable in the English context. Nonetheless, we consider that the progress of this new concept in sentencing should continue to be watched.

Conclusion

21. Our review of the practice in other jurisdictions revealed two underlying themes with which we have considerable sympathy. The first is the recognition (evidenced particularly by the case of Canada as seen by the Law Reform Commission) that English-style high maxima are irrelevant to a modern penal policy, and should be abolished in favour of greatly reduced penalties. We hope that our own proposals will promote further discussion in those countries whose practice has developed from the English system and who have doubts about its continuing viability. Secondly, we were struck by the evidence from countries like the Netherlands where a policy of reducing the length of prison sentences has been carried out successfully without damage to the fabric of society. It is in our view hardly surprising that the maximum penalties in such countries are on average much lower than our own.

167

Article from Judicature, The Journal of the American Judicature Society Vol. 60, No. 5. December 1976[1]

Is the end of judicial sentencing in sight?

by Jack M. Kress, Leslie T. Wilkins and Don M. Gottfredson[2]

There is a rising call throughout the land, from liberal and conservative alike, to take away the judge's sentencing discretion. In its place, critics would substitute legislative sentencing in the form of "flat-time" or "presumptive sentencing" or, most often, "mandatory sentencing."

This call to eliminate judicial discretion stems from the growing recognition that the sentencing process must be made more rational and consistent. Fairness demands that individuals who have similar backgrounds and similar criminal histories should receive similar sentences when they are convicted of the same crime. But up until now, judges have not had the tools with which to achieve this level of equity. Hence, the thrust towards a legislative solution.

While a serious problem does exist, abolition of judicial sentencing discretion is not the answer. For almost two years, the authors have been co-directing a sentencing study under the sponsorship of the Law Enforcement Assistance Administration.[3] We propose a middle course between retaining the disparity inherent in present indeterminate practices and legislatively mandating sentences which will ignore justifiable distinctions among offenders. We have devised a guideline system to provide trial court judges with the tools which will enable them to put their own house in order. First, however, let us examine the alternatives.

Indeterminate sentences

Early in this century and until recently, enhancing the discretionary powers of both judges and parole boards was hailed as a major reform. Indeterminate sentencing seemed to offer "the best of both worlds—long protection for the public yet a fully flexible opportunity for the convict's rehabilitation."[4] The judge could render a probationary sentence when the experts' presentence report showed that to be in the best interests of both the defendant and the public. The indeterminacy of the prison sentence would leave the eventual release of the defendant to the "experts"—correctional and paroling authorities who could diagnose the offender's problems, treat them, and best decide when (and under what circumstances) the offender should be released.

Today, almost no one defends the totally indeterminate sentence. Prisoners' rights groups such as the Prisoner's Union denounce the concept as wholly unfair to the defendant in both a psychological and a material sense.[5] "Law and order" advocates, on the other hand, argue that the offender-orientation of indeterminacy often ignores the cruel facts of the specific offense.

Judicial discretion, critics contend, has led to sentencing disparity. Numerous studies have demonstrated great disparity, at least to the satisfaction of the growing body of

[1] We are grateful to the publishers of *Judicature* for permission to reproduce this article in its entirety.
[2] Jack Kress is a Director of the Criminal Justice Research Centre at Albany, New York. Leslie Wilkins is professor at the Graduate School of Criminal Justice at the State University of New York at Albany, and a former member of the Home Office Research Unit. Don Gottfredson is Dean of the Rutgers University School of Criminal Justice.
[3] The research discussed in this article was undertaken under the auspices of "Sentencing Guidelines: Structuring Judicial Discretion," a research project funded by the National Institute of Law Enforcement and Criminal Justice, Law Enforcement Assistance Administration, United States Department of Justice. The viewpoints and opinions expressed do not necessarily represent those of the funding agency.
[4] Ramsey Clark, CRIME IN AMERICA (New York: Simon and Schuster, 1970), Chapter 13.
[5] See the attack on indeterminate sentencing by the American Friends Service Committee, STRUGGLE FOR JUSTICE (New York: Hill and Wang, 1971).

judicial critics.[1] Hence, the almost universally proposed reform: End sentencing disparity by taking discretion away from the judges and lodging it instead with state legislators (as if, for some unstated reason, legislators are incapable of institutionalizing disparity).

In short, the philosophical pendulum has swung away from the rehabilitative undergirding of the indeterminate sentence toward a retributive view now trendily packaged as "just deserts."[2]

Mandatory sentences

At present, the proposal for a "mandatory minimum sentence" for given offenses is getting wide play in the press since its advocates are as diverse as President Gerald Ford and Senator Edward Kennedy.[3] This measure fixes a minimum sentence that must be served for conviction of a crime within an offense category, without regard to the circumstances of the offense or the backgrounds of the offenders. However, the actual time served may still remain discretionary with the parole board.

The "flat-time" concept tells judges to specify a definite sentence if they impose a prison sentence at all. Prisoners sometimes may shorten their sentences through "good behavior" in prison, but they cannot be paroled. Only when the sentence is complete is the prisoner released. One widely quoted variant proposed by David Fogel supplies the judge with a legislatively prescribed length for any prison sentence the judge chooses to impose, but permits the judge a wide range of upward or downward deviation if the judge finds specific aggravating or mitigating factors.[4] Hence, neither of these versions of flat-time is truly mandatory and, therefore, neither can "end" disparity, although both eliminate indeterminate sentencing and parole.

Another variation on the "prescriptive sentencing" theme, described in a recent Twentieth Century Fund report, is a more moderate version of legislative sentencing. In addition to setting the outer bounds of judicial sentencing powers, as it presently does, the legislature would establish a "typical" or "presumptive" sentence to be served unless the court finds specified circumstances that would raise or lower the penalty according to fixed formulae.[5] This proposal, like David Fogel's, attempts to introduce a modicum of individualization by offering some (albeit mechanical) consideration for factors surrounding the criminal act in question.

All three proposals, however, err in their reliance upon *a priori* establishment of the "right" sentence with little or no factual support. In each, there is a tendency to try to run before one can walk, to prescribe solutions before possessing any adequate capability to measure or describe the present process.

Two kinds of disparity

Under a completely indeterminate sentencing system, the legislature totally abdicates its authority to either the judge or the parole board. More typical of present legal structures, however, is a "quasi-indeterminate" model, which specifies minima and maxima—often with a wide range in between—within which sentences must be set. Gross disparities do arise within such structures, because both judge and parole board lack appropriate information about a specific case or sufficient information about the range of cases generally.

---

[1] See, for example, John Hogarth, SENTENCING AS A HUMAN PROCESS (Toronto: University of Toronto Press 1972); Frank Remington and Donald J. Newman. *The Highland Park Institute on Sentence Disparity*, 26 FEDERAL PROBATION 1 (March 1962); and Stuart Nagel, *Disparities in Criminal Procedure*, 14 U.C.L.A. LAW REVIEW 1272 (1967).

[2] Andrew von Hirsch, DOING JUSTICE: THE CHOICE OF PUNISHMENTS (New York: Hill and Wang, 1976). See also Norval Morris, THE FUTURE OF IMPRISONMENT (Chicago: University of Chicago Press, 1974).

[3] See various speeches by President Ford, including his 1975 message to Congress on crime, and his 1976 State of the Union address calling for mandatory imprisonment of all persons convicted of carrying a hand gun while committing a federal crime. Senator Kennedy proposed a similar measure in an article printed in the *Boston Globe* of November 9, 1975. (Each of these men have indicated subsequently, however, that they view the sentencing guidelines approach as a possible and desirable compromise between indeterminate and mandatory sentences.)

[4] David Fogel, "WE ARE THE LIVING PROOF": THE JUSTICE MODEL FOR CORRECTIONS (Cincinnati: W. H. Anderson Co., 1975). It should be noted that the State of Maine adopted a version of "flat-time" sentencing on March 1, 1976.

[5] REPORT OF THE TWENTIETH CENTURY FUND TASK FORCE ON CRIMINAL SENTENCING, FAIR AND CERTAIN PUNISHMENT (New York: McGraw-Hill Book Company, 1976).

Under a mandatory or presumptive system, the legislature pretends omniscience and —years before the crime in question occurs—sets the precise duration of imprisonment for a general class of crime. These mandatory systems lead to disparity of a more dangerous sort, a *hidden* disparity resulting from ignoring valid and justifiable individual variations which judges presently consider. The presumptive sentencing proposal attempts to rescue legislatively imposed sentencing by ameliorating the worst aspects of the mechanistic equality it espouses. Its central flaw is that it depends upon purely speculative reasoning to establish what the "fairly typical first offender" would receive as a sentence, what fixed percentage increase would be meted out for each prior conviction, and what legislatively specified factors would allow a judge to lower or raise presumptive sentences by fixed degrees.

Each of these legislative sentencing proposals places the sentencing decision at a point too far removed in thought and action from the human being who is being sentenced. Worse, if the legislature makes its decision only on the basis of theoretical argument and the skimpy factual information it now possesses, it will inevitably draw unrealistic conclusions which will ensure the wholesale discretionary avoidance of the legislative mandate by police, prosecutors and judges which has rendered so many reform efforts nugatory. Instead, primary sentencing responsibility must continue to reside with the trial judge, who is more than an automaton, and reform must be based upon a careful review of actual sentencing practices.

Sentencing guidelines

Feasibility: We believe that sentencing guidelines can structure judicial discretion and avoid the pitfalls of the indeterminate sentence without going so far as the above proposals.

The judiciary is entitled to the presumption of innocence. We should assume that sentencing disparities are not due to design on the part of judges but to their inability to see the full picture. Now that sentencing guidelines can provide the courts with a tool to curb disparity from within, judges should be offered this opportunity for self-improvement before legislators attempt to impose mandatory solutions upon an independent branch of government. The research and procedures we have been developing work towards this end.

Recognition of the evidence regarding disparity does not require that we accept the facile view that *all* variation is "disparity." There is scope for legitimate and necessary moral variations in sentencing practice. The goal is equity in sentencing practices as realized by achieving consistency over time and over an entire court system.

The sentencing guidelines research project grew out of the successful completion of a decision-making study which developed guidelines for the United States Board of Parole. The Board of Parole was so pleased with the results of the study that it incorporated the guidelines as a major part of its operational procedures.[1] Seeing value in the guideline concept, the authors asked trial judges in several American jurisdictions whether they would be willing to engage in collaborative research and action for a similar project to be applied to sentencing.

Then, through a study of actual—not hypothetically "typical"—cases coming before cooperating trial court judges in Colorado and Vermont,[2] we extracted and examined the underlying offense/offender characteristics which appeared to account for justifiable sentencing variations. We did not employ our own prescriptive notions as to what would be a "right" sentence, but we studied the data to see what underlying factors informed actual sentencing decisions and what value judges gave each of these factors.

---

[1] The Parole Decision-making Project which developed the parole guidelines was conducted in collaboration with the United States Board of Parole, supported by a grant from the National Institute of Law Enforcement and Criminal Justice of the Law Enforcement Assistance Administration, and was administered by the Research Center of the National Council on Crime and Delinquency. *See* Don M. Gottfredson, Peter B. Hoffman, Maurice H. Sigler, and Leslie T. Wilkins, *Making Paroling Policy Explicit*, 21 CRIME AND DELINQUENCY 34 (January 1975). *See also* William J. Genego, Peter D. Goldberger, and Vicki C. Jackson, *Parole Release Decision-making and the Sentencing Process*, 84 YALE LAW JOURNAL 810 (March 1975). The parole guidelines have been incorporated in 28 C.F.R. 2.13 (1975), as amended.

[2] We studied two primary judicial jurisdictions, the County of Denver, Colorado and the State of Vermont. We have also been fortunate to have the input of judges representing our "observer courts," Essex County (Newark), New Jersey and Polk County (Des Moines), Iowa.

We first collected all factors that authorities in the literature or the judiciary on our Steering and Police Committee considered relevant to reaching the sentencing decision. Some 205 items of information from 200 randomly selected sentencing decisions in each of the two participating courts were collected. We also tried to gather all the information which was available to the judge for consideration in deciding upon an actual sentence.

Next, we analyzed that information statistically to find those offense/offender characteristics which accounted for the largest percentage of variation in the sentencing decision. Our analyses indicated that the two most influential groupings of information items were those measuring the seriousness of the current offense and the extent of the offender's criminal record.

Our initial analysis allowed us to design various preliminary guideline models to be considered by our Steering and Policy Committee. (A model in social science terms is essentially a simplification of a complex system designed to facilitate understanding and prediction.) These models attempted to demonstrate what the average or "modified" average sentence of all the judges in that particular jurisdiction would have been in a particular case. By tapping the same data base available to the judges in constructing our models, we made valuable use of the experiences of veteran sentencing judges.

We tested these models on a validation sample of cases and then formulated one synthesis model for further evaluation by Denver District Court judges. This is as far as we managed to go in our preliminary study, but we believe that we demonstrated the feasibility of a sentencing guidelines approach. Indeed, at this point, the Denver judiciary has moved forward and is making full use of an implemented guideline system.[1]

The tentative guideline sentences we developed were readily computed by assigning values to characteristics of both the crime and the criminal, and locating those values on a sentencing grid. The values that resulted in an offense score (seriousness of the offense) were located on the Y axis and the offender score values (prior record and social stability dimension) were located on the X axis. The intersection of the offense score and the offender score is the cell of the grid containing the guideline sentence. An example of a feasibility study sentencing grid for Felony 4 offenses in Denver County, Colorado, is shown in the table [*overleaf*].

Implementation: Close study of these descriptive results—tentative though they are —has allowed us to begin to develop a series of sentencing guidelines which will provide a model or suggested sentence to each trial court judge. Through analysis of the relevant variables, this model sentence may be specifically tailored to the defendant's case rather than to a general class or category. This guideline model is intended as a mathematical aid and in no way provides a binding, prescriptive sentence to be imposed automatically. It acts as one additional—but very significant—piece of information for the sentencing judge explaining what the "average" sentence of all the judges in that jurisdiction in the recent past would have been in the actual case before that judge.

By this means, judicial discretion is not obliterated and judicial experience is not ignored. Indeed, local trial court expertise thoroughly informs the guideline model and the police determinations which underlie it. The sentencing judge, as human decision-maker, still retains the discretion to override any guideline, although departures from guidelines are expected to occur only in unusual cases where the judge presents written reasons. Such an explanation, at a minimum, is due to the judge's own colleagues as well as to the defendant. Further, by restricting written reasons to the approximately 5 to 15 per cent of cases expected to fall outside the guidelines, this method avoids the trivialization of the reason-giving process whereby some meaningless phrase such as "in the interests of justice" is unthinkingly repeated.

---

[1] On July 1, 1976, the sentencing guidelines project entered an implementation phase involving four participating jurisdictions including Denver County, Colorado; Essex County (Newark), New Jersey; and Cook County (Chicago), Illinois. A number of other fully participating courts are involved, although their funding is from local sources. The Philadelphia, Pennsylvania, Court of Common Pleas was the first of these.

171

Suggested sentencing guidelines for Denver, Colorado
(Felony 4 Offenses)
Offender Score

		−1 −7	0 2	3 8	9 12	13+
Offense score	10–12	Indet. Min. 4–5 year max.	Indet. Min. 8–10 year max.	Indet. Min. 8–10 year max.	Indet. Min. 8–10 year max.	Indet. Min. 8–10 year max.
	8–9	Out	3–5 month work project	Indet. Min. 3–4 year max.	Indet. Min. 8–10 year max.	Indet. Min. 8–10 year max.
	6–7	Out	Out	Indet. Min. 3–4 year max.	Indet. Min. 6–8 year max.	Indet. Min. 8–10 year max.
	3–5	Out	Out	Out	Indet. Min. 4–5 year max.	Indet. Min. 4–5 year max.
	1–2	Out	Out	Out	Out	Indet. Min. 3–4 year max.

The Colorado Penal Code contains five levels of felonies (Felony 1 is the most serious) and three levels of misdemeanors. The Felony 4 category includes crimes such as manslaughter, robbery and second degree burglary.

The legislated maximum sentence for a Felony 4 offense is ten years. No minimum period of confinement is to be set by the court.

"Out" indicates a non-incarcerative sentence such as probation, deferred prosecution or deferred judgment.

We anticipate that judicial councils (or sentencing panels) may someday consider all proposed guideline departures before final sentence is imposed. But, whether a council or an individual judge provides the articulated reasoning for departures, the system we envision would use those departures as a data base to construct better guidelines in a continuous self-improvement process. The structure for accomplishing this would be a regular review (say, every six months) of the overall performance of the guidelines, and of departures from them, by a "college" of the same judiciary. The articulated reasoning which this system fosters would transform most of the explained departures from the guidelines into the raw material for modifications of overall sentencing policy. The final stage would be the normal appellate review process, which we favor for sentencing, and which would ensure that the now explicit underlying sentencing policy of the particular court system is fair and proper as well as consistent and equitable. Over time, a common law of sentencing policy should develop which will far more cogently and clearly explain specific factors considered (as well as their weights or values) rather than be mere repetitions of the often meaningless generalities which seem to make up much of so-called reasons for sentencing today.

If the judiciary themselves come to grips with these problems, then they should be less threatened by attacks on their discretion. There is no way for judges in this country, at this time, to defend their right to an individual exercise of unbridled discretionary power.[1] If they choose instead a policy of articulated reasoning and structured discretion, they should be able to withstand all onslaughts upon their authority. Our aim is to provide the means for establishing just such a system of structured discretion and articulated reasoning, with the structure to be determined not by external fiat but by the judges themselves who can allow for legitimate local variations.

Judicial sentencing can survive only if it reforms itself by institutionalizing a self-monitoring process. Judges must retain that quantum of discretion they need so that each sentence will be just and humane, but they must create a sentencing framework so that separate decisions can accurately reflect their collective wisdom and sense of justice.

---

[1] *See generally*, Marvin Frankel, CRIMINAL SENTENCES: LAW WITHOUT ORDER (New York: Hill and Wang, 1973); and Kenneth Culp Davis, DISCRETIONARY JUSTICE: A PRELIMINARY INQUIRY (Baton Rouge: Louisiana State University Press, 1969).

APPENDIX D (Chapter 3)

THE REDUCTION OF SENTENCE LENGTHS 1884–93

1. Letter from Sir Edmund Du Cane to the Permanent Under-Secretary of State, Home Office, 4 February 1884

PRISON DEPARTMENT, HOME OFFICE,

WHITEHALL, S.W.

4th February, 1884.

SIR,

I beg leave to request that you will call the attention of the Secretary of State to certain points connected with the terms of the sentences awarded by the various criminal courts, as I venture to think that, if the subject were duly brought under consideration of those who are responsible for the administration of justice, a considerable amount of unnecessary suffering might be saved without any diminution of the efficiency of the law; and that a very appreciable economy in the cost of our penal establishments might be effected.

I refer to the traditional practice, by which certain particular periods are usually assigned for the duration of sentences to the almost entire exclusion of the intermediate periods, and which would, there is little doubt, be quite as effective.

The traditional practice above referred to is exhibited in the following tables, which give the sentences of the population both of convict and local prisons on a certain day last year.

STATEMENT A, showing the sentences of PRISONERS in Convict Prisons on 31st March, 1883.

Sentence.	Males.	Females.	Total.
Life	245	39	284
Twenty-five years	13	—	13
Twenty-four years	3	—	3
Twenty-three years	—	—	—
Twenty-two years	—	—	—
Twenty-one years	—	—	—
Twenty years	257	8	265
Nineteen years	—	—	—
Eighteen years	8	—	8
Seventeen years	—	—	—
Sixteen years	—	—	—
Fifteen years	360	13	373
Fourteen years	166	1	167
Thirteen years	2	—	2
Twelve years	173	3	176
Eleven years	1	—	1
Ten years	1,606	127	1,733
Nine years	5	—	5
Eight years	351	27	378
Seven years	2,742	374	3,116
Six years	78	9	87
Five years	3,231	354	3,585
Total	9,241	955	10,196

STATEMENT B, showing the NUMBER of PRISONERS under each Period of Sentence of Imprisonment by Ordinary Courts in the Local Prisons on the last Tuesday of the Year ended 31st March, 1883.

Sentence.	Number of Prisoners.		
	Males.	Females.	Total.
Two years and two years	1	—	1
Eighteen months and eighteen months	2	—	2
Two years	232	23	255
Twenty-three months	—	—	—
Twenty-two months	3	—	3
Twenty-one months	10	1	11
Twenty months	31	—	31
Nineteen months	—	1	1
Eighteen months and one day	1	—	1
Eighteen months	960	110	1,070
Seventeen months	1	—	1
Sixteen months	22	—	22
Fifteen months	424	67	491
Fourteen months	13	1	14
Thirteen months	—	—	—
Twelve months	1,475	292	1,767
Eleven months	1	—	1
Ten months	32	9	41
Nine months and three weeks	1	—	1
Nine months	570	127	697
Eight months	141	42	183
Seven months and seven days	1	—	1
Seven months	20	7	27
Six months and twenty-one days	1	—	1
Six months and fourteen days	1	—	1
Six months and seven days	2	—	2
Six months	1,415	288	1,703
Twenty-four weeks	3	—	3
Five months	36	4	40
Four months and twenty-one days	1	—	1
Three months and six weeks	1	—	1
Four months	382	101	483
Sixteen weeks	—	1	1
Three months and twenty-one days	—	1	1
Three months and fourteen days	4	—	4
Fourteen weeks	1	—	1
Three months	1,612	386	1,998
Twelve weeks	42	17	59
Two months and twenty-one days	2	—	2
One month and one month and fourteen days ...	—	1	1
Two months and fourteen days	5	—	5
One month and six weeks	1	—	1
Ten weeks	8	2	10
Seventy days	1	—	1
Two months and seven days	4	—	4
Sixty-six days	1	—	1
Two months and three days	1	—	1
Nine weeks	2	—	2
Two months	910	207	1,117
Eight weeks	41	5	46
Seven weeks, or seven days and forty-two days ...	6	1	7
Forty-five days	2	—	2
One month and fourteen days	4	—	4
Six weeks	327	66	393
Forty days	39	—	39
One month and seven days	4	2	6
Thirty-six days or five weeks	31	2	33
One month or thirty days	1,076	468	1,544
Four weeks or twenty-eight days	145	35	180
Three weeks	287	53	340

174

Sentence.					Number of Prisoners.		
					Males.	Females.	Total.
Twenty days	...	...	...	...	7	—	7
Seventeen days	...	...	...	...	1	—	1
Sixteen days	...	...	...	...	1	—	1
Two weeks ...	...	...	...	...	819	273	1,092
Twelve days	...	...	...	...	1	—	1
Ten days	...	...	...	...	81	16	97
Eight days ...	...	...	...	...	—	1	1
One week	...	...	...	...	370	168	538
Five days	...	...	...	...	17	18	35
Four days	...	...	...	...	6	1	7
Three days ...	...	...	...	...	9	5	14
Total	...	...	...		11,651	2,802	14,453

The return marked A shows, as regards penal servitude, that, out of a total of 10,196 the great bulk of the sentences are for five, seven, and ten years, which, with a comparatively small number of eight years, account for 8,812; that, beyond these, the usual periods are twelve, fourteen, fifteen, twenty years, and life, which account for 1,265, the intermediate periods comprising thirteen different periods of years having been assigned only in 119 cases.

It is impossible not to feel that some more exact measurement is possible than is exhibited in the above figures, and, if it is possible, that the present arbitrary practice is incapable of justification.

The practice of selecting these particular periods of years is, no doubt, derived from the time of the transportation system, but a person sentenced to transportation passed a much shorter time in prison than one now sentenced to penal servitude. For instance, fifteen years penal servitude involves *at least* eleven years five months and eight days in prison, whereas a person sentenced to fifteen years transportation, if not sent to Australia, would ordinarily be released at the end of six years two months and eight days, and, if sent to Australia, even earlier, and so with other periods of sentence.

In those times also "supervision" by the Police, which is now by statute a definite sentence and serves some of the objects of a long confinement, did not exist.

The return of the sentences of the population of the Local Prisons (marked B) suggests similar remarks in regard to the sentences of imprisonment which are awarded.

It shows that about one-half of the criminal population of the local prisons were under sentences of various periods not exceeding three months, and that, as regards the remainder who were under various sentences up to two years, 5,975 were under sentences of four, six, nine, twelve, eighteen, and twenty-four months, the number under the intermediate fifteen periods of months being only 866.

Here again it is impossible to doubt that many prisoners might have been spared some weeks of punishment and yet that the object of the punishment might have been completely secured.

I have referred to these questions as worthy of consideration because of the needless suffering which is inflicted on a person subjected to a sentence longer than is absolutely necessary for its object, but, his family, who being innocent, suffer and undergo privations because he is taken from them, are even more to be taken into account, and the burden thrown on the public, when they are unable to support themselves is an important element in the consideration.

175

It is obvious, too, that if enquiry should justify the correctness of the suggestions I have made as to the possibility of many of the sentences being shortened, and should lead to such a result, a very appreciable diminution in the cost of our penal establishments might be effected. In order to give some idea of the magnitude of the financial question, I will suppose that, by assigning shorter sentences followed by " supervision," and making more use of the intermediate periods of six years, to which only eighty-seven were sentenced, and nine, eleven, thirteen, sixteen, seventeen, eighteen, nineteen, twenty-one, twenty-two, twenty-three, and twenty-four years, to which only nineteen prisoners altogether had been sentenced, the term of maintenance of the convicts should be diminished by an average of six months, the annual gross saving might be put at about £20,400. If the average diminution amounted to twelve months the saving would be £40,700; and, if to eighteen months, it would be £61,000 per annum.

It is not unreasonable to assume that a saving approaching this might also be made in regard to the local prisons, so that the financial question is one involving a very large total.

I venture to think that if only a portion of this result could be anticipated it would be well worthy of consideration.

In bringing this subject before the Secretary of State, I have not entered upon the question of the principles by which the duration of sentences should be regulated, nor would I suggest that any too rigid restriction should be placed on the discretion of those whose office it is to carry out these principles. I have only ventured to point out, and to illustrate, the necessity which seems to me to be obvious, of an authoritative investigation of the subject, and the advantages which would result from the adoption of such changes in practice as I believe could not fail to follow from such an investigation.

> I am,
>
> SIR,
>
> Your obedient servant,
>
> (Signed) E. F. DU CANE.

THE UNDER-SECRETARY OF STATE
  FOR THE HOME DEPARTMENT.

---

2. Letter from Sir William Harcourt, Home Secretary, to the Lord Chancellor, 10 December 1884

WHITEHALL,

10*th December*, 1884.

MY DEAR LORD CHANCELLOR,

I desire to direct your Lordship's attention to the statistics of crime in England, as displayed in the recent Report of the Commissioners of Prisons and the Directors of Convict Prisons.

The latter of these establishments indicate the condition of the more serious crime, and the former that of ordinary offences throughout the country in recent times.

It has been my good fortune to be connected with the Home Office during a period of four years and a half, which has been contemporaneous with the most marked and continuous diminution in the prison population, of which we have any experience. I may ask your consideration of the following most satisfactory passages from the Report of the Directors of Convict Prisons for the current year:—

"5. The following paragraphs from our last Report may be repeated, *mutatis mutandis*:—

"The steady decrease in the number of sentences of penal servitude, on which we have previously commented in our reports, is therefore still continuing. The following table shows the remarkable decrease of serious crime in late years as evidenced by the decrease in the number of sentences of penal servitude between 1854 and 1883, although the population of the country has in that time so largely increased."

Average Number of Sentences of Penal Servitude for Indictable Offences in England and Wales.		Estimated Average Population of England and Wales.
During 5 years ended 1859	2,589	19,257,184
„ 5 years ended 1864	2,800	23,369,938
„ 5 years ended 1869	1,978	21,680,874
„ 5 years ended 1874	1,622	23,087,947
„ 5 years ended 1879	1,633	24,700,326
„ 4 years ended 1883	1,447	26,213,629

"The following table of the number of sentences of ordinary imprisonment for indictable offences shows during 1883 an increase on the preceding three years, but the average of the four years, viz., 9,997, is about the same as in the two previous periods of five years beginning 1874, and much below the period between 1859 and 1873":—

Average Number of Sentences of Imprisonment for Indictable Offences in England and Wales.	
During 5 years ended 1859	12,536
„ 5 years ended 1864	11,406
„ 5 years ended 1869	12,058
„ 5 years ended 1874	9,848
„ 5 years ended 1879	9,950
„ 4 years ended 1883	9,997

"6. The very large decrease in our convict prison population during recent years is shown by the following figures, which have been compiled by collecting the

177

statistics of persons maintained by the public under sentence of transportation or penal servitude at the end of each year since 1869 (*see* Appendix, No. 8):"—

	Total Number in Custody under Sentence of Penal Servitude.
1869	11,660
1870	11,890
1871	11,712
1872	11,488
1873	11,061
1874	10,867
1875	10,765
1876	10,725
1977	10,763
1878	10,671
1879	10,884
1880	10,839
1881	10,676
1982	10,587
1883	10,529
1884	9,942
Number, July, 1884	9,574

In December, 1884, the numbers are still further reduced.

"7. These statistics, which have never been thus collected before, have not been easy to procure, as the prisoners referred to have been in establishments controlled by several independent authorities. They certainly do not fully represent the decrease in the number of prisoners under sentence of penal servitude, because so long as any considerable number of convicts have been undergoing sentences in Australia, the number maintained by the public has been less than it would have been if (as in recent years) they had all been kept in England, by reason of the practice of releasing such prisoners on ticket-of-leave in the Colony earlier than they would have been released if retained in England; so that, for purposes of comparison, the fall in number of the convict population since 1869, which is represented in the return by 2,086, might well be somewhat increased."

"8. The population of the convict prisons in this country has fallen during the year under report by no less than 556, a diminution which would have been still greater, if there had not been during 1882 and 1883 about 61 prisoners more than the average sentenced by court-martial; but this is, it is believed, not likely to be repeated. We had also 46 soldiers under sentence of penal servitude transferred to us from prisons in Ireland, as related in our last report, and 20 other penal servitude prisoners temporarily transferred from Ireland in February last."

You will perceive from these tables, that, whilst during the last twenty-five years the population of England and Wales has increased by seven millions, the annual average number of sentences of penal servitude, representing the graver crimes, which in the five years ending 1859 amounted to 2,589, in the four years ending 1883 had declined to 1,447. These facts are the more remarkable, when we remember the grave apprehensions, which were entertained during the first quinquennial period to which I have referred, lest the absorption of the criminal population into the social system of this country (which was the natural consequence of the abolition at that period of the system of transportation) should aggravate the condition of the criminal population at home. So far from that having been the case, since the substantial abolition of transportation in the year 1854 and the treatment of the more serious criminals at home, the improvement in the returns of the criminal classes is most striking and satisfactory. You will agree with me, that, whilst the ever increasing density of our population, especially in the great cities, brings with it many evils in its train, a consolatory evidence of the success of the efforts which have been made in the last half century to improve the condition of the people is furnished in the fact, that the sentences of penal servitude in 1883, when the population of England is about twenty-seven millions, amount to about one-half the corresponding sentences in the year 1836, when the population did not exceed fifteen millions.

Amidst much that is dark, this at least may be regarded as a bright and encouraging light on our social horizon.

No. 7.

RETURN showing the Population of England and Wales, with the Number of Sentences to Imprison ment, Transportation, and Penal Servitude, and the Number actually transported; also showing the Number of Persons sentenced to Death, and the Number executed, from 1836 to 1883, inclusive.

Year.	Population.	Sentenced to Imprison- ment for Indictable Offences.	Sentenced to Transportation and Penal Servitude.		Number Transported to Australia.	Number Transported to Bermuda.	Number Sentenced to Death.			Number Executed.	Number Sentenced to Transportation or Penal Servitude for Life.
			By Ordinary Courts.	By Courts Martial, from 1866.			For Murder.	For Other Crimes	Total.		
1836	14,928,477	10,125	3,611	—	4,273	—	20	474	494	17	740
1837	15,103,778	12,294	3,785	—	4,068	—	11	427	438	8	636
1838	15,287,699	12,927	3,696	—	3,805	—	25	91	116	6	266
1839	15,514,255	12,927	3,696	—	2,732	—	12	44	56	11	205
1840	15,730,813	15,110	3,105	—	2,573	—	18	59	77	9	238
1841	15,911,757	15,747	3,800	—	2,926	—	20	60	80	10	156
1842	16,130,326	17,871	4,481	—	4,166	—	16	41	57	9	191
1843	16,332,228	16,275	4,488	—	2,993	—	22	75	97	13	225
1844	16,535,174	14,969	3,651	—	3,279	—	21	36	57	16	180
1845	16,739,136	14,052	3,247	—	2,542	—	19	30	49	12	79
1846	16,944,092	14,902	3,157	—	1,708	—	13	43	56	6	101
1847	17,150,018	18,312	3,262	—	1,222	—	19	32	51	8	46
1848	17,356,882	19,175	3,600	—	1,897	296	23	37	60	12	67
1849	17,564,656	17,761	3,202	—	1,609	—	19	47	66	15	60
1850	17,773,324	17,602	3,173	—	2,465	284	11	38	49	6	84
1851	17,927,609	18,418	3,338	—	2,440	230	16	54	70	10	124
1852	18,193,206	18,441	2,896	—	2,541	245	16	45	61	9	43
1853	18,404,368	18,130	2,709	—	600	—	17	38	55	8	48
1854	18,616,310	20,388	2,742	—	280	—	11	38	49	5	31
1855	18,829,000	17,397	2,590	—	485	346	11	39	50	7	48
1856	19,042,412	11,885	2,715	—	498	—	31	38	69	16	59
1857	19,256,516	12,507	2,841	—	532	300	20	34	54	13	35
1858	19,471,291	10,834	2,419	—	550	640	16	37	53	11	17
1859	19,686,701	10,060	2,383	—	224	281	18	34	52	9	17
1860	19,902,713	9,656	2,436	—	296	—	16	32	48	12	21
1861	20,066,224	11,233	2,678	—	306	—	26	24	50	15	16
1862	20,371,013	11,944	3,369	—	*782	—	28	1	29	15	25
1863	20,625,855	12,251	3,071	—	727	—	29	—	29	22	20
1864	20,883,889	11,948	2,445	—	261	—	32	—	32	19	12
1865	21,145,151	12,358	2,081	—	845	—	20	—	20	7	4
1866	21,409,684	11,582	2,016	13	410	—	26	—	26	12	2
1867	21,677,525	11,801	1,846	10	451	—	27	—	27	10	3
1868	21,948,713	12,546	1,939	7	—	—	21	—	21	12	18
1869	22,223,299	12,002	2,006	7	—	—	18	—	18	10	8
1870	22,501,316	10,908	1,788	1	—	—	15	—	15	6	6
1871	22,712,266	10,083	1,627	5	—	—	13	—	13	4	4
1872	23,095,819	9,318	1,514	11	—	—	30	—	30	15	14
1873	23,407,317	9,141	1,493	8	—	—	18	—	18	11	8
1874	23,723,017	9,793	1,690	11	—	—	25	1	26	16	16
1875	24,042,974	9,282	1,639	12	—	—	33	—	33	18	16
1876	24,367,247	10,020	1,753	19	—	—	32	—	32	†22	13
1877	24,695,894	9,793	1,639	9	—	—	34	—	34	22	11
1878	25,028,973	10,218	1,634	11	—	—	20	—	20	16	14
1879	25,366,544	10,440	1,502	9	—	—	34	—	34	15	10
1880	25,708,666	9,663	1,523	13	—	—	28	—	28	13	8
1881	25,974,439	9,266	1,525	9	—	—	23	—	23	11	17
1882	26,406,820	9,715	1,364	50	—	—	22	—	22	12	7
1883	26,770,744	11,347	1,378	31	—	—	23	—	23	13	10

* 192 from Bermuda, 590 from England.

† One of these persons was not executed until Jan. 1877, although convicted in Dec. 1876.

NOTE.—The population for the years other than Census years is of course estimated.

So much for the statistics of the more serious crime as displayed in the Report of Convict Prisons. The facts are not less satisfactory in regard of the offences of the second order, revealed in the report for the current year of the Commissioners of ordinary prisons:—

"9. The decrease in the prison population in recent years is very remarkable, on account of the length of the period during which it has continued to fall or to stand at a low level, in which respect it is quite unprecedented. The average population (17,194) has never since 1861 been so low as during the year 1883–84, but at the former date the population of the Kingdom was only 20 millions, whereas now it is 26¾ millions, i.e., some 30 per cent. more. In no other series of years within record has the average prison population continued to fall for more than three years successively, after which a marked and continuous rise has been usual, but since 1878, when it was 20,833, it has fallen down to its present number 17,194, as the following figures show:"—

Half-year ended 31 March 1878		...	...	...	...	20,833
Year ended 31 March	1879	...	...	...	...	19,818
,, ,, ,,	1880	...	...	...	...	19,835
,, ,, ,,	1881	...	...	...	...	18,027
,, ,, ,,	1882	...	...	...	...	17,798
,, ,, ,,	1883	...	...	...	...	17,876
,, ,, ,,	1884	...	...	...	...	17,194

"10. The numbers in May, June, and July of the current year were lower than in the same months of any of the years since we have had charge of the prisons."

A certain portion of this reduction, perhaps about 500, is due to removal of military prisoners elsewhere.

The diagram [see pages 182–3] which accompanies this Report gives a very interesting and satisfactory view of the recent rapid and continuous decrease in the prison population, and I am happy to know that according to the latest reports it is still on the decline. You will observe that at this moment the prison population does not exceed that of the year 1850 when the population of the country was less by nine millions.

There is another feature which is revealed by the comparative diagrams, which show the relations of pauperism to crime. You will observe that in the periods antecedent to 1870 the rise and fall of the prison population corresponded tolerably closely with the increase and the decrease of adult able-bodied pauperism.

Since the year 1877, at all events, that relation has ceased in a very remarkable degree to obtain. In the year 1877, when owing to the prosperity of the preceding six years, pauperism had reached its lowest point, the prison population had reached its highest level. Since that period the unfortunate declension of trade in all its branches has brought pauperism to a higher summit, and the rise in the number of adult able-bodied paupers, from 1877 to 1883 has been rapid and continuous, but contemporaneously with this you will observe that the fall in the numbers of the prison population from its highest summit in 1877, to its lowest level in 1884, has been equally marked and continuous.

To my mind these remarkable figures carry the conviction of a solid and stable improvement in the moral staple and fibre of the population, which enables it to resist the temporary pressure of want and crime. In a great degree crime has ceased to be the inevitable concomitant of want.

Nor is it only in the numbers, but in the character and conduct of the criminal population in prisons, that a marked improvement is to be observed. There is no better test of the effective discipline of prisons, than that which is supplied in the rapid and marked diminution of the punishments which it is found necessary to inflict upon the prisoners.

"35. As regards the discipline of the prisons, our returns show that the number of prison offences was smaller than last year, and the occasions on which the more severe forms of punishment were found necessary are less in a marked degree than formerly. The average population having been 17,194 against 17,876 in the previous year, the punishment cells have been used only on 1,438 occasions instead of on 1,869, and dietary punishment inflicted only on 16,969 occasions instead of 19,114. The great contrast these figures afford to those of former years is shown by the following table":—

Year.	Daily average number of Prisoners in the year. Males and Females.	Punish-ment Cells.	Dietary Punish-ment.	Loss of Stage or Privilege.	Total Punish-ments.	Daily Average number of Punish-ments per 1,000 Prisoners.
Year ended 29th September 1868 ...	18,677	17,109	43,884	,,	60,993	8·9
,, ,, ,, 1869 ...	20,080	18,014	47,668	,,	65,682	8·9
,, ,, ,, 1870 ...	19,830	17,984	46,692	,,	64,676	8·9
,, ,, ,, 1871 ...	18,465	15,234	37,392	,,	52,626	7·7
,, ,, ,, 1872 ...	17,505	14,994	37,401	,,	52,395	8·1
,, ,, ,, 1873 ...	17,680	15,388	38,709	,,	54,097	8·3
,, ,, ,, 1874 ...	17,896	16,331	40,378	,,	56,709	8·6
,, ,, ,, 1875 ...	18,487	17,853	39,482	,,	57,335	8·4
,, ,, ,, 1876 ...	18,986	16,212	42,922	,,	59,134	8·5
,, ,, ,, 1877 ...	20,361	18,263	39,159	,,	57,422	7·7
Six months ended 31st March 1878 ...	20,833	9,245	21,986	,,	31,231	8·2
Year ended 31st March 1879 ...	19,818	5,164	36,830	16,908	58,902	8·1
,, ,, ,, 1880 ...	19,835	2,320	24,693	22,550	49,563	6·8
,, ,, ,, 1881 ...	18,027	2,407	21,846	18,886	43,139	6·5
,, ,, ,, 1882 ...	17,798	1,767	18,895	17,621	38,283	5·8
,, ,, ,, 1883 ...	17,876	1,869	19,114	21,400	42,383	6·4
,, ,, ,, 1884 ...	17,194	1,438	16,969	18,688	37,095	5·8

The decrease of punishments of 1884 is cumulative upon that of 1883, upon which the Commissioners in their Report of 1883, made the subjoined well-founded remarks.

"50. The decrease in the total number of punishments of all kinds from about 60,000 to 42,000, and of the dietary punishments from about 40,000 to 19,000 cases in the year, will be admitted to be remarkable. Those who know the interior working of these establishments are aware that this remarkable decrease is not due to any relaxation of subordination and regularity, nor to any diminution in the industry or good order in the prisons, but that, on the contrary, these qualities much more generally and uniformly characterise them than in former years. We think, therefore, we may be justified in believing that the system under which the prisons are now carried on constitutes a real advance on that which prevailed formerly; and we hope also that we may be allowed to point out how much the public are indebted to the magistrates who undertake the duty of supporting the governors in administering the discipline of the prisons for the assistance they have given in carrying out the system which has been established."

It might be difficult, and it is not necessary to analyse all the causes which have led to these satisfactory results; they are certainly not due to a greater laxity in the pursuit, or the punishment of crime. Within the epochs referred to in these tables, there has been a larger increase in the numbers of the Police, and I believe also in their vigilance and activity in the detection and prosecution of crime. One great and para-mount influence has been no doubt the salutary operation of the Education Act, and of the Reformatory and Industrial Schools upon the younger portion of the population, from which the army of crime is mainly recruited, and probably also the advance of temperance amongst the masses of the people.

The Prison Commissioners in their Report of 1882 called attention to this most material element in the diagnosis of crime:—

"10. It may be of interest again to repeat the observations we have already made on the subject of the ages of the prison population, and to refer to the statistics of the year we are now reporting on in connection with them.

" '9. The statistics of the fluctuations in, and the composition of the prison population are of great interest, as the only certain guides to the discovery of the best mode of diminishing crime, for by means of these observations we can gain a clue to sources of crime, and to the conditions under which it is fostered and developed. Among these statistics the table in Appendix 8 of the third Report of the Commissioners, which records the ages of the prison population, is of high value.

181

DIAGRAM SHOWING FLUCTUATIONS IN THE DAILY AVERAGE LOCAL PRISON POPULATION SINCE 1849 AS COMPARED WITH THE PAUPER POPULATION.

ADULT ABLE-BODIED PAUPERS IN RECEIPT OF RELIEF INDOOR.

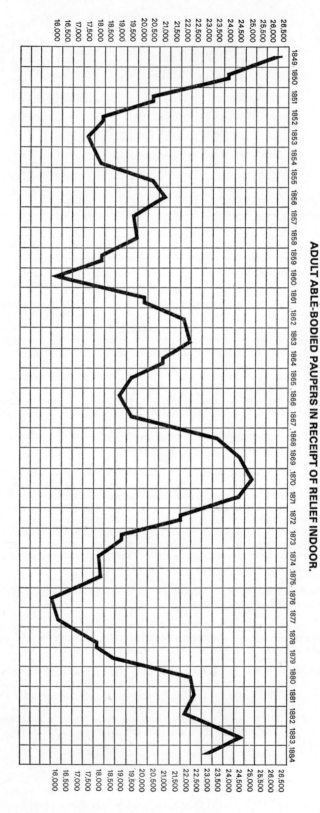

DAILY AVERAGE NUMBER OF PRISONERS IN THE LOCAL PRISONS IN ENGLAND AND WALES.

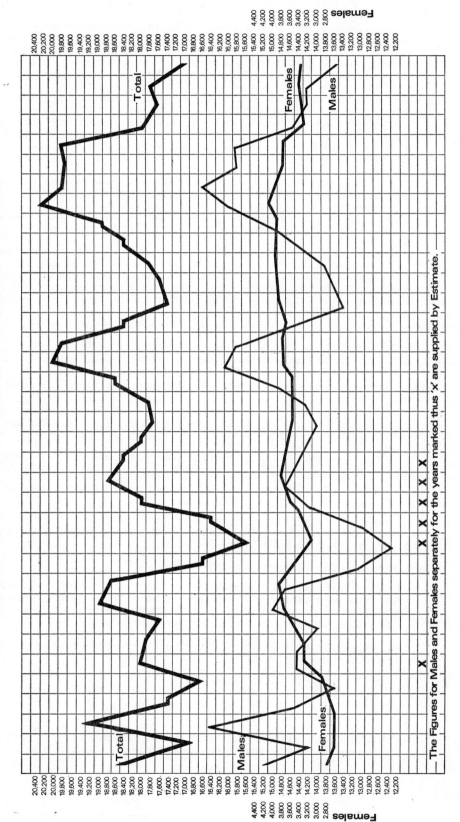

The Figures for Males and Females separately for the years marked thus 'x' are supplied by Estimate.

183

" '10. It appears that there was on the 31st March, 1880, in all the local prisons united, a population of 15,352 males and 3,627 females. Of these, 32 males were under 12, 338 between 12 and 16, and 3,181 between 16 and 21, making altogether no less than 3,551 who were under 21. There were also 5,854 between 21 and 30 years of age; so that 58·9 per cent. of the whole male prison population were between 16 and 30 years of age. As the proportion of males in England and Wales between 16 and 30 is only 41·4 per cent. of the total male population above 15 (that being the nearest corresponding age given in the census) the proportion of younger criminals to the total number of criminals is largely in excess. The number who are between 30 and 40 is not much more than half the number between 21 and 30, and is about equal to the total number of those who are 40 and upwards.

" '11. These figures cannot but be regarded as affording a demonstration that men take to crime in the earlier rather than in the more mature periods of life, and that means for its effective repression are to be sought much more among the agencies for securing a good training of the neglected part of our population in their early years than in any form of punishment which can be devised.'

"11. Last year we pointed out that the larger proportion of the decrease in the prison population by which that year was characterised had occurred among the younger criminals. This year, although the population has risen as a whole, the younger part has risen considerably less than the older, so that the percentage of prisoners under 30, which on 31st March, 1879, was 59·4 of the whole, has gradually fallen, until on 31st March, 1882, it was 56·6."

Year ended.	Under 30.	30 and over.	Total.	Per-centage of whole under 30.	Per-centage of whole 30 and over.
	M. F.	M. F.	M. F.	M. F.	M. F.
31 Mar. 1879	9,584 1,807	6,038 1,739	15,622 3,546	61·3 50·9	38·7 49·1
	11,391	7,777	19,168	59·4	40·6
„ 1880	9,405 1,868	5,947 1,759	15,352 3,627	61·3 51·5	38·7 48·5
	11,273	7,706	18,979	59·4	40·6
„ 1881	8,334 1,643	5,755 1,597	14,089 3,240	59·1 50·7	40·9 49·3
	9,977	7,352	17,329	57·6	42·4
„ 1882	8,613 1,791	6,181 1,807	14,794 3,598	58·2 49·8	41·8 50·2
	10,404	7,988	18,392	56·6	43·4

This reduction in the population of criminals under 30 years of age is still progressing and in the year 1884 it has declined from 59·4 to 54·4.

In the Report for 1883 the Prison Commissioners state:—

"9. The decrease between the population of the prisons at the end of the year 1881–2 and of the year now under report has occurred chiefly among the younger criminals. The decrease among those under 30 years of age formed 55·1 per cent. of the whole, and among those over 30 formed 44·9 per cent."

"10. The number in prison under 16 years of age has been as follows on the last day of each of the years named":—

On 31 March 1880	...	...	...	429
„ „ 1881	...	...	...	275
„ „ 1882	...	...	...	329
„ „ 1883	...	...	...	268

It may therefore, I think, be safely concluded, that we have successfully tapped the fountains of crime, and that the labour and the expense to which we have gone in the

184

improvement of the Social Soil, has not been without its results. Something also I think may fairly be claimed for the immense advance which has been made in the science and practice of Prison Discipline.

The question of reconvictions must always be an important one. You will observe from the following table, that the number of sentences to penal servitude on reconviction for crimes of violence, such as robbery with violence, wounding and cutting, manslaughter, and violent assault hardly amount to a dozen, and those for burglary and housebreaking to forty-eight, a total which is not considerable on a population of twenty-six millions.

STATEMENT of CONVICTS RECONVICTED, and of LICENCES REVOKED, during the Year ended 31st March, 1884, showing the Crimes for which the Convicts were reconvicted, and the Offences for which the Licences were revoked.

	M.	F.	Total.
Reconvictions { during the currency of a former sentence ...	96	35	131
not during the currency of a former sentence	215	35	250
Totals	311	70	381
Revocations of licence	170	60	230

Reconvictions.	M.	F.	Total.	Revocations.	M.	F.	Total.
Arson	4	—	4	Arson	1	—	1
Assault with intent to rob ...	2	1	3	Assault, breach of the peace, &c.	17	—	17
Assaulting police	1	—	1	Brothel-keeping	—	1	1
Bigamy	1	—	1	Burglary, house, shop, and			
Burglary, house, shop, and				counting-house breaking, &c.	3	—	3
counting-house, breaking, &c.	48	—	48	„ attempted ...	1	—	1
Coinage offences	13	3	16	Coinage offences	9	—	9
Forgery, uttering forged instru-				Drunkenness	1	4	5
ments, &c.	2	—	2	Failing to produce licence, not			
Fraud, embezzlement, &c. ...	12	1	13	notifying change of resi-			
Fraudulent enlistment	1	—	1	dence to police, failing to			
Felonious possession of plates				report to police, and other			
for forged notes	1	—	1	breaches of the Penal Servi-			
Horse, cattle, and sheep stealing,				tude Acts	51	12	63
&c.	6	—	6	Found on enclosed premises ...	7	—	7
Larceny, receiving stolen pro-				Fraud, embezzlement, &c. ...	2	—	2
perty, &c.	175	60	235	Frequenting public places with			
Manslaughter	1	—	1	intent to commit a felony ...	8	5	13
Possession of house-breaking				Indecent behaviour	2	2	4
implements	5	—	5	Larceny, receiving stolen pro-			
Robbery with violence	8	—	8	perty, &c.	47	24	71
Sacrilege	1	—	1	Larceny, attempted	5	—	5
Wounding, cutting, shooting, &c.	1	—	1	Malicious damage and injury			
Other offences	29	5	34	to property	3	—	3
				Poaching...	2	—	2
				Prostitute, being a	—	5	5
				Unlawful possession	2	1	3
				Vagrancy	6	2	8
				Wounding, cutting, shooting,			
				&c.	—	2	2
				Other offences	3	2	5
Totals	311	70	381	Totals	170	60	230

I am sure that you will share with me the satisfaction inspired by this view of the solid and rapid progress in the social improvement of the country in relation to crime; but it is with a practical object that I address this letter to you, as the chief judicial authority in the country. You will remember with what apprehension the great mitigation of the Criminal Code more than half a century ago was viewed by many, even wise and prudent men, who believed that life and property would not be secure if the severity of punishments were relaxed. Those anticipations of evil have not been fulfilled; our criminal jurisprudence has been greatly mitigated in its rigour. In a population which has nearly doubled, fewer persons are hanged, far fewer are imprisoned, yet life and property are not less safe, but safer than they were. There have been periods, as in the years immediately preceding 1863, when an apparent recrudescence of crime, due in the opinion of The Royal Commission of 1864 (*sic*), to the mismanagement of our penal system in the period immediately following the abolition of transportation, led to an increase of terms of punishment, but if it is reasonable to augment punishment, where crime appears to be on the increase, it is surely not less reasonable to consider whether severity may not be relaxed, when crime over long periods of time is shown to be steadily on the decrease. My experience and observation now extending over nearly five years, and embracing the whole criminal administration of Great Britain, has led me to the same conclusion at which Sir E. Du Cane has arrived, that the time has come when a sensible mitigation of punishment may be safely introduced into the administration of our Criminal Law by materially shortening the length of sentences imposed in ordinary cases. I am happy to observe that the Lord Chief Justice has expressed himself recently to this effect on more than one occasion. In connection with this matter, I would again call your attention to an important letter, addressed to me during the present year by Sir E Du Cane (which I think you have previously seen), and which in connection with the whole of this subject, I would ask you to bring under the consideration of Her Majesty's judges. Sir E. Du Cane's observations on this subject seem to me to be just, and I believe that a great diminution in the average length of imprisonment might be made by taking more account of the intervals which exist between terms of five, ten, and fifteen years Penal Servitude, in like manner of the spaces between a week, a month, three months, six months, twelve months, eighteen months, and two years' imprisonment.

I must express to you, and ask you to communicate to the Judges in the most respectful manner my concurrence in the opinion of Sir E. Du Cane, that the deterring and reformatory effect of imprisonment (subject, of course, to special exceptions) would be as well and even more effectually accomplished if the average length of sentences were materially shortened.

There is one other subject of the highest importance in the treatment of crime, though I am well aware of the difficulties which surround it. One of the main objects which was contemplated, and which, I think, has been accomplished by the consolidation of the local prisons under the central control of the Home Office, was to secure greater uniformity in the administration of prison discipline, and consequently greater equality and identity in the punishment of crime.

There remains, however, behind a still greater difficulty, viz., the means of securing somewhat more of harmony and uniformity in the extent of punishment, and the amount of the sentences pronounced in similar cases.

That sentences do vary extremely in their magnitude without such difference in the circumstances as should seem to account for the diversity, is a matter which comes under my constant observation.

I should be very glad, if in consultation with the Judges you found it possible, if any general rules in this matter, subject of course to the necessary exceptions in particular cases, should be safely laid down so as to lead to greater uniformity of practice.

I have the honour to remain,

My dear Lord Chancellor,

Yours faithfully,

W. V. HARCOURT.

3. Letter to *The Times* from Charles Hopwood QC, Recorder of Liverpool, **12 January 1892**

EXCESSIVE SENTENCES

TO THE EDITOR OF THE TIMES

Sir,—It is with hesitation that I ask your leave to place before the public some facts and inferences on the subject of sentences on convicted offenders. For my action has been the subject of approval and disapproval, but as it is possible to separate personal considerations from the interesting and important public question, my motive is neither defence nor self-assertion, but the service of public interests.

The question of how much or of the proper punishment is one upon which everybody feels himself at all times competent to express an opinion without limitation or restraint, and with or without the precise knowledge of the facts. In consequence a tempest rages frequently between the public and the criticized Judge or magistrate—a most salutary restraint if it be exercised under strict sense of responsibility.

In this way public opinion changes from mercy at one time to severity at another. Though mercy has the greater power in the end, yet severity at times secures the passing of legislative measures introducing new punishment, making new crimes, enforcing greater hardships in the prison, and longer terms of penal servitude.

The ruling idea at such times is that by severity the crime, obnoxious for the moment, may be stamped out.

When mercy is in the ascendant, recourse is not had in so full or frequent a degree to the Legislature, but the public visits with condemnation some sentence as excessive which merely follows routine and bad example.

I hope to show that sentences harsh or mild have little effect in reducing crime, and if the latter will be as effective as the former we may indulge our own feelings by the pleasanter alternative. Here I expect the acute reader will see his opportunity, and, while he reserves his own opinion, will challenge mine with "Oh! then logically you are driven to advocate no imprisonment at all." I shall content myself with anticipating this stroke by saying that some other course may be taken than is afforded by the present law, or it may be allowed to me that if one advises a great eater or great drinker to eat or drink less one does not enforce upon him that he should neither eat nor drink.

I would admit that much has been done in this century, and even in the present reign, to get rid of barbarous and savage penalties of death and compulsory terms of penal servitude.

Still, in the matter of theft, we have been for part of that period in the hands of theorists who have in respect of successive offences by the same man been advocates of heaping terms of penal servitude upon unhappy wretches whose offences have been, as the humane Chief Constable of Liverpool says, the result "of the pressure of extreme want."

At the same time we have made imprisonment more rigorous, more secluded, imposed a dietary barely sufficient for the ordinary poor helpless wretch, and approaching starvation for those who require more or have been accustomed to satisfy their appetites. Cut off from the enjoyments of life, with no recreation, no amusement, permitted rarely to communicate with relatives outside, and even that privilege liable to be taken away for slight offences at the will of a severe gaoler, the unhappy subject is reduced to a despairing and spiritless creature. As for reform from such a process, which its shortsighted and severe inventors prophesied, no one now would assert that it is in any case realized.

This terrible system has been administered unflinchingly and logically by Recorders and chairmen of quarter sessions according to their lights. Their example has descended to the Courts of summary jurisdiction, where unnecessary imprisonment is resorted to, and disproportionate long sentences to the extent of their power are inflicted.

187

The Judges—some of them—and notably the Lord Chief Justice and Mr. Justice Mathew, have protested against the system, and have set examples of moderation.

Following such high authority, in my humbler sphere I have endeavoured to be more moderate to all offenders, but especially to those who have only repeated small offences.

Take one example out of many instances which have occurred.

A poor woman pleaded guilty before me, charged with stealing a duck. I looked at her record. She had already endured, for stealing meat, 12 months'; again, for stealing butter, seven years' penal servitude; again, for stealing meat, seven years'; again, for stealing meat, seven years'; or 22 years of sentences for stealing a few shillings' worth of food! My sentence for the duck was one month, and I regret it now as too much. I have never since seen her.

Mr. Tallack, the well-known secretary of the Howard Association, has collected a list of similar examples. They are, however, examples of a large class, for uniformity of severity has been the rule.

By self-imposed practice Judges, too, have inflicted sentences in Post-office and base coin cases which have shocked every thinking man.

As to sentences generally, the popular notion is that the Secretary of State submits them to revision by himself. It is an absolute misconception. He does in particular cases brought to his attention by petition, but not otherwise, and he is very slow to comply even in those cases.

The recent suggestion of Lord Justice Bowen and Mr. Justice Mathew to the Lord Chief Justice, and by him to the Lord Chancellor, that this should be considered by a meeting of the Judges and a mode of revision created is of immense importance.

I have now as shortly as possible to give some statistics of the course pursued by me at the Liverpool Quarter Sessions, and to show by independent testimony that my action has had no effect in encouraging or increasing crime, though I might claim many indirect beneficial results for it, too long to enter into in this communication.

Of 3,162 prisoners dealt with in the past six years, 464 were acquitted, 1,960 pleaded guilty, a very large proportion owing to reliance on lenity of treatment.

The average length of sentence per convicted prisoner before my appointment in 1886 was one year one month and six days.

The average sentence inflicted by me has been two months and 22 days.

If I had continued the old system the imprisonment in the six years I have presided would have reached a total of 2,967 years, whereas mine was in fact 618 years, showing a remission, or decrease, of 2,349 years of imprisonment, or 391 years annually.

Let the observant reader make the sum of saving of human misery for himself.

But have the bad consequences ensued oft foretold, constantly threatened by some, though not by the enlightened part of the local Press—notably, the *Mercury* and the *Daily Post*, who have constantly supported what must be admitted to have been experimental? Let the Head Constable of Liverpool answer the question. In his report to the Watch Committee, dated October 19, 1891, he says:—

"I have the great satisfaction of being able to congratulate you upon the fact that never since the first publication of returns of crime in Liverpool—*i.e.*, since 1857—have the statistics disclosed so small an amount of crime, or so large a success in making criminals amenable to justice, as those for the year ended September 29, 1891. The number of indictable offences committed during the year was 3,320, being 907 less than last year, and 967 less than the year previous.

"Each class of crime shares in the general improvement. Burglary, housebreaking, &c., continue to decrease, there having been only 385 cases during the year, against 610 last year and 633 the year previous.

"Serious crimes of violence—*i.e.*, indictable offences—have been 201, while last year they were 347, and the year previous 323."

188

I may interpolate here that housebreaking and violence, stabbing, &c., are within my jurisdiction, and are treated by me much on the same lines.

He adds, referring to his report in 1888, "Many of the minor larcenies are without doubt due to the pressure of extreme want."

This accords with my views, and has largely prompted my treatment of the offenders.

Of course I do not claim the credit of the decrease, though doubtless I should have had the discredit of the increase, had there been one. For present purposes what I do claim is to have proved that moderate sentences are as effective as excessive ones in the repression of crime.

If in six years we may remit two thousand and more years of imprisonment and yet leave property and person even safer than before in Liverpool, we may be encouraged to employ similar moderation in every Court of the country.

I have no hesitation in affirming that at least two-thirds of the imprisonment now being inflicted may be safely dispensed with.

Yours obediently,

CHAS. H. HOPWOOD, Recorder of Liverpool.

Temple, Jan. 8.

(The correspondence continued, largely concentrating on the question of the increase or decrease in crime, in *The Times* in the ensuing weeks as follows:

January 18	Letter from W. D. Morrison.
January 25	Letter from J. W. Nott Bower, Head Constable of Liverpool. *The Times* leading article.
January 28	Further letter from C. H. Hopwood.
February 2	Further letter from W. D. Morrison.)

---

4. Parliamentary Question. 8 December 1893 (see footnote[4] on page 27)

THE LIVERPOOL RECORDER AND SHORT SENTENCES

MR. S. SMITH (Flintshire): I beg to ask the Secretary of State for the Home Department whether his attention has been drawn to a protest signed by the Bishop of Liverpool and many other of the leading citizens against the sentence passed by the Recorder of Liverpool on the manager of the infamous Trocadero Club, wherein they deplore the imposition of a mere fine in this case; whether he is aware of the feeling of indignation which has been aroused in Liverpool with regard to the leniency of this sentence; and whether the Government can do anything, by legislation or otherwise, to secure the infliction of more severe sentences for such offences?

MR. HANBURY (Preston): Before the right hon. Gentleman answers the question, I should like to ask whether it is a fact that this sentence was one of a series of very light punishments for grave offences passed by the same Judge; and whether the Government intend to take any steps to remedy a scandal to the administration of justice generally caused by the disparities in the sentences passed in different Courts for similar offences?

MR. SNAPE: Have not the short sentences passed by the Recorder of Liverpool been attended by a diminution of crime?

MR. REES DAVIES (Pembrokeshire): At the same time, may I ask whether it is not the case that short sentences have been very strongly recommended by some Judges of the High Court?

MR. ASQUITH: The supplementary questions which I am asked refer to a matter of great delicacy and gravity, and they ought, therefore, to be put down on the Paper. With reference to the question on the Paper, my attention has been called to the protest referred to by my hon. Friend, and I gather from its terms and from the number and character of the signatures appended to it that there is a widespread feeling in Liverpool that this sentence was inadequate. I have no jurisdiction to interfere where the only complaint against a sentence is that it is too lenient, and as I have no title to take action in such a case I think it better not to express any opinion of my own upon it. The law, in my opinion, does not need strengthening, and its enforcement must of necessity be left largely to the discretion of those whose duty it is to administer it.

MR. HANBURY: I beg to give notice that I will repeat this question tomorrow.

MR. S. SMITH: I should like to further ask whether the right hon. Gentleman is aware that the evidence given against the Trocadero Club was of so abominable a character as to be unfit for publication; whether the manager of the club, a foreigner called Grossi, has been convicted before of similar offences——

MR. SPEAKER: Did the hon. Gentleman give notice of this question?

MR. S. SMITH: Well, the Home Secretary is quite aware of the facts of the case.

(Parliamentary Debates, Fourth Series, Vol. 19, Cols. 817–8. A further question was asked about the case—see Parliamentary Debates, Fourth Series, Vol. 19, Cols. 1175–6. 12 December 1893.)

THE ALVERSTONE MEMORANDUM 1901

Royal Courts of Justice

2 July 1901

The Right Honourable
The Home Secretary

Sir,

I have the honour to enclose a memorandum on normal punishments which has been agreed by his Majesty's Judges subject to certain observations, which you will find, by individual Judges, in the body of the Report. The Report has not been signed by Mr Justice Day as he was taken ill on Circuit while it was in course of signature and I have thought it better not to send it to him at present.

I need scarcely say that if you desire any further information on the matter I place myself entirely at your disposal

I am, Sir,

Your obedient servant

Alverstone.

MEMORANDUM ON NORMAL PUNISHMENTS
IN CERTAIN KINDS OF CRIME.

The extent of divergence in the assessment of punishment by Judges of the High Court, sitting in Courts of criminal jurisdiction, has been much exaggerated. In almost every class of crime, and pre-eminently in the case of manslaughter, the Judge, in fixing the punishment, has to discriminate between widely different degrees of moral culpability, and to weigh an infinite variety of circumstances and situations. The Legislature has wisely provided a large latitude in punishment. Justice demands, at times, that this latitude should be boldly used; and demands constantly the use of it in a slighter degree. Any attempt to mete out punishment to offenders in the same class of crime at a rigidly uniform rate could result only in the frequent perpetration of injustice. If due allowance is made for these essential considerations, there is nothing in the sentences of Judges of the High Court of Justice which are recorded in the criminal statistics (apart from the question of the advisability of flogging as a punishment) to indicate the existence of any established difference of principle or of general practice in the sentences of Judges of the High Court of Justice.

At the same time, the Judges of the King's Bench Division are agreed that it would be convenient and of public advantage in regard to certain classes of crime to come to an agreement, or, at least, to an approximate agreement, as to what may be called a "normal" standard of punishment: a standard of punishment, that is to say, which should be assumed to be properly applicable, unless the particular case under consideration presented some special features of aggravation or of extenuation.

They have, accordingly, considered carefully the Report of a Committee which was early in last year entrusted with the duty of investigating this subject, as well as the written comments upon that Report which have been made by Members of the Bench, and a scheme of punishment in certain cases drawn up by Mathew, J.; and the result of their deliberation is embodied in this Memorandum. It will be seen that in some cases it has not been found practicable to do more than recommend a range of punishment within certain limits.

I.—OFFENCES AGAINST PROPERTY, WITHOUT VIOLENCE.

The inclination of the Court towards leniency of punishment which has marked the last 20 years has, on the whole, been justified by results.

But, as the Reports published annually by the Home Office and the Statistics of Crime which they contain seem clearly to indicate, the leniency has gone too far in regard to those who are habitual criminals. In the case of such criminals, alike for the protection of property and as the best chance of reclaiming the offender, the Judges are of opinion that, as is indicated below, a sentence of penal servitude should, as a general rule, be passed upon such persons as have already been convicted of similar offences and appear to be seeking regularly to make a livelihood out of crime.

It is, however carefully to be borne in mind that there are offenders who have been previously convicted of dishonesty who are not professional criminals; and the mere repetition at intervals of acts of dishonesty ought not to be treated as in itself sufficient to stamp the convict as a member of the class to which reference has just been made. There are, for example, persons who from one cause or another have been temporarily disabled from earning wages and yield to the pressure of want; and again, persons, who, although leading a generally honest life of work, do at times commit acts of dishonesty, owing to a special temptation, or, as often happens, under the influence of drink. For such occasional criminals imprisonment* seems to us to be, as a rule, sufficient punishment.

Juvenile offenders under 16 years of age should not be sentenced to any term of imprisonment unless there has been a previous conviction.

NORMAL SENTENCES.

Larceny.

(a) In the case of a first offence—

For juveniles under 16, no term of imprisonment.

For adults, a discharge upon recognizances, or a short term of imprisonment.

(b) In the case of subsequent convictions—

If intervals of honest conduct, imprisonment for from 6 to 12 months.

If the prisoner whilst at liberty has been making crime his source of livelihood, penal servitude from 3 to 5 years.

Embezzlement.

(a) In the case of a first offence—

Same treatment as for convictions for larceny (*supra*).

(b) In the case of subsequent convictions—

In ordinary cases imprisonment, 4 to 12 months.

If the offence is systematic, and/or the amount embezzled is large, penal servitude, 3 to 5 years.

---

* NOTE.—The term "imprisonment" in this Memorandum is to be understood as covering both imprisonment with, and imprisonment without, hard labour.

False Pretences.

(*a*) In the case of a first offence—

Same treatment as for convictions for larceny (*supra*).

(*b*) In the case of subsequent convictions—

Imprisonment, 4 to 12 months. If the prisoner has been getting his living by crime, penal servitude, 3 to 5 years.

Forgery.

For first offences, when the offence is akin to larceny, or obtaining by false pretences, as *e.g.* forging an order for goods or an endorsement to a cheque—

Same treatment as for convictions for larceny (*supra*).

(*b*) *In the case of subsequent convictions:*

Where the offence is of the same sort and is not effected systematically, imprisonment, 6 to 12 months.

Where the offence is effected systematically, penal servitude, 3 to 5 years.

Forgery or uttering of Bank Notes, Bills or Deeds, or where there is a conspiracy to defraud and/or to a large amount by forged documents.

Penal servitude, 3 to 10 years.

Fraudulent personation of Pensioners.

In the case of adult convicts, imprisonment, 3 to 9 months.

In the case of convicts under 16, same treatment as in case of larceny (*supra*).

Post Office cases (stealing of or from letters).

Imprisonment, 8 to 15 months.

Fraudulent personation of owners of Stocks or public funds, or of personal representatives of deceased persons.

Penal servitude, 7 to 12 years.

II.—OFFENCES AGAINST PROPERTY, WITH VIOLENCE TO PROPERTY.

Burglary, Housebreaking, Shopbreaking, &c.

These offences, as is stated in the official Home Office Report, are mostly the work of professional criminals, and, where the offence is of a serious kind and is not a first offence, the normal sentence should be one of penal servitude, 3 to 5 years. But it is mportant to bear in mind that an offence which really differs little or nothing in point of gravity from thieving, may technically constitute in law one or other of these offences, and may be set down as such in the Judge's private Calendar at the Assizes if the convict is charged with a subsequent offence. A burglary, a housebreaking, or a shop-breaking, may be really a petty offence against property, and should, in such a case, be treated, in the matter of punishment, as an ordinary larceny would be treated.

Arson.

Stack burning, from 12 months' imprisonment to 3 years' penal servitude.

Setting fire to house, penal servitude, 5 years; and, where human life is endangered, 10 years.

III.—OTHER OFFENCES RELATING TO PROPERTY.

Coining or uttering base coin.

On first conviction, imprisonment, 1 to 6 months.

On second conviction, imprisonment, 9 to 12 months.

On a third conviction, penal servitude, 5 to 7 years.

IV.—OFFENCES AGAINST PROPERTY, WITH VIOLENCE TO THE PERSON.

Robbery with violence.

After a previous conviction for a similar offence, penal servitude; and if serious bodily hurt has been inflicted, or the crime has been committed by several in concert, for a period not less than 5 years.*

V.—OFFENCES AGAINST THE PERSON.

Manslaughter.

Where the death arises from an assault, and there is no intent to kill, the person should be punished as if he had been convicted for the infliction of such an injury as might reasonably be expected to result from the assault.

Attempts to murder where life is endangered.

Penal servitude, 7 to 12 years.

Felonious wounding or inflicting grievous bodily harm, with intent, &c.

Imprisonment for 18 months, or penal servitude, not exceeding 5 years.

Shooting with intent, &c.

Penal servitude, 5 to 10 years.

Administering poison.

The same.

Throwing vitriol.

Penal servitude, not less than 3 years.

Assaults, other than those above-mentioned, causing bodily harm, or unlawful wounding.

Imprisonment, 6 to 18 months.

Rape on females over 13 years of age.

A period of from 5 to 7 years' penal servitude gives a reasonable range of punishment; to be increased if there are accompanying circumstances of aggravation, such *e.g.* as rape by a gang or by a parent or a master, or with brutal violence, and to be reduced if there are extenuating circumstances.

[Mathew, J., has suggested a more detailed normal scale, as follows:—

> Where temptation and no great violence, imprisonment for 18 months, or penal servitude for 3 years. Where violent assault, penal servitude for 5 years. When done by several in concert, penal servitude for 10 years.]

---

*NOTE.—As to flogging, see note *ad fin.*

It is agreed, however, that rape is an offence which, covers varying degrees of wickedness, and the just punishment for which requires varying degrees of severity.

Rape on children under 13 years of age, and felonious carnal knowledge under the Criminal Law Amendment Act, 1885:—

If by a parent, in the absence of exceptional brutality or intimidation or cruelty, penal servitude, 10 years.

If by an adult stranger, penal servitude for 7 years.

If by a youth under 18, and upon a child nearly 13 years of age, and with consent in fact, imprisonment for 3 to 12 months.

If by a youth over 18 years of age, under the same circumstances, imprisonment from 12 to 18 months.

If the convict is under 15 years of age, and there is no evidence of earlier wrongdoing of the like kind, and there has been no grave physical injury to the sufferer—

No imprisonment, but a whipping, as authorized by the Criminal Law Amendment Act, 1885, s. 4.

[Wills, J, in cases of assaults of this nature, committed by fathers upon their children, approves of 12 to 16 years' penal servitude as a normal standard of punishment; and where helpless children have been forced by strangers, approves of 10 to 15 years' penal servitude as a normal standard of punishment.]

Indecent assault.

Imprisonment, 1 to 12 months.

Misdemeanor under the Criminal Law Amendment Act.

Imprisonment, 1 to 12 months.

Procuring abortion.

5 years' penal servitude.

Sodomy.

As to the punishment of this crime there is some difference of opinion amongst the Judges of the King's Bench Division. The recommendation of the Report, of which the majority approve, has suggested, in the case of an adult convict, that, where there is no violence, and the other party is also adult, a sentence of penal servitude for 3 years, would, in the absence of special circumstances, be sufficient; that in the case of juvenile offenders under 16 years of age, the punishment should not exceed 6 months' imprisonment; and that, when the offence is committed by an adult upon a youthful and unwilling victim, a punishment of penal servitude up to a maximum of 10 years would be just. In the opinion of Wright, Bruce, and Phillimore, JJ., this scale of punishment is too low.

VI.—OTHER OFFENCES.

Bestiality.

The punishment for a first offence should not except under very special circumstances exceed 12 months' imprisonment, and if the offender is not over 16 years of age should not exceed 6 months' imprisonment. [Wright, J., and Phillimore J., are of opinion that this scale of punishment is unnecessarily high.]

Bigamy.

If woman not deceived and/or prosecution vindictive, imprisonment not exceeding 6 months.

If woman deceived, imprisonment from 12 to 18 months, or penal servitude, in rather worse cases, from 3 to 5 years. [Wright, J., suggests a normal sentence of 6 months' imprisonment when the woman is not deceived, and 3 years' penal servitude where the woman is deceived. Bruce, J., suggests 3 months as the minimum sentence.]

Perjury.

Generally, imprisonment from 3 to 12 months.

Where a deliberate attempt to injure character, or to defraud, or to pervert justice, penal servitude from 5 to 7 years.

Concealment of birth.

Imprisonment for 2 months.

[Suggested by Bruce, J.]

FLOGGING AS A PUNISHMENT.

As to the wisdom of inflicting in any case this form of punishment, there is a considerable divergence of opinion. But it is, at all events, the decided view of almost all, if not all, of the Judges of the King's Bench Division that, if flogging forms part of a sentence, (1) it should be only a single flogging, and (2) that it should be administered at the commencement of the term of punishment; and they are also of opinion that its infliction should be confined to cases where the criminal has either inflicted serious bodily hurt, or has made the assault in concert with others.

Grantham, Wright, Ridley, Bigham, Darling, Phillimore, and Bucknill, JJ., are in favour of the extension of this form of punishment to cases of the grosser criminal assaults on women and children. Lawrance, J., is of opinion that flogging is a punishment which might advantageously be adopted in some cases of assaults on children, but that, unless it were universally adopted it would be unwise to extend it to such cases. Ridley, J., has suggested that, wherever a person under the age of 17 years has been convicted of a criminal assault under section 4 of the Criminal Law Amendment Act 1885, the legislature should empower the Judge to order a whipping with the birch-rod in lieu of imprisonment, and Channell J. is in favour of this suggestion.

(Signed)	Alverstone C.J.	William R. Kennedy
	J. C. Mathew	Edward Ridley
	Alfred Wills	John C. Bigham
	Wm. Grantham	Charles Darling
	J. C. Lawrance	A. M. Channell
	N. S. Wright	Walter G. F. Phillimore
	Gainsford Bruce	T. T. Bucknill

NOTES ON THE
MEMORANDUM ON NORMAL PUNISHMENTS,
By BRUCE, J.

Larceny.

(a) In the case of a first offence—For Juveniles under 16, no term of imprisonment.

I do not think that this should be laid down as a general rule. The Prison Commis-

196

sioners have lately made special arrangements for the training and discipline of boys under 16, and I believe that there are many cases where it would be distinctly mischievous to allow an act of theft to pass without punishment. In many cases it is important to remove the boy from the influence of vicious parents for a time, and it is not always a good thing to send a boy to a Reformatory for a long term. The Memorandum says nothing about whipping as an alternative to imprisonment in the case of boys under 16. In some cases, whipping is, I think, the proper punishment, but I cannot regard it as a substitute for imprisonment in all cases.

Forgery.

For first offences—forging an order for goods or an endorsement to a cheque.

I do not agree that as a general rule a person who is for the first time convicted of an offence of this kind should be discharged upon recognizances. I think forgery is a much more serious crime than larceny, and in the case of forgery I think only special circumstances can render a discharge upon recognizances a right determination.

Manslaughter.

I do not agree that an assault that causes death is to be punished just in the same way as the assault would have been punished if death had not ensued. The loss of life is, I think, always an element to be taken into consideration in awarding punishment.

Felonious wounding with intent—Shooting with intent, &c.

The intent is the essence of the offence, whether committed by means of one instrument or another. I doubt whether it is right to make the punishment for wounding with intent so much lighter than for shooting with intent.

Perjury.

I do not understand the force of the phrase to pervert justice; all perjury tends to pervert justice. I suppose the phrase to defraud means to obtain gain or advantage personal to the accused.

Concealment of birth.

What is the opinion of the Judges on this matter? I think we ought to be able to agree upon a normal sentence.

197

APPENDIX F (Chapter 3)

THE CHURCHILL SCALE OF OFFENCES 1910

The following is an extract from two minutes written by Winston Churchill, when Home Secretary, in May and September 1910

The general scale of crimes is as follows in my judgment;

I. <u>Offences of the First Degree</u>: (Against Life.)

(a) Offences against the State
High treason and treason felony.

(b) Offences against Life
Murder

Attempts to murder where life is endangered
Shooting with intent
Felonious wounding
Administering poison

Throwing vitriol

Rape (1) where life is endangered

Arson (1) where life is endangered

II. <u>Offences of the Second Degree</u>: (Against the person.)

(a) Offences of dangerous violence
Rape (2)
Rape (3) by fraud, e.g., bigamy (1)
Rape (4) (unnatural.)

Burglary, armed.
Robbery with violence
Blackmail
Perjury, malicious

(b) Offences of violence
Abortion where death results
Brutal assault without danger to life upon a woman, child or weak man.
Cruelty, wilful, to children.

III. <u>Offences of the Third Degree</u>: (Against property.)

Larceny
Receiving
Coining
Forgery
Fraud

198

Obtaining by false pretences

Arson (2) where no life endangered

These with their different degrees should be carefully set out in their order of gravity, putting the most serious first.

IV. Offences of the Fourth Degree: (Against morals.)

    Offences against minors

    Offences against decency

    Bestiality

    Abortion

    Bigamy

    Incest

These are the four main degrees of crime against life, the person, property and morals. It is clear that the same offence may appear in more than one category according to circumstances, but I think the classification should, subject to further consideration, be taken as a guide. No doubt very considerable refinement and numerous sub-divisions will be necessary, and, of course, my outline does not pretend to be complete . . . .

The second part of the Memorandum should deal with Petty Crime. The title may, perhaps, be "Offences against Social Order". There are two primary divisions: (1) Occasional; (2) Habitual. The occasional will include all the existing Police Court crimes . . . when considered as isolated acts. For these imprisonment, or fine leading certainly to imprisonment, should very rarely be imposed, and usually only when the offence is so serious as to make a sentence of a month's imprisonment not excessive. All other isolated offences should be dealt with by probation, admonition, disciplinary probation (juveniles), and by suspensory sentences. The habitual commission of minor offences of a particular character or of a variety of minor offences without long intervals of blamelessness, should make the offender liable to be prosecuted upon the occasion of a fresh offence not on the individual offence, but on his general record.

199

APPENDIX G (Chapter 4)

SENTENCING POWERS AND PRACTICE OF THE COURTS

1. The maximum powers of imprisonment respectively of the Crown Court and of magistrates' courts are controlled statutorily in different ways. In the case of a purely summary offence (where the maximum penalty is often less than six months' imprisonment) there is an overriding limit on magistrates of six months' imprisonment which cannot be exceeded even where two or more sentences are ordered to run consecutively. In the case of an indictable offence tried summarily, there is a similar limit of six months' imprisonment for an offence, but with an overriding maximum of 12 months imprisonment on consecutive sentences.[1] In the Crown Court the maximum is always that provided for by the statute for the particular offence, with no overriding limit on consecutive sentences.

2. Whenever the magistrates' court considers that its powers of sentence are inadequate, having regard to the character and antecedents of the offender, it may commit him for sentence in respect of any indictable offence tried summarily.[2] The powers of the Crown Court on such committal are then the same as they would have been had the conviction taken place before the Crown Court. The magistrates' courts also have power to commit to the Crown Court for sentence young offenders who are eligible for borstal training, provided that certain conditions are satisfied.[3] The purpose of such a committal is to enable the Crown Court to pass a sentence of borstal training, which a magistrates' court has no power to do. If the Crown Court does not think that borstal training is appropriate, its power in passing any sentence of imprisonment is limited to that which a magistrates' court could itself have exercised had it not committed the offender for sentence.

3. An appeal against sentence may be made from the decision of the magistrates' court to the Crown Court.[4] On the hearing by the Crown Court of any appeal, or in proceedings on committal for sentence, the professional judge in the Crown Court sits with not less than two, nor more than four, magistrates. There is no direct appeal from the magistrates' court to the Court of Appeal (Criminal Division), although on a point of law a magistrates' court may be called upon to state a case for the opinion of the Queen's Bench Divisional Court, which has a similar membership to the Court of Appeal (Criminal Division). A person sentenced by the Crown Court after committal to it for sentence by a magistrates' court may, with the leave of the Court of Appeal, appeal to that Court against sentence if that sentence exceeds six months' imprisonment, or is one which the magistrates' court could not itself have passed, and in certain other instances.[5] But on appeal against the sentence of a magistrates' court to the Crown Court there is no further right of appeal to the Court of Appeal.[6] Any person convicted in the Crown Court may appeal against his sentence to the Court of Appeal, with the leave of that Court.

4. Thus, while the annual number of offenders imprisoned by the magistrates' courts is large (nearly half of all persons sentenced to immediate imprisonment) the lengths of those sentences are by definition short, and in practice are rarely interfered with, or indeed directly influenced by the higher courts. Such interference or influence, moreover, is almost exclusively effected by the Crown Court. The numbers sentenced to immediate imprisonment in 1976 were:

---

[1] Magistrates' Courts Act 1952, section 108 (as to subsection (3), see Criminal Law Act 1977, section 27(1) and (2)).
[2] Magistrates' Courts Act 1952, section 29, as amended by the Criminal Law Act 1977, Schedule 12 (not yet in force).
[3] Magistrates' Courts Act 1952, section 28.
[4] *Ibid.*, section 83 (as amended).
[5] Criminal Appeal Act 1968, section 10.
[6] *Ibid.*, section 10(1).

	Magistrates' Courts	Crown Court	Total
Indictable offences	12,263 (35%)	22,468 (65%)	34,731
Non-indictable offences	4,934 (87%)	750 (13%)	5,684
Total	17,197 (43%)	23,218 (57%)	40,415

5. Appeals from the magistrates' court to the Crown Court differ markedly from appeals that go from the Crown Court to the Court of Appeal. When hearing appeals from magistrates' courts the Crown Court comprises a number of lay magistrates, each of whom has an equal vote with the professional judge and can therefore outvote him. By contrast, the Court of Appeal is composed of three senior High Court judges. An appeal to the Crown Court is, moreover, a rehearing, whereas in the Court of Appeal it is a review based on the transcript of the proceedings before the court of trial. This makes little practical difference, since the Court of Appeal always has power to hear fresh evidence and base its judgment on the situation as at appeal and is not bound to be satisfied that the trial judge was wrong before it can intervene. But there is a natural tendency in the Court of Appeal to lean towards upholding the sentences of the professional judiciary. That tendency is less marked in the Crown Court in relation to lay magistrates. The Court of Appeal, since 1966, has not been able to increase the severity of a sentence appealed against, whereas the Crown Court has power, within the limits governing the magistrates' courts' sentencing powers, to increase the sentence on appeal. Finally, the Crown Court, in exercising its appellate powers, does not establish principles of sentencing. As with its original jurisdiction to pass sentence, it is bound to apply the principles laid down by the Court of Appeal. It is only by this hierarchy of courts that the principles of sentencing established by the Court of Appeal percolate down, through the Crown Court, to the magistracy.

6. The Crown Court can ordinarily do little more than provide guidance to magistrates by demonstrating, through its own sentencing, the observance of principles of sentencing. The direct association of lay magistracy with the professional judge at the Crown Court in appeals from magistrates' courts, however, is vital, since only in that way can the magistracy keep in touch with the changing policy of the Court of Appeal. Magistrates sitting at the Crown Court can thus take back with them to their own courts the prevailing judicial attitudes to sentencing.

7. The replacement of the present system of maximum penalties by new maxima, based firmly on the sentencing practice of the higher courts, should provide a valuable additional guide to magistrates as to how to exercise their function as sentencers. While maximum penalties for indictable offences will remain well beyond the limits imposed on magistrates, the less remote the maxima are to the upper limits of magisterial power, the greater the impact they will doubtless make, and the more they will help magistrates to gauge their own range of appropriate penalties.

APPENDIX H (Chapter 4)

APPEALS TO THE COURT OF APPEAL[1] 1956–76

TABLE 1

Appeals heard 1956–76

Year	Number sentenced in the Crown Court	Number sentenced to immediate imprisonment	Number of appellants	Number of appeals heard	Result of appeals heard					Legal aid granted for appeals heard	
					Conviction and sentence affirmed	Conviction affirmed[2] sentence varied	Conviction quashed other conviction substituted	Conviction quashed	Retrial ordered	Number	Percentage of appeals heard
1956	20,209	9,721	1,094	157	52	84	—	21	—	37	24
1957	23,700	10,731	1,302	190	74	96	3	17	—	64	34
1958	28,454	12,254	1,446	206	59	134	1	12	—	65	32
1959	30,168	13,359	1,940	294	132	134	10	18	—	71	24
1960	31,275	13,692	2,292	288	119	127	4	38	—	109	38
1961	34,669	14,714	2,930	423	186	175	2	60	—	194	46
1962	33,881	14,518	2,607	486	198	212	3	73	—	357	73
1963	28,040	12,409	2,531	424	179	164	6	75	—	379	89
1964	27,985	11,900	2,741	388	179	135	6	66	2	335	86
1965	30,891	12,421	2,906	444	196	179	7	57	5	381	86
1966	34,679	14,347	4,431	473	193	204	2	70	4	390	82
1967	36,225	14,354	5,820	573	211	282	7	66	7	513	90
1968	39,125	14,068	7,927	826	362	365	7	91	1	787	95
1969	44,554	16,079	8,660	905	427	352	5	117	4	657	73
1970	51,640	19,097	8,321	978	441	423	4	104	6	828	85
1971	53,534	18,928	6,349	1,052	405	460	6	173	8	881	84
1972	55,711	19,085	6,308	1,037	464	444	4	124	1	891	86
1973	56,591	17,984	6,187	1,116	412	544	7	149	4	941	84
1974	60,744	18,488	4,853	954	300	543	6	102	3	705	74
1975	70,023	21,753	5,561	1,130	438	547	6	130	9	920	81
1976	72,834	23,218	6,203	1,305	549	598	8	146	4	1,152	88

The table does not include appeals against findings of unfit to plead or not guilty by reason of insanity.

[1] To the Court of Criminal Appeal up to 1966 and to the Court of Appeal (Criminal Division) thereafter.
[2] Conviction affirmed includes cases where there was no appeal against conviction.

TABLE 2

Applications for leave to appeal October 1969–October 1970

	1969													1970													
Fortnight ending	3 Oct.	17 Oct.	31 Oct.	14 Nov.	28 Nov.	12 Dec.	31 Dec.	9 Jan.	23 Jan.	6 Feb.	20 Feb.	6 Mar.	20 Mar.	3 Apr.*	17 Apr.	1 May	15 May	12 June	26 June	10 July	24 July	7 Aug.	21 Aug.	4 Sep.	18 Sep.	2 Oct.	16 Oct.
Number of applications	387	445	405	414	462	484	458	252	377	442	371	438	429	354	203	174	212	187	242	255	234	230	268	188	99	130	225

*The Practice Note (Crime: Applications for leave to appeal) [1970] 1 W.L.R. 663, which announced that henceforth single Judges would exercise freely their power to direct loss of time in respect of hopeless applications, was made on 17 March 1970 and took effect on 7 April.

PRINCIPLES OF SENTENCING

Judgment of Lawton L.J. in R v Sargeant (1975) 60 Cr. App. R. 74

(The appellant pleaded guilty at the Central Criminal Court on 20 May 1974 to affray and was sentenced to two years' imprisonment.)

"We have thought it necessary not only to analyse the facts, but to apply to those facts the classical principles of sentencing. Those classical principles are summed up in four words: retribution, deterrence, prevention and rehabilitation. Any judge who comes to sentence ought always to have those four classical principles in mind and to apply them to the facts of the case to see which of them has the greatest importance in the case with which he is dealing.

I will start with retribution. The Old Testament concept of an eye for an eye and tooth for tooth no longer plays any part in our criminal law. There is, however, another aspect of retribution which is frequently overlooked: it is that society, through the courts, must show its abhorrence of particular types of crime, and the only way in which the courts can show this is by the sentences they pass. The courts do not have to reflect public opinion. On the other hand courts must not disregard it. Perhaps the main duty of the court is to lead public opinion. Anyone who surveys the criminal scene at the present time must be alive to the appalling problem of violence. Society, we are satisfied, expects the courts to deal with violence. The weapons which the courts have at their disposal for doing so are few. We are satisfied that in most cases fines are not sufficient punishment for senseless violence. The time has come, in the opinion of this Court, when those who indulge in the kind of violence with which we are concerned in this case must expect custodial sentences.

But we are also satisfied that, although society expects the courts to impose punishment for violence which really hurts, it does not expect the courts to go on hurting for a long time, which is what this sentence is likely to do. We agree with the trial judge that the kind of violence which occurred in this case called for a custodial sentence. This young man has had a custodial sentence. Despite his good character, despite the excellent background from which he comes, very deservedly he has had the humiliation of hearing prison gates closing behind him. We take the view that for men of good character the very fact that prison gates have closed is the main punishment. It does not necessarily follow that they should remain closed for a long time.

I turn now to the element of deterrence, because it seems to us the trial judge probably passed this sentence as a deterrent one. There are two aspects of deterrence: deterrence of the offender and deterrence of likely offenders. Experience has shown over the years that deterrence of the offender is not a very useful approach, because those who have their wits about them usually find the closing of prison gates an experience which they do not want again. If they do not learn that lesson, there is likely to be a high degree of recidivism anyway. So far as deterrence of others is concerned, it is the experience of the courts that deterrent sentences are of little value in respect of offences which are committed on the spur of the moment, either in hot blood or in drink or both. Deterrent sentences may very well be of considerable value where crime is premeditated. Burglars, robbers and users of firearms and weapons may very well be put off by deterrent sentences. We think it unlikely that deterrence would be of any value in this case.

We come now to the element of prevention. Unfortunately it is one of the facts of life that there are some offenders for whom neither deterrence nor rehabilitation works. They will go on committing crimes as long as they are able to do so. In those cases the only protection which the public has is that such persons should be locked up for a long period. This case does not call for a preventive sentence.

Finally, there is the principle of rehabilitation. Some 20 to 25 years ago there was a view abroad, held by many people in executive authority, that short sentences were of little value, because there was not enough time to give in prison the benefit of training. That view is no longer held as firmly as it was. This young man does not want prison training. It is not going to do him any good. It is his memory of the clanging of prison gates which is likely to keep him from crime in the future.

In the light of that analysis of the classical principles to be applied in sentencing, what is the result on the facts of this case? The answer is that this sentence is much too long. It was submitted that a suspended sentence should have been passed. For the reasons I have already given, we do not agree. But we are satisfied, having regard to the facts of this case and the social inquiry and prison reports which the Court has been given that we can deal with this case by substituting for the sentence which was passed such a sentence as will enable him to be discharged today. To that extent the appeal is allowed."

APPENDIX J (Chapter 4)

THE LENGTH OF PRISON SENTENCES 1913–76

Analysis of receptions into prison by effective length of sentence (males and females)

	1913		1938		1951		1961		1966		1971		1976	
	Receptions on sentence	Percentage of total	Receptions on sentence	Percentage of total	Receptions on sentence	Percentage of total	Receptions on sentence	Percentage of total	Receptions on sentence	Percentage of total	Receptions on sentence	Percentage of total	Receptions on sentence	Percentage of total
Up to 5 weeks	111,320	80·5	16,295	53·2	8,726	26·7	8,802	22·0	10,169	20·3	8,332	17·7	8,321	16·5
Over 5 weeks and up to 3 months	16,862	12·2	7,043	22·3	8,659	26·5	10,250	25·6	13,989	27·9	10,015	21·3	12,294	24·4
Over 3 months and up to 6 months	5,070	3·7	3,947	12·9	6,065	18·6	8,255	20·6	12,210	24·3	7,751	16·4	8,353	16·6
Over 6 months and up to 12 months	2,873	2·1	1,881	6·1	4,401	13·5	5,969	14·9	5,743	11·4	8,695	18·5	7,825	15·5
Over 12 months and up to 2 years	1,341	1·0	987	3·2	3,090	9·5	4,191	10·5	4,622	9·2	7,462	15·8	7,401	14·7
Over 2 years and up to 4 years	602	0·4	374	1·2	1,346	4·1	1,927	4·8	2,576	5·1	3,753	8·0	4,755	9·4
Over 4 years and up to 7 years	196	0·1	106	0·3	358	1·1	494	1·2	659	1·3	839	1·8	1,066	2·1
Over 7 years	19	—	13	—	36	0·1	64	0·2	142	0·3	164	0·3	259	0·5
Life sentences (including H.M.P.)	12	—	0	—	0	—	51	0·1	87	0·2	114	0·2	165	0·3
TOTAL	138,295	100	30,646	100	32,681	100	40,003	100	50,197	100	47,125	100	50,439	100

Sources: Figures for 1913–61 extracted from *The Machinery of Justice in England* by R. M. Jackson (Cambridge University Press, 1964), Table IX, page 217.

Figures for 1966–76, Home Office Statistical Department.

Note: As a result of the rounding of the figures, the percentages do not total 100 in every case.

APPENDIX K (Chapter 5)

EXTENDED SENTENCES

TABLE 1

Persons given extended sentences, by offence 1967-76

Offence group	Year									
	67*	68	69	70	71	72	73	74	75	76
Violence against the person	1	—	2	2	4	3	1	4	2	—
Sexual offences	2	2	2	4	5	2	—	2	1	—
Burglary	2	6	35	65	34	42	15	8	17	5
Robbery	2	2	5	16	10	5	4	1	—	—
Theft and handling stolen goods	—	6	10	12	16	10	3	6	3	1
Fraud and forgery	—	—	3	8	8	7	7	5	3	3
Criminal damage	—	—	1	1	3	1	1	—	2	—
Other	—	—	1	2	—	—	—	—	1	—
TOTAL (Trial)	7	16	59	110	80	70	31	26	29	9
Sentenced after summary conviction	—	11	15	19	17	9	1	2	4	5
TOTAL	7	27	74	129	97	79	32	28	33	14

*Section 37 of the Criminal Justice Act 1967, which introduced the power to impose an extended sentence, came into force on 1 October 1967.

TABLE 2

Persons given extended sentences, by offence 1974-76

Offence	Number of persons
Manslaughter	1
Wounding	2
Other wounding	3
Buggery	1
Rape	1
Indecent assault on a female	1
Burglary in a dwelling	22
Burglary in other type of building	10
Aggravated burglary in other building	1
Robbery	1
Theft by an employee	2
Theft from mail	1
Shoplifting	2
Theft of motor vehicle	1
Other theft	5
Handling stolen goods	1
Other fraud	10
Arson	2
Other forgery and uttering	6
Other offence	2
TOTAL	75

TABLE 3

Persons given extended sentences, by length of sentence 1967-76

Length of sentence	Year									
	67*	68	69	70	71	72	73	74	75	76
2 years and under	1	2	4	4	5	2	3	3	—	—
Over 2 years and up to 3 years	—	2	8	10	11	19	5	2	13	2
Over 3 years and up to 4 years	2	3	12	12	12	9	3	5	7	1
Over 4 years and up to 5 years	1	3	22	36	31	19	9	9	4	6
Over 5 years and up to 7 years	1	7	16	35	23	19	10	8	6	5
Over 7 years and up to 10 years	2	9	11	26	12	10	2	—	3	—
Over 10 years	—	1	1	6	3	1	—	1	—	—
TOTAL	7	27	74	129	97	79	32	28	33	14

*Section 37 of the Criminal Justice Act 1967, which introduced the power to impose an extended sentence, came into force on 1 October 1967.

APPENDIX L (Chapter 9)

PERIODICITY OF RECONVICTION

TABLE 1

Rates of reconviction within two years of release in 1965 for a sample of prisoners having served over 18 months, according to sentence length

Sentence length	Number	Percentage reconvicted (brackets indicate base figures of less than 16)
Less than 2 years	74	60
2 years and under 3 years	451	56
3 years and under 4 years	324	54
4 years and under 5 years	129	58
5 years and under 6 years	87	41
6 years and under 7 years	9	(67)
7 years and under 8 years	28	46
8 years or more	32	59
Life	4	(0)
TOTAL	1,138	54

Source: Parole in England and Wales, Home Office Research Study No. 38 (HMSO, 1977).

TABLE 2

Reconvictions: adult male prisoners discharged during 1973 from sentences of over 3 months— two-year follow-up from date of discharge

Result of follow-up	Length of sentence from which discharged							
	Over 3 months up to 6 months	Over 6 months and under 18 months	18 months	Over 18 months up to 4 years	Over 4 years up to 10 years	Over 10 years	Life	TOTAL
Percentage reconvicted	53	50	48	48	39	18	9	49
Number discharged	4,896	7,676	2,749	5,852	917	22	45	22,157

Source: Report on the work of the Prison Department 1976, Statistical Tables, Cmnd. 6884.

TABLE 3

Proportion of male prisoners discharged during 1973 who were first reconvicted within specified periods from the date of their release

Time between release and first reconviction	Percentage (of those at risk)	
	Adult male prisoners with sentence over 3 months	Young male prisoners with sentence over 3 months
Up to 3 months	8	12
Over 3 months up to 6 months	11	21
Over 6 months up to 9 months	11	17
Over 9 months up to 12 months	9	11
Over 12 months up to 15 months	8	14
Over 15 months up to 18 months	7	12
Over 18 months up to 21 months	5	7
Over 21 months up to 24 months	5	7

Source: Report on the work of the Prison Department 1976, Statistical Tables, Cmnd. 6884.

APPENDIX M (Chapter 10)

CONSECUTIVE SENTENCES

An account of the principal case-law

1. A court, in sentencing an offender on the same occasion for more than one offence (whether charged in the same indictment or not) should pronounce a specific sentence in respect of each of them, but may make any such sentence either concurrent with or consecutive to any other of them.[1] There is no rule of law requiring that the aggregate length of consecutive sentences so passed shall not exceed the maximum that could have been imposed for the most serious of the offences.[2] Similarly, a sentence of imprisonment passed upon an offender already subject to a sentence may be made concurrent with, or to commence on the expiration of, that existing sentence.[3]

2. There are two established principles that currently guide the use of the power to impose consecutive sentences:

(*a*) In general, sentences for offences arising out of the same transaction or series of transactions should be concurrent,[4] although there are a number of true exceptions, and some apparent ones which on consideration prove to be instances where the right view is that the individual offences ought to be regarded as separate. Thus, in *R* v *Britten*,[5] a true exception, consecutive sentences were held appropriate for offences against section 1 of the Official Secrets Act 1911 because of the exceptional category of the offences, and notwithstanding that each of them could properly be described as one of a series. By contrast, the ground on which consecutive sentences were upheld in cases of robbery and, on the occasion of that robbery, possessing firearms with intent to commit that offence,[6] plainly was that each was an offence of a different kind, carrying a sentence in its own right. The same principle was applied in *R* v *Costas*[7] where the Court of Appeal upheld consecutive sentences of three years' imprisonment (the then maximum) for each of the offences of possessing firearms and of selling them. Lord Denning M.R. pointed out that each was a serious offence and said "We think that Parliament must have realised that a man might be guilty of the double offence—the two offences of possessing and selling—and have regarded the maximum for each separately as three years, and for the two together as six years".

---

[1] *R* v *Wilkes* (1796) 19 How. St. Tr. 1075, 1136; *Castro* v *R* (1881) 6 App. Cas. 229.

[2] *R* v *Blake* [1962] 2 Q.B. 377.

[3] *R* v *Greenberg* [1943] K.B. 381. In relation to bringing into effect a sentence previously suspended, these powers are expressly conferred by the Powers of Criminal Courts Act 1973, section 23(2). As to magistrates' courts, the Magistrates' Courts Act 1952, section 108, as amended by the Criminal Law Act 1977, empowers the court to order a sentence of imprisonment imposed by it to commence on the expiration of any other term imposed either by it or by any other court, but with the limitation that when a magistrates' court imposes two or more terms to run consecutively the aggregate of them must not exceed six months, or (with a minor exception) in the case of offences triable either on indictment or summarily but in fact dealt with summarily, 12 months.

[4] For example, burglary and, on the same occasion, going equipped to steal—*R* v *McGould* [1965] Crim. L.R. 561; seven counts for theft by an employee—*R* v *Brown* (1970) 54 Cr. App. R. 176. In the latter case, the Court of Appeal indicated that the correct approach was to decide what the overall sentence should be, and then to pass a concurrent sentence of that length for each offence.

[5] [1969] 1 W.L.R. 151.

[6] For example, *R* v *Faulkner* (1972) 56 Cr. App. R. 594; *R* v *Lydon* [1974] Crim. L.R. 265. The principal was again approved in *R* v *Knowles* [1977] Crim. L.R. 433, described in paragraph 4.

[7] (1968) 52 Cr. App. R. 115 (the words quoted are at page 117).

211

(b) When the question arises whether a sentence should be ordered to be served consecutively to another, the court in deciding that question and the question of length of term should ensure that the totality of imprisonment is not excessive.[1]

3. This applies whether:

(i) the sentences are passed on the same occasion; or

(ii) a subsequent sentence is ordered to commence at the expiration of a term to which the offender is already subject; or

(iii) a sentence previously passed but suspended may be ordered to take effect consecutively to a sentence passed for an offence or offences, committed during the operational period of the suspended sentence, and so rendering it liable to be enforced.

4. Instances of (i), where really serious offences were involved, are *R* v *Knowles*[2] and *R* v *Turner*.[3] In the former case, sentences of seven years' imprisonment for wounding by shooting, and five years' consecutive for possessing a firearm with intent, were varied on appeal to run concurrently, on the ground that the total of 12 years was too high, although the Court of Appeal affirmed the general principle of passing consecutive sentences for such offences. In the latter case, Lawton L.J., delivering the judgment of the Court of Appeal on sentence, stated that since the abolition of the death penalty, "the only sentence which can be imposed for the most serious crime known to the English law, treason apart, is that of life imprisonment"; that very few persons convicted of murder are kept in custody after about 15 years; and that it is not in the public interest that even for grave crimes, sentences should be passed which do not correlate sensibly and fairly with the time in prison likely to be served by somebody who has committed murder in circumstances in which there were no mitigating circumstances. He divided grave crimes into two distinct categories—the wholly abnormal, with horrifying circumstances and possibly endangering the State; and those which, although grave, are of common occurrence and should not be treated as abnormal crimes. The former would include bad cases of espionage, the notorious train robbery, cases of horrid violence such as occurred in *Richardson*[4] ("the Torture Case"), bomb outrages and acts of political terrorism. The case then before the court—of bank robberies in which firearms were carried and sometimes fired, but in general violence, although threatened, was not inflicted—fell into the latter category, and in such instances the normal sentence should be 15 years. A number of the appellants in that case had each committed and been sentenced for more than one such robbery, and in considering their cases Lawton L.J. said:

"What, if anything, should be added to the basic sentence of 15 years to cover the fact that they had committed more than one robbery? The Court is alive to the problems arising when men are kept in prison for very long periods of time. On the other hand it seems to the Court only just that those who are making a career of crime should receive more severe punishment than those who have been convicted of only one grave offence. We have come to the conclusion that something must be added to the basic sentence passed on those who committed more than one robbery, but the maximum total sentence should not normally be more than 18 years. That is about the maximum sentence which should be passed for crimes which do not come into the category of offences on which we have put the description 'wholly abnormal'."

5. An example of (ii) is *R* v *Cox*,[5] where an offender sentenced in 1973 as follows:
February—18 months' imprisonment for handling stolen property;
May—12 months' consecutive for impeding the apprehension or prosecution of another person; and
July—nine months' consecutive for handling stolen property,
had the last of these sentences ordered by the Court of Appeal to run concurrently

---

[1] *R* v *Bocskei* (1970) 54 Cr. App. R. 519.
[2] [1977] Crim. L.R. 433.
[3] (1975) 61 Cr. App. R. 67 (sentence is dealt with at pages 88 *et seq.*).
[4] *R* v *Richardson* (1967) 51 Cr. App. R. 381.
[5] No. 2629/C/73, 12 February 1974.

with those previously passed, so reducing the total term from three years and three months to two years and six months, on the ground that if all those matters had been dealt with at the same time he would not have received consecutive sentences on each.

6. The principle stated at (*b*) is applied also to two other types of case falling under (ii). In *R* v *Hennessey and Bowers*[1] the Court of Appeal stated that sentences on an absconder from prison for offences, not of a grave character, committed while "on the run", although they ought to be consecutive to the total term to which he is already subject, should not be heavy. When a person released on licence from prison under section 60 of the Criminal Justice Act 1967 (applicable to fixed terms) is being dealt with for an offence punishable with imprisonment, committed during the currency of his licence, section 62(7) gives the Crown Court power to revoke his licence whether or not it passes a fresh sentence on him; and a Practice Direction of 19 December 1975[2] indicated that in such cases the court should consider all the facts and decide whether the offender should be returned to custody for a term of not less than the remaining effective period of his licence. If so, the court should revoke his licence. It should then consider whether any sentence of imprisonment it may pass for the fresh offence should be concurrent or consecutive to that in respect of which it has revoked the licence.

7. In cases falling within (iii) the general principle that, in the absence of special circumstances, the suspended sentence should be made to run consecutively to that for the new offence, was established soon after the suspended sentence became legally possible,[3] but it is clear that that principle is subject to that set out at (*b*) above. This is illustrated by the recent case of *R* v *Clarke*,[4] where concurrent sentences amounting to four years, with a suspended sentence of 15 months activated consecutively, on a man of only 24 years old, were varied so as to make the suspended sentence concurrent, thus reducing the total to four years.

---

[1] (1970) 55 Cr. App. R. 148.
[2] (1976) 62 Cr. App. R. 130.
[3] *R* v *Brown*, *The Times*, 12 November 1968, approved in *R* v *Ithell* [1969] 1 W.L.R. 272.
[4] [1977] Crim. L.R. 430.

APPENDIX N (Chapter 11)

OFFENCES CARRYING A LIABILITY TO LIFE IMPRISONMENT

Piracy Act 1698
Mutiny   Section 8

Piracy Act 1721
Trading with pirates   Section 1

Incitement to Mutiny Act 1797
Incitement to mutiny   Section 1

Unlawful Oaths Act 1812
Unlawful oaths to commit treason or murder   Section 1

Slave Trade Act 1824
Slave trading   Section 9

Piracy Act 1837
Piracy *jure gentium**   Section 2

Treason Felony Act 1848
Treason felony   Section 3

Forgery Act 1861
Making false entries in the books of public funds   Section 5
Destruction of registers of births etc.   Section 36
Making false entries in copies of registers sent to
   registrar   Section 37

Malicious Damage Act 1861
Placing anything upon a railway with intent to
   obstruct an engine   Section 35
Exhibiting false signals   Section 47

Offences against the Person Act 1861
Manslaughter*†   Section 5
Wounding with intent to do grievous bodily
   harm†   Section 18
Attempting to choke or strangle in order to
   commit an indictable offence   Section 21
Administering a drug with intent to commit an
   indictable offence   Section 22
Causing bodily injury by explosions   Section 28
Causing grievous bodily harm by explosives or
   corrosives   Section 29
Placing anything upon a railway with intent to
   endanger passengers   Section 32
Endangering railway passengers by throwing
   anything at railway carriages   Section 33
Procuring a miscarriage   Section 58

India Stock Certificate Act 1863
Personation of owner of India stock — Section 14

Explosive Substances Act 1883
Causing explosions likely to endanger life
or property — Section 2
Attempting to cause an explosion or possessing
explosives with intent to cause an explosion — Section 3

Forgery Act 1913
Forgery of banknotes, bonds, will etc. — Section 2
Forgery of a document stamped with the Great
Seal — Section 3(1)
Forgery of the Great Seal — Section 5(1)

Infant Life (Preservation) Act 1929
Child destruction — Section 1

Coinage Offences Act 1936
Counterfeiting — Section 1
Gilding or altering coins — Section 2
Buying or selling counterfeit coins — Section 6
Making coining implements — Section 9
Conveying coining implements or coins out of
the Mint — Section 10

Infanticide Act 1938
Infanticide — Section 1

Sexual Offences Act 1956
Rape*† — Section 1 and 2nd Schedule
Sexual intercourse with a girl under 13† — Section 5 and 2nd Schedule
Incest with a girl under 13† — Section 10 and 2nd Schedule
Buggery with a boy under 16, a woman or an
animal† — Section 12(1) and 2nd Schedule
Permitting a girl under 13 to use premises for
intercourse — Section 25 and 2nd Schedule

Murder (Abolition of Death Penalty) Act 196
Murder*† — Section 1

Firearms Act 1968
Possessing firearms with intent to endanger life — Section 16 and Schedule 6
Using firearms with intent to resist arrest — Section 17(1) and Schedule 6

Theft Act 1968
Robbery or assault with intent to rob† — Section 8
Aggravated burglary† — Section 10

Genocide Act 1969
Genocide — Section 1

Criminal Damage Act 1971
Criminal damage with intent to endanger life† — Sections 1(2) and 4(1)
Arson† — Sections 1(3) and 4(1)

Hijacking Act 1971
Hijacking aircraft in flight — Section 1

Protection of Aircraft Act 1973
Destroying, damaging or endangering aircraft   Sections 1–4

Biological Weapons Act 1974
Biological weapons offences   Section 1

---

 * In these cases, the substantive offence is a common law offence. There are other common law offences for which no statutory maximum penalty has been provided in the past; they include:
  Affray
  Conspiracy to corrupt morals or outrage public decency
  Conspiracy to defraud
  Contempt
  Fabrication of evidence, causing a person to be wrongly convicted, interference with witnesses
  False imprisonment
  Incitement to commit crime
  Indecent exposure
  Kidnapping†
  Misprision of treason
  Public nuisance
  Riot
  Seditious words and libels
  Unlawful assembly.
 † Offences in respect of which a sentence of life imprisonment has been passed in the years 1967–76 inclusive.

APPENDIX O (Chapter 11)
STATISTICS OF LIFE IMPRISONMENT
TABLE 1

Persons sentenced* to life imprisonment for homicide and non-homicide offences 1958–76 (excluding H.M.P. and detention for life†)

OFFENCE	1958	1959	1960	1961	1962	1963	1964	1965	1966	1967	1968	1969	1970	1971	1972	1973	1974	1975	1976
HOMICIDE																			
Murder	20	35	33	40	27	39	37	40	70	60	68	69	87	87	72	82	105	101	97
Attempted murder	1	—	—	—	1	1	1	—	—	5	—	5	3	4	2	2	1	7	5
Manslaughter (diminished responsibility)	10	9	11	9	7	14	9	12	5	8	2	6	11	12	7	10	19	14	20
Other manslaughter	—	—	—	—	—	—	—	—	—	3	—	2	1	1	1	1	3	2	1
TOTAL	31	44	44	49	35	53	46	52	75	76	70	82	102	104	82	95	128	124	123
NON-HOMICIDE																			
Violence against the person		1	1						4	8	4	8	1	1	2	14	7	4	5
Buggery					1	1	1	1							2	2	1	3	4
Rape							1	1	3	8	2	2	3	2	3	2	8	5	5
Unlawful sexual intercourse with a girl under 13										1	2		1						
Incest									1	2	3	3	6	5		2		1	1
Aggravated burglary																			
Robbery	1	1				2	1	1	2	7	3	5	2	1	2	2	2	7	7
Arson											7	1	3	2		4			
Criminal damage endangering life																	2		
Kidnapping																		1	1
TOTAL	1	2	1	—	1	3	3	3	10	26	21	19	16	11	9	24	20	21	23
Total of homicide and non-homicide offences	32	46	45	49	36	56	49	55	85	102	91	101	118	115	91	119	148	145	146
Non-homicide offences as a percentage of the total	3	4	2	—	3	5	6	6	12	26	23	19	14	10	10	20	14	15	16

*The figures in the table relate to sentencing at the Crown Court and do not take into account the results of appeals.
† Detention for life cannot be distinguished from the *Criminal Statistics* but the figures for H.M.P. cases are as follows:

OFFENCE	1958	1959	1960	1961	1962	1963	1964	1965	1966	1967	1968	1969	1970	1971	1972	1973	1974	1975	1976
Murder	1	1	1	4	—	3	—	2	2	3	6	6	10	10	7	8	7	6	7

Source: Criminal Statistics.

TABLE 2

Persons serving life sentences in prisons in England and Wales on 31 December 1957 to 1976 (including persons sentenced to death whose sentences were commuted to life imprisonment and persons detained during Her Majesty's Pleasure or for life under the Children and Young Persons Act 1933 but excluding persons recalled to prison)

Year	Population
1957	122
1958	139
1959	173
1960	210
1961	250
1962	281
1963	329
1964	365
1965	413
1966	471
1967	536
1968	596
1969	656
1970	749
1971	833
1972	888
1973	975
1974	1,070
1975	1,176
1976	1,228

Source: Home Office Criminal Department records.

(The latest population estimate for 31 December 1977 is 1,350.)

TABLE 3

Persons serving life sentences (including H.M.P. and detention for life but excluding recall cases) on 31 December 1976 by offence and complete years served*

Complete years served	Murder M	Murder F	Manslaughter M	Manslaughter F	Attempted murder M	Rape etc.† M	Buggery M	Arson M	Robbery with violence or while armed M	Grievous bodily harm, wounding with intent M	Causing an explosion M	Kidnapping M	Incest M	TOTAL
24	1													1
19	4		1											5
18			1											1
17	2		1											3
16			1						1					2
15	4		2			1								6
14	7		4			1								10
13	12		3			1								14
12	10	1	4			7	1							14
11	24	1	6	1		3	1							30
10	37	1	2			4				1				44
9	44	1	9	1	2	5	2	2	1	2				65
8	63	1	8		3	4	5	4	2	4				81
7	71		12	1	2	1	2	3	1	2				98
6	91	3	10		3		1	2	1	2				118
5	79	2	6		2				1	2				105
4	75	4	17		3	3	1	6	1	4	4			95
3	94	8	19		2	8	3	4		3	1			124
2	130	1		2	10	6	2	6	2	2		1		182
1	91			4	4	1				2				141
Less than 1 year	58		13		5	5	1	4	2				1	89
TOTAL	898	23	120	9	36	49	19	31	12	24	5	1	1	1,228

OFFENCE

* At 31 December 1976 in addition to the above there were 29 life-sentence prisoners in custody whose licences had been revoked. (This figure excludes two cases who were convicted and sentenced to life imprisonment, while on licence and whose licences were subsequently revoked.) The periods served by these 29 prisoners since their recall varied between 22 years and one month.

† Rape etc. covers:—Rape, attempting to choke with intent to rape, burglary with intent to rape and unlawful sexual intercourse with a girl under the age of 13.

Source: Home Office Criminal Department records.

TABLE 4

Persons released on licence from life imprisonment (including H.M.P. and detention for life) 1949–76, by time served (excluding the release of recalled life-sentence prisoners)

Year	Complete years served																	TOTAL
	1	2	3	4	5	6	7	8	9	10	11	12	13	14	15	16–19	20 or more	
1949					1	2		1										4
1950		1	1	1					2	1					1			5
1951		2	1					2	1									5
1952				1				2	1	1								9
1953	1			1			1		1									2
1954	1				1			3	5									11
1955						2		5	3	2								10
1956		2				1	1	1	7									13
1957	1						2	3	7	5	4						1[20]	16
1958					3		2		6		1							17
1959	1			1		1	2	3	5									12
1960		1		1		1	1	2		1								9
1961	1	1		1	1		1	3	9									17
1962						1	1	2	2	1								7
1963					1		3	3	2					1	1			9
1964			1		1	1	1	4	8	1							2[20][21]	20
1965	1				1		3	11	3	1								20
1966	1					1	5	5	14	3								22
1967							2	6	8		1	2						25
1968			1	1	1		1	5	13	4	4	1						27
1969				1	1		1	8	13	6	1	1	1	4				29
1970			1	1		1	4	3	14	5	3	2						29
1971			1	1	1	2	4	6	5	4	5	2	1		1		1[24]	26
1972		1	1	1	1	4	3	8	7	4	3	3	1	2				28
1973			1	1			4	6	8	7	5	4	1	1	2			39
1974			1	1		4	8	4	14	10	3	6	2	1	2			48
1975				1	1	2		6	10	10	11	2	3	2	2			44
1976				1	4	2	8	14	18	13	11	2	3	2	2	7		87
TOTAL	5	7	10	11	17	19	49	112	186	71	39	23	8	11	10	8	4	590

Source: Home Office Criminal Department records.

TABLE 5

Number and proportion of persons convicted of murder (excluding H.M.P.) who were given life sentences with a recommended minimum period of detention, by minimum period recommended 1965–76

Year	Minimum periods recommended (years)											TOTAL	Number of persons sentenced to life imprisonment	Percentage of life sentences with a recommended minimum period
	10	12	14	15	17	18	20	25	30	35	Life			
1965	—	—	—	2	—	—	—	—	—	—	—	2	40	5
1966	—	—	—	1	—	—	1	1	3	—	—	6	70	9
1967	—	—	—	—	—	—	—	—	—	—	—	—	60	—
1968	—	—	—	—	—	—	3	—	—	—	—	3	68	4
1969	1	1	—	3	—	—	2	—	2	—	—	9	69	13
1970	—	—	—	2	—	—	5	—	1	—	—	8	87	9
1971	—	1	—	4	1	—	2	2	—	—	1*	11	87	13
1972	—	1	—	1	—	—	2	1	2	—	—	6	72	8
1973	—	1	—	1	—	—	5	1	—	—	—	8	82	10
1974	—	2	—	2	—	1	3	—	—	—	—	8	105	8
1975	—	—	—	2	—	—	2	—	1	1	—	6	101	6
1976	—	2	1	2	—	—	5	1	—	—	—	11	97	11
TOTAL	1	7	1	20	1	1	30	6	9	1	1	78	938	8

*This was probably not a legal recommendation (see footnote[1] on pgae 100).

Source: Criminal Statistics and Home Office Criminal Department records.

NON-MANDATORY LIFE IMPRISONMENT

Description of the sentencing policy of the Court of Criminal Appeal and of the Court of Appeal (Criminal Division).[1]

1. There are a number of criminal offences other than murder for which the prescribed penalty is life imprisonment, but only as a maximum sentence. In respect of these offences there has been an increasing use made by the courts in the last decade of the indeterminate sentence of life imprisonment in preference to a sentence for a definite number of years. Broadly speaking, this has happened in relation to offences of manslaughter, causing grievous bodily harm or wounding with intent, rape, buggery and arson.

2. Table 1 (Persons sentenced to life imprisonment for homicide and non-homicide offences, 1958–76, excluding H.M.P. and detention for life) in Appendix O shows the trends in sentencing practice during the two decades. Of 453 persons receiving life sentences in the years 1958–66, 341 (75%) were for murder, 86 (19%) were for manslaughter on the grounds of diminished responsibility and 26 (6%) for all other offences for which life imprisonment was imposed by the courts in their discretion. During the next decade the figures for the three categories of offences were respectively 828 (71%), 109 (9%) and 239 (20%). The bulk of the 239 life sentences in the third category was made up of offences of wounding with intent, rape and arson.

3. The Criminal Justice Act 1948 is a convenient starting point for any examination of the courts' discretionary power to pass life sentences. By that Act the two previous forms of custodial penalty—imprisonment (typically limited to a maximum of two years[2]) and penal servitude (usually with a minimum of three years, but in many cases with a maximum of life)—were merged into the generic sentence of imprisonment. The Act provided for the release on licence at any time of a person sentenced to life imprisonment.

4. From 1948 until the Parole Board came into operation on 1 April 1968, by virtue of section 61(1) of the Criminal Justice Act 1967, persons serving life sentences were released under the provision of the 1948 Act (re-enacted in section 27(1) of the Prison Act 1952). This provision empowered the Home Secretary to release the prisoner on licence at such time as he thought fit, subject always to the executive power to recall any such person to prison if there had been a breach of his licence. Apart from the introduction of parole in 1968, which provided an independent review of the release of prisoners serving life sentences, and the introduction of the hospital order under sections 60 and 65 of the Mental Health Act 1959 (which allowed courts to place an offender in the mental health system in lieu of any prison sentence) there were no other legislative changes that could have affected the use of the non-mandatory life sentence by the courts.

5. The principles of sentencing applicable to the passing of life sentences for offences other than murder first emerged in a trilogy of cases in the Court of Criminal Appeal in 1955,[3] at which time the Court possessed the power to increase sentences. In the event the Court varied three long fixed-term sentences—of 18, 15 and 10 years' imprisonment—to sentences of life imprisonment. The sentences were explained on the basis that they would provide at one and the same time for the long-term detention of the offender so long as he remained a potential danger and for possible

---

[1] We are indebted to Mr. David Thomas for drawing our attention to many of the cases in this Appendix.

[2] After 1948, a sentence of imprisonment of more than two years could be passed where the offence was a common law misdemeanour—see *R* v *Morris* [1951] 1 K.B. 394 and *R* v *Higgins* [1952] 1 K.B. 7.

[3] *R* v *Cunningham*, *R* v *Grantham*, *R* v *Holmes* [1955] Crim. L.R. 193, 386 and 578 respectively.

earlier release if the conditions that prompted a prediction of dangerousness had improved. The courts specifically referred to the release mechanism under the current legislation, and in two of the cases[1] expressed the view that a life sentence was more merciful[2] than a long determinate sentence. (At that time a prisoner serving a sentence other than life imprisonment was released automatically after two thirds of his sentence, but was not eligible for any other earlier release such as has been available since 1968 under which a prisoner is eligible for parole after one third.) In the third case[3] the court expressed the view that in the circumstances of that case (the rape of an 11 year old girl in the presence of the accused's wife) it was the duty of the court to leave it to the Home Secretary to decide when the offender should be released from prison.

6. *Grantham* is a typical example of the case that qualifies for the imposition of a life sentence. A young National Serviceman was convicted of shooting (twice, deliberately) a fellow serviceman with intent to murder; he had two previous convictions, one for housebreaking and the other for an assault when he was armed with a knife. The Court of Criminal Appeal said:

> "we do not know what view the Medical Officers . . . might take of the state of his mind, his general make-up and his ability to control his temper at the end of five years. If he was allowed out then he could get hold of another rifle and he might easily do this sort of thing again. On the other hand, so he might if the sentence stands at 15 years if he has to stay in prison for ten years . . . the only proper sentence to pass is one of imprisonment for life . . . If after a considerable period the Secretary of State comes to the conclusion that it is a case in which this man can be safely released, he can release him . . . We think in view of the gravity of the case which would justify a sentence of imprisonment for life . . . we are giving him the sentence in mercy to him in order that there may be an unfettered exercise of discretion of the Secretary of State."

7. The gravity of the offence remained an important criterion for the imposition of the life sentence. In 1960 in the case of *O'Connor*[4] a young man was convicted of manslaughter (not by reason of diminished responsibility) of a woman whom he struck with his fist causing her to fall and fatally strike her head on a stone. The trial judge, adopting the principle laid down in *Grantham* passed a life sentence. The Court of Criminal Appeal, however, said that since there was "no question of mental disease or of anything requiring mental treatment" the sentence was "quite wrong in principle".[5] It was a case of no exceptional gravity and the punishment for the crime warranted a sentence of five years' imprisonment.

8. The other criterion for imposing a sentence of indefinite detention was the offender's propensity to dangerous crime. To assume dangerousness it was unnecessary to show that the offender was suffering from any mental disorder within the meaning of the Mental Health Act 1959 (indeed if that were shown, the proper disposal would be a hospital order). A life sentence could be imposed on a person suffering from such a psychological or personality disorder not within the meaning of mental disorder if the overwhelming consideration were the protection of the public.[6]

9. Through the 1960s the Court of Criminal Appeal (and its successor the Court of Appeal (Criminal Division)) maintained the twin criteria of gravity of the crime and the propensity to dangerousness exhibited by the offender's disorder of the mind or personality, or instability of character. Where the offender was treatable within the mental health system, ordinarily the court would make a hospital order; in the

---

[1] *Cunningham* and *Grantham*.
[2] Life sentences are often stated to be preferable to long determinate sentences "in mercy" to the offender, but this can hardly be a basis for selecting a penalty of indeterminate length—see, for example, *R v Skelding* (1974) 58 Cr. App. R. 313 at page 318 and *R v Handoll* No. 4858/B/77, 9 February 1978, quoted in footnote [2] on page 99.
[3] *Holmes*.
[4] *R v O'Connor* [1960] Crim. L.R. 275.
[5] Followed in *R v Knight* (1967) 51 Cr. App. R. 466.
[6] *R v Beever* [1971] Crim. L.R. 492; *R v McCann* [1970] Crim. L.R. 167; *R v Costelloe* (1970) 54 Cr. App. R. 172; *R v Bland* No. 1018/C/71, 21 September 1971.

alternative, if hospital accommodation were not available or thought insufficiently secure, the court would impose a life sentence with the hope that the Home Secretary might consider exercising his powers under section 72 of the Mental Health Act 1959 and transfer the prisoner to hospital.[1]

10. Shortly after the Court of Appeal (Criminal Division) came into existence in 1966, there is discernible for the first time in the decisions, but not until 1973 in the reasoning, of the courts a divergence in the attitudes of the judges towards the imposition of a life sentence. The traditional approach was reflected in a judgment of the Court (Lord Denning, Mr. Justice Widgery and Mr. Justice MacKenna) delivered by Mr. Justice MacKenna in R v Hodgson.[2] The accused was convicted of two acts of rape and one of buggery committed on two women whom he had attacked late at night in public places. There were two other offences of assaulting women for which he was given short prison sentences. In upholding sentences of life imprisonment for the other offences, the Court laid down the conditions that had to be satisfied. A life sentence might be passed—

(a) where the offence or offences were in themselves grave enough to require a very long sentence;

(b) where it appeared from the nature of the offence or from the defendant's history that he was a person of unstable character likely to commit such offences in the future; and

(c) where, if the offences were committed, the consequences to others might be specially injurious, as in the cases of sexual offences or crimes of violence.

In R v Picker [3] the appellant aged 17 was convicted in July 1967 of the manslaughter of a woodman aged 76. The verdict was on the ground that the appellant had no intention to kill or to do grievous bodily harm; there was no question of diminished responsibility. Nearly three years after his trial, when he was sentenced to life imprisonment, he applied for leave to appeal out of time against his sentence because, although the sentence was said to have been imposed in mercy to him, no review of his case for release had been undertaken. The Lord Chief Justice, in substituting a sentence of four years' imprisonment (which meant immediate release) said that a life sentence could be imposed where the nature of the offence and the make-up of the offender were of such a nature that the public required protection for a considerable time unless there were a change in his condition. But where no such condition existed it was not right for a judge to pass to others the difficult matter of sentencing and the length of detention. But even where such a condition persisted life imprisonment could be resorted to only where the offence was grave. In R v Turemko in 1965 life sentences were set aside on the ground that the offences—burglary and two counts of robbery with violence—were insufficiently grave to justify a life sentence and eight years' imprisonment was substituted, although the appellant was in need of psychiatric treatment.[4] In 1970, in R v Scott [5] the Court again set aside a life sentence on the ground that the offence, in that case of burglary accompanied by an attempted rape, was not grave enough to satisfy the test and a sentence of seven years was imposed instead. In R v Williams in 1973 the Court, in substituting five years' imprisonment for a life sentence, said that life imprisonment could not be used to deal with cases posing medical problems.[6]

11. Parallel to this line of judicial authority some courts began to develop a principle that the gravity of the instant offence and the degree of probability of offences in the

---

[1] R v Gunnell (1966) 50 Cr. App. R. 242 (a series of rapes and attempted rapes by a psychopath with a long record of mental disorders). The Court upheld a sentence of life imprisonment mainly on the grounds that the offender had frequently absconded from mental hospitals and needed more security than even a special hospital provided. The case is strongly criticised by Professor Cross in his book The English Sentencing System (Butterworths, 1975), pages 65–6 and 143–4; see also R v Horan No. 3023/A/73, 24 April 1974, R v Officer [1976] Crim. L.R. 698 and R v Keelan No. 1/8/77, 18 November 1977.
[2] (1968) 52 Cr. App. R. 113.
[3] [1970] 2 Q.B. 161; followed in R v Blythin No. 9288/69, 15 June 1970, R v Beever [1971] Crim. L.R. 492 and R v Atkinson No. 5761/A/72, 5 April 1973.
[4] [1965] Crim. L.R. 319.
[5] No. 8885/69, 15 May 1970.
[6] [1974] Crim. L.R. 376.

future were inter-related factors and were not separate stages in the process of satisfying the conditions for imposing a life sentence. A high degree of probability of future offences could justify the use of life imprisonment where the instant offence was not in the first order of gravity. In *R v Ashdown*[1] the appellant was convicted of an offence that the Court readily acknowledged would ordinarily have justified a sentence no longer than five years' imprisonment (life imprisonment was imposed solely in respect of one offence of robbery with a toy pistol). The Court cited *Hodgson* and *Picker* but not *Turemko, Scott* or *Williams*. The case of *Ashdown* seems to have established the principle that life imprisonment is justified by reference to the dangerousness of the offender for the future rather than to the inherent gravity of his most recent offence. In *R v Thornton*[2] the appellant was convicted of arson and sentenced to life imprisonment. He had set fire to curtains in rooms at a hospital where he had been a patient; the fires were easily put out. He suffered from brain damage and had been diagnosed as psychopathic. The Court agreed that the instant offence was at the lower end of the scale of gravity but that "the gravity of the offence need not be so serious where the likelihood of repetition was high as where it was remote".[3]

12. Underlying the decision in *Ashdown* there appears to be a general unwillingness on the part of the Court to include "dangerousness" as a factor to be taken into account in selecting the appropriate length of the fixed-term sentence. That element is accommodated by judges the more easily in the indeterminacy of the life sentence, to be given effect to in the release powers of the Executive. There is a distinct dislike among the judges of passing very long prison sentences; there comes a point where the alternative to life imprisonment would be so long that life imprisonment is to be preferred.

13. The case of *R v Rose*[4] strikingly illustrates the point. Rose pleaded guilty to a serious manslaughter; he attacked a very old lady whose house he had broken into. The psychiatric evidence and the gravity of the offence amply qualified him for a sentence of life imprisonment. Indeed the Court of Appeal said that had Rose been given a life sentence it would have been entirely appropriate. But the trial judge selected a sentence of 18 years' imprisonment. In assessing the propriety of that sentence, the Court felt bound to apply the principles appropriate to fixed-term sentences, of which the most important is that the length of sentence must be related to the gravity of the offence, in isolation from the peculiar characteristics of the offender. The Court said "once the judge had decided to pass a determinate sentence then this Court has to consider whether in all the circumstances the sentence was of the appropriate length and it has come to the conclusion that it was not ... the plea shows that this young man did not intend to cause Mrs. Palmer really serious injury. In all those circumstances one has to look at the quality of the acts which he did and, grave though they were, in the judgment of this Court, they did not attract a sentence of eighteen years' imprisonment." The Court substituted a sentence of 10 years' imprisonment.

---

[1] No. 3001/C/72, 1 November 1973.
[2] [1975] Crim. L.R. 51.
[3] Followed in *R v Chaplin* [1976] Crim. L.R. 320 and *R v Anderson* [1977] Crim. L.R. 489.
[4] [1974] Crim. L.R. 266; cf. *R v Cunningham* [1955] Crim. L.R. 193 where, during the time when the appeal court had power to increase sentences, the Court substituted for 18 years' imprisonment a sentence of life imprisonment. See also *R v Handoll* No. 4858/B/77, 9 February 1978.

APPENDIX Q (Chapter 13)

SUSPENDED SENTENCES

Note by the Home Office Statistical Department

1. The general effect on sentencing patterns of the introduction in 1968 of ordinary suspended sentences can be seen in Graph 1, which shows the proportionate use of different sentences over the period 1964 to 1976. A substantial change occurred in the sentencing pattern between 1967 and 1968, following the Criminal Justice Act 1967. It is evident that the total of immediate imprisonment and suspended sentences was in 1968, and also in later years, higher than the level that immediate imprisonment alone might have been expected to reach. Consequently the suspended sentence must have displaced not only immediate imprisonment but also some non-custodial penalties, and it is noticeable in Graph 1, that the proportionate use of both fines and probation orders fell sharply between 1967 and 1968.

2. Table 1 records the numbers of persons who received immediate or suspended imprisonment sentences over the period 1964 to 1976 and the proportion of all sentences of imprisonment that was suspended.

TABLE 1

Persons aged 17 and over sentenced at all courts: numbers given immediate imprisonment or suspended sentences 1964–76

Year	Immediate imprisonment	Suspended sentence	
		Number	Percentage
1964	36,039		
1965	37,517		
1966	41,993		
1967	39,883		
1968	30,443	32,002	51
1969	34,010	32,169	49
1970	38,263	33,909	47
1971	36,926	31,720	46
1972	35,196	32,404	48
1973	31,379	26,200	46
1974	32,293	29,499	48
1975	37,158	32,920	47
1976	40,415	34,666	46

3. Further examination of Graph 1 shows that the proportionate use of immediate imprisonment declined generally over the period 1964 to 1974 but increased slightly in 1975 and 1976; the use of suspended sentences also declined up to 1973 but rose in 1974 and 1975. Table 1 shows that the proportion of suspended sentences to all imprisonment (immediate plus suspended) decreased from its initial level of 51% in 1968 and since 1970 has fluctuated only narrowly between 46% and 48%.

4. Table 2, below, gives for the years 1968 to 1976 the numbers who received suspended sentences and the numbers who had a suspended sentence activated; the numbers activated relate to suspended sentences imposed in the calendar year and in earlier years.

TABLE 2

Persons aged 17 and over sentenced at all courts 1968-76: suspended sentences imposed and activated

Year	Number of suspended sentences imposed	Number of suspended sentences activated
1968	32,002	4,222
1969	32,169	8,742
1970	33,909	10,313
1971	31,720	9,601
1972	32,404	8,470
1973	26,200	6,656
1974	29,499	6,401
1975	32,920	7,425
1976	34,666	7,789

Allowing for suspended sentences imposed in 1975 and 1976 but activated after 1976, it is estimated that 27% of suspended sentences have been activated.

5. An examination of the numbers of persons received into prison under sentence (Table 3) reveals a dramatic change, following the Criminal Justice Act 1967, in the distribution of effective sentence lengths (which take account of concurrent and consecutive sentences).

TABLE 3

Receptions into prison under sentence of persons aged 17 and over (excluding fine defaulters), by length of sentence 1967-76

Total effective* sentence length	1967	1968	1969	1970	1971	1972	1973	1974	1975	1976
Up to 6 months	21,625	12,772	12,334	12,935	12,340	10,900	9,493	10,051	11,512	13,136
Over 6 months up to 4 years	12,820†	13,770†	17,576†	20,811†	19,791	18,998	16,517	17,047	19,196	19,873
Over 4 years	772	805	823	1,161	1,116	1,141	1,149	1,127	1,268	1,462
TOTAL	35,217	27,347	30,733	34,907	33,247	31,039	27,159	28,225	31,976	34,471

* Taking into account whether sentences (including activated suspended sentences) are consecutive or concurrent.
† Includes a small number of persons aged under 21 serving sentences of over 4 years.

There was a reduction in the total number received into prison owing to a substantial fall in the number with short sentences, clearly a result of the substitution of suspended sentences for immediate imprisonment. This reduction in short sentences has been largely maintained and the total number of receptions has remained below the 1967 level; thus some offenders have been kept out of prison by the use of suspended sentences. On the other hand, between 1968 and 1970, there was a large rise in the number receiving medium-length sentences, and since 1970 the proportion of such cases has not changed greatly. This change in sentence length pattern can probably be attributed to activated suspended sentences which are usually consecutive to sentences for fresh offences.

Graph 1 Proportionate use of different sentences for persons aged 17 and over found guilty of indictable offences: 1964-1976

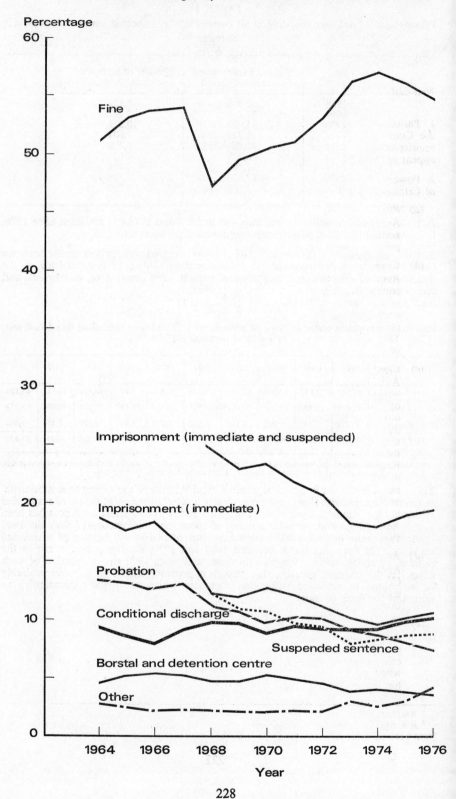

Percentage

Fine

Imprisonment (immediate and suspended)

Imprisonment (immediate)

Probation

Conditional discharge

Suspended sentence

Borstal and detention centre

Other

Year

APPENDIX R (Chapter 14)

COMBINED SENTENCES

Non-custodial sentences and orders available to the courts for combination with imprisonment.

1. Paragraph 2 of this Appendix lists those powers and orders which, it appears to the Council, might in appropriate circumstances be combined with a sentence of imprisonment. Paragraph 3 lists, briefly, those powers which it would not normally appear appropriate to combine.

2. Powers which appear appropriate for combination (references are to the Powers of Criminal Courts Act 1973 unless otherwise stated) are:—

(a) *Fines*

Available, in any case where the penalty is not fixed by law, in lieu of or in addition to dealing with the offender in any other way in which the court has power to deal with him (section 30(1)). The sanction is imprisonment.

(b) *Community service orders*

Available in the case of any person who has attained the age of 17 and is convicted of an offence punishable with imprisonment, subject to availability of the necessary facilities, the suitability of the offender and his consent, but only "instead of dealing with him in any other way" (section 14). Use in combination with any other sentence would therefore require statutory power. The sanction is either a fine, or sentencing for the offence after revocation of the community service order (section 16).

(c) *Compensation orders*

Available in any case, in addition to dealing with the offender in any other way (section 35(1)). The power is very wide, although it excludes loss by reason of death and (generally) injury, loss or damage due to any accident arising out of the presence of a motor vehicle on a road (subsection (3)). Such an order may be made in relation to any offence taken into consideration when sentencing the offender (subsection (1)). No such order may, however, be combined with the making of a criminal bankruptcy order (for which see (e) below) (section 39(1)). Regard must be had to the offender's means (subsection (4)), and the order must be a realistic one bearing in mind the importance of rehabilitation.[1] However, lack of immediate means to pay does not preclude the making of an order in a reasonable sum, which the offender is fit to earn.[2] The sanction is imprisonment by order of a magistrates' court (Administration of Justice Act 1970, section 41 and Schedule 9, part I; Powers of Criminal Courts Act 1973, section 56(1) and Schedule 5, paragraph 40).

(d) *Restitution orders*

Ancillary orders, under the Theft Act 1968, section 28 as extended by the Criminal Justice Act 1972, section 6, in any case when goods have been stolen and the offender is convicted of any offence with reference to the theft. Such an order can be combined with any sentence and any other order.

(e) *Criminal bankruptcy orders*

Available in addition to dealing with the offender in any other way (except by compensation order) provided that it appears to the court that as a result of offences of which the offender is convicted, or which are taken into consideration when sentencing him, loss or damage (not attributable to personal injury) has been suffered by one or more persons whose identity is known to the court,

---

[1] *R* v *Oddy* (1974) 59 Cr. App. R. 66.
[2] *R* v *Bradburn* (1973) 57 Cr. App. R. 948, where payments were to begin after release from a sentence of borstal training imposed for the same offences.

and the aggregate amount of it exceeds £15,000 (section 39). The figure of £15,000 can be varied by order of the Secretary of State (subsection (6)).

(*f*) *Deprivation of property*
Available on conviction of an offence punishable with not less than two years' imprisonment, depriving the offender of any interest in property in his possession or control at the time of his apprehension, and used or intended by him to be used for committing or facilitating the commission of any offence (section 43). Such an order can be made in addition to passing any sentence.

(*g*) *Disqualification from holding or obtaining a driving licence*
Available on conviction of an offence punishable with not less than two years' imprisonment, if a motor vehicle were used (whether by the offender or by another person) for committing or facilitating the commission of that offence (section 44). Such an order can be made in addition to passing any sentence.

(*h*) *Disqualification of directors*
Available (Companies Act 1948, section 188) on conviction on indictment of any offence in connection with the promotion, formation or management of a company or where, in the course of winding up a company, it appears that a person has been guilty of any offence of fraudulent trading (*ibid.* section 332) for which he is liable (whether he has been convicted or not) or has otherwise been guilty while an officer of the company of any fraud in relation to the company or of any breach of his duty to the company. The disqualification may be for any period not exceeding five years from the date of conviction[1] and may be made by the court before which the offender is convicted as well as any court having jurisdiction to wind up the company. A person acting in contravention of an order is liable on conviction on indictment to imprisonment for a period not exceeding two years.

(*i*) *Orders as to costs* (*against the offender*)
(i) Costs of the prosecution—the offender on conviction may be ordered to pay the whole or any part of the costs of the prosecution (including costs of the proceedings before the examining justices) (Costs in Criminal Cases Act 1973, section 4);
(ii) A contribution order may be made against the offender, at the conclusion of the hearing, in an amount having regard to his resources and commitments (Legal Aid Act 1974, section 32).

3. Powers which do not appear to be normally suitable for combination are:—
(*a*) Attendance centre orders (Criminal Justice Act 1948, section 19), in general available only to magistrates' courts for those aged under 21.
(*b*) Supervision orders and care orders for those under 17 (Children and Young Persons Act 1969, sections 1, 7, 11–19 and 70).
(*c*) Absolute and conditional discharges—available only when it is inexpedient to inflict punishment (Powers of Criminal Courts Act 1973, section 7).
(*d*) Probation orders (*ibid.* section 2(1)). A probation order cannot be used in combination with an immediate custodial sentence,[2] nor with a suspended sentence of imprisonment imposed on the same occasion for another offence (*ibid.* section 22(3)).
(*e*) Bind over (Justices of the Peace Act 1968, section 1(7) or common law and Courts Act 1971, section 6(4)); guardianship order (Mental Health Act 1959, section 60), recommendation for deportation (Immigration Act 1971, section 6(1)).

4. It should perhaps be mentioned that when the court exercises the power (under section 1(1)) to defer sentence, it is precluded until sentence is in fact passed from making any order consequent upon conviction.[3]

---

[1] *R* v *Bradley* (1961) 45 Cr. App. R. 97.
[2] *R* v *Emmett* (1969) 53 Cr. App. R. 203.
[3] *R* v *Dwyer* [1974] Crim. L.R. 610.

APPENDIX S (Chapter 15)

CRIMINAL BANKRUPTCY CASES 1973–78

TABLE 1

List of criminal bankruptcy orders in respect of which receiving orders had been obtained up to 28 February 1978

	Offence	Sentence	Date of receiving order	Liabilities under criminal bankruptcy order (in £s)	Estimated assets (in £s)
1	Conspiracy to defraud and dishonest handling	7 years	4.10.73	36,164	Nil
2	Conspiracy to defraud and dishonest handling	3 years' probation	4.10.73	16,200	1
3	Conspiracy to defraud	3 years	15.11.73	26,749	2,050
4	Theft	3 years	3.12.73	15,221	6,612
5	Burglary	10 years	20. 2.74	33,789	146
6	Burglary	10 years	20. 2.74	19,508	54
7	Burglary	6 years	13. 3.74	32,916	Nil
8	Robbery	8 years	14. 3.74	28,000	Nil
9	Robbery	12 years	14. 3.74	28,000	Nil
10	Theft	3 years	4. 4.74	28,578	2,729
11	Conspiracy to defraud	7 years	10. 4.74	98,909	1,986
12	Conspiracy to defraud	3 years	1. 5.74	126,488	755
13	Conspiracy to defraud	4½ years	1. 5.74	126,488	336
14	Conspiracy to defraud	7 years	1. 5.74	98,578	97,202
15	Conspiracy to defraud	5 years	1. 5.74	78,198	18,049
16	Robbery	17 years	7. 5.74	144,580	11,745
17	Robbery	21 years	23.10.74	375,847	60,000
18	Robbery	21 years	23.10.74	138,111	500
19	Robbery	13 years	28.10.74	138,111	8,100
20	Robbery	Proceedings annulled after successful appeal	28.10.74	138,111	876
21	Robbery	21 years	28.10.74	375,847	16,000
22	Conspiracy to defraud	3 years	21.11.74	159,236	7,989
23	Burglary	10 years	5.12.74	19,733	3,850
24	Robbery	22 years	9.12.74	319,733	9,000
25	Robbery	17 years	31. 1.75	237,736	3,000
26	Robbery	16 years	31. 1.75	237,736	50
27	Robbery	16 years	31. 1.75	296,451	—
28	Robbery	16 years	31. 1.75	296,451	12
29	Robbery	Proceedings annulled after successful appeal	31. 1.75	—	—
30	Robbery	16 years	4. 2.75	296,451	—
31	Theft	4 years	14. 3.75	81,119	Nil
32	Theft	5 years	19. 5.75	21,583	15,000
33	Conspiracy to defraud	5 years	11. 6.75	56,213	3,027
34	Conspiracy to defraud	3 years	11. 6.75	56,213	774
35	Conspiracy to defraud	2 years suspended	11. 6.75	56,213	125
36	Conspiracy to defraud	2 years	1. 7.75	56,213	1

TABLE 1—*continued*

	Offence	Sentence	Date of receiving order	Liabilities under criminal bankruptcy order (in £s)	Estimated assets (in £s)
37	Conspiracy to defraud	12 months	2. 7.75	35,887	—
38	Conspiracy to defraud	3 years	30. 7.75	35,887	Nil
39	Obtaining by forged instrument	5 years	6. 8.75	22,700	800
40	Theft	2 years	23.10.75	49,657·74	—
41	Theft	5 years	4.11.75	32,020	Nil
42	Theft	3 years	4.11.75	32,020	Nil
43	Conspiracy to defraud and obtaining property by deception	21 months suspended	7.11.75	24,027	Nil
44	Conspiracy to defraud and obtaining property by deception	2 years suspended	7.11.75	22,943	—
45	Conspiracy to defraud and obtaining property by deception	2 years	7.11.75	26,734	95
46	Conspiracy to defraud and obtaining property by deception	21 months suspended	28.11.75	53,447	700
47	Obtaining by deception and conspiracy to defraud	5 years	5. 2.76	33,676	187
48	Theft	18 months	27. 2.76	17,850	495
49	Obtaining pecuniary advantage and theft	5 years	26. 3.76	30,021	Nil
50	Obtaining by deception	12 months	7. 5.76	16,000	Nil
51	Theft	3 years	10. 5.76	36,346	3,209
52	Theft	3 years	13. 5.76	34,100	15,666
53	Conspiracy to steal	8 years	16. 6.76	150,441	396
54	Conspiracy to defraud	5 years	25. 6.76	22,063	5,610
55	Obtaining by deception	2 years	25. 6.76	22,063	25,318
56	Obtaining by deception	2 years	28. 6.76	16,390	210
57	Theft	10 years	12. 7.76	54,863	4,582
58	Obtaining by deception	2 years	23. 7.76	38,896	731
59	Conspiracy to obtain pecuniary advantage and conspiracy to defraud	7 years	23. 8.76	72,025	Nil
60	Conspiracy to defraud	2 years suspended	27. 9.76	44,694	4,550
61	Conspiracy to defraud	4 years	27. 9.76	44,694	Nil
62	Conspiracy to defraud	4 years	27. 9.76	44,694	Nil
63	Conspiracy to defraud	7 years	27. 9.76	44,694	Nil
64	Theft	4 years	4.10.76	41,941	14,667
65	Theft and obtaining by deception	7 years	5.10.76	46,818	137,185
66	Theft and obtaining by deception	2 years suspended	5.10.76	24,967	7,347
67	Obtaining by deception	3 years	6.10.76	20,000	16,327
68	Dishonest handling	6 years	18.10.76	83,678	Nil
69	Theft	4 years	19.10.76	21,024	Nil
70	Fraudulent trading	3 years	1.11.76	55,935	77,564
71	Fraudulent trading	18 months	17.11.76	28,663	123
72	Conspiracy to defraud	7 years	1.12.76	34,626	Nil
73	Conspiracy to defraud	5 years	1.12.76	34,626	Nil
74	Conspiracy to defraud	5 years	13.12.76	203,984	Nil
75	Conspiracy to defraud	5 years	13.12.76	203,984	200
76	Conspiracy to defraud	21 months	13.12.76	203,984	Nil
77	Obtaining by deception	$2\frac{1}{2}$ years	16.12.76	15,923	Nil
78	Theft	3 years	20.12.76	18,379	170
79	Theft	6 years	30.12.76	186,697	Nil

TABLE 1—*continued*

	Offence	Sentence	Date of receiving order	Liabilities under criminal bankruptcy order (in £s)	Estimated assets (in £s)
80	Conspiracy to steal	6 years	16. 2.77	130,000	11,767
81	Conspiracy to steal	6 years	16. 2.77	130,000	17,057
82	Theft	5 years	23. 2.77	49,870	6,710
83	Obtaining by deception and theft	4 years	8. 3.77	41,672	5,102
84	Forgery and uttering	2½ years	20. 4.77	25,000	25
85	Robbery	18 years	4. 5.77	485,982	15,730
86	Robbery	20 years	4. 5.77	485,982	4,631
87	Conspiracy to steal	6 years	5. 5.77	150,441	Nil
88	Conspiracy to steal	6 years	5. 5.77	150,441	—
89	Theft and forgery	3½ years	5. 5.77	39,100	5,868
90	Robbery	11 years	9. 5.77	61,466	2,208
91	Obtaining by deception	4 years	20. 5.77	100,000	17,437
92	Conspiracy to defraud	6 years	20. 5.77	1,277,668	2,393
93	Conspiracy to defraud	6 years	20. 5.77	1,277,668	2,474
94	Obtaining by deception	18 months	28. 6.77	25,500	1,535
95	Robbery	15 years	4. 7.77	19,513	855
96	Robbery	20 years	4. 7.77	61,466	8,782
97	Robbery	15 years	4. 7.77	41,953	2,055
98	Obtaining by deception	4 years	15. 7.77	32,104	Nil
99	Conspiracy to defraud	4½ years	15. 7.77	142,068	21,122
100	Conspiracy to defraud	4½ years	15. 7.77	142,068	Nil
101	Obtaining by deception	33 months	20. 7.77	235,000	5,600
102	Obtaining by deception	6 years	20. 7.77	235,000	Nil
103	Forging valuable securities	7 years	26. 7.77	18,552	396
104	Conspiracy to defraud	4 years	26. 7.77	20,378	Nil
105	Conspiracy to defraud	4 years	26. 7.77	20,378	517
106	Conspiracy to defraud	3 years	27. 7.77	62,334	—
107	Obtaining by deception	4 years	27. 7.77	33,687·61	—
108	Conspiracy to defraud	5 years	27. 7.77	62,335	Nil
109	Conspiracy to defraud	4 years	27. 7.77	62,335	Nil
110	Conspiracy to defraud	2½ years	12. 9.77	39,475	Nil
111	Conspiracy to defraud	3½ years	12. 9.77	40,942	5,250
112	Conspiracy to defraud	2 years	12. 9.77	40,941	37
113	Robbery	12 years	28. 9.77	103,164	1,200
114	Conspiracy to defraud	4 years	28. 9.77	21,000	11,000
115	Obtaining money on forged instrument	8 years	4.10.77	77,853	—
116	Obtaining property by deception	2 years	10.10.77	58,371	65,460
117	Obtaining property by deception	3 years	14.10.77	37,900	2,640
118	Conspiracy to defraud and theft	15 months	2.11.77	31,810	6,868
119	Theft and conspiracy to defraud	2½ years	2.11.77	52,816	5,500
120	Procuring execution of valuable security and obtaining by deception	4 years	14.12.77	26,754	7,085
121	Theft and obtaining property by deception	18 months	11. 1.78	22,421·13	20,000
122	Obtaining property by deception	12 months	15. 2.78	26,345	—
123	Obtaining property by deception	4½ years	28. 2.78	34,261·22	—
124	Obtaining property by deception	5 years	28. 2.78	16,721·88	—

TABLE 2

List of courts making criminal bankruptcy orders (those orders in respect of which a receiving order had been obtained, or a decision taken by the Director of Public Prosecutions not to institute proceedings, up to 28 February 1978)

Court	Number	Court	Number
Barnstaple	1	Liverpool	5
Bedford	3	Maidstone	2
Birkenhead	1	Manchester	6
Birmingham	7	Merthyr Tydfil	2
Caernarvon	2	Middlesex	2
Cardiff	4	Mold	2
Central Criminal Court	66	Northampton	4
Chelmsford	3	Norwich	3
Chester	3	Plymouth	2
Derby	1	Portsmouth	1
Inner London Sessions	3	Preston	1
Ipswich	1	Sheffield	2
Kingston	1	Shrewsbury	1
Knightsbridge	1	Snaresbrook	2
Leeds	2	Stoke on Trent	1
Leicester	2	Taunton	1
Lewes	3	Winchester	6
		TOTAL	147

234

THE JUDGMENT IN *REGINA* v *KEITH ANTHONY ANDERSON*—
15 NOVEMBER 1977

LORD JUSTICE ORMROD: In addition to the sentence of imprisonment, with which this court dealt yesterday, in this case, the learned Judge below, after some considerable discussion with counsel, decided to make a criminal bankruptcy order under what is now section 39 of the Powers of Criminal Courts Act, 1973. That was a course which at the time, Mr. Bagnall, who was appearing for the defence, agreed with in preference to a compensation order being made. The learned Judge then went in considerable detail into the background of criminal bankruptcy orders, and was at great pains to make sure that the criminal bankruptcy order which he intended to make should be factually right.

It was accepted in the course of that discussion that the total amount involved in this case—and I use that phrase deliberately—was of the order of £29,000, although in fact it was subsequently reduced to a figure of about £26,000, for reasons which do not matter so far as this judgment is concerned, and the court proceeded on that footing. Difficulties then arose when it came to drawing the actual order. Two outstanding difficulties have been brought to the attention of this court. The first one, which is the important one, goes directly to the jurisdiction to make a criminal bankruptcy order, and in those circumstances, in spite of the fact that there is an express statutory provision which precludes a right of appeal against criminal bankruptcy orders, it is plain that where the suggestion is that the order is a nullity, this court can adjudicate upon that matter as has been held in relation to other similar problems. So no question arises so far as this court's jurisdiction is concerned, to deal with the problem.

The problem which has arisen is that the aggregate sum involved in the actual counts in the indictment in this case does not amount to the minimum figure fixed by section 39(1). That is the figure of £15,000. The total of the items or counts which were specifically charged, and of which the Appellant was specifically found guilty, amount to £7,112 and therefore is less than £15,000. So, the first question here is: Had the court below jurisdiction, in the sense of power, to make a criminal bankruptcy order? That takes us to section 39(1) of the 1973 Act, which is the jurisdiction section. That section reads as follows: "Where a person is convicted of an offence before the Crown Court and it appears to the court that—(a) as a result of the offence, or of that offence taken together with any other relevant offence or offences, loss or damage (not attributable to personal injury) has been suffered by one or more persons whose identity is known to the court; and (b) the amount, or aggregate amount, of the loss or damage exceeds £15,000; the court may, in addition to dealing with the offender in any other way ... make a criminal bankruptcy order against him in respect of the offence or, as the case may be, that offence and the other relevant offence or offences."

In subsection (2) "other relevant offence or offences" is defined as meaning: ". . . an offence or offences of which the person in question is convicted in the same proceedings or which the court takes into consideration in determining his sentence." The crux of the matter, therefore, lies in the meaning to be given to the words "or which the court takes into consideration in determining his sentence." There are two points of view which have been argued most helpfully by all three counsel in this case, and we are indebted to them all for the assistance they have given in what is undoubtedly a difficult point.

Before saying anything about the construction of that phrase in this section, it is wise to bear in mind the particular nature of this section and those immediately following it which deal with criminal bankruptcy orders, and for this reason: that this section and the earlier one, section 35, dealing with compensation are really attempts to bridge a gap which has always existed, and has never been bridged before, between the criminal law, or criminal code if one uses a more general phrase, and the civil code. These two sections are clearly designed by Parliament to make it easier and cheaper and more practicable in certain cases to bring into the criminal procedure an element of civil remedy, or alternatively to bring some part of the criminal law into the civil procedure. So far as section 39 is concerned, it creates this new concept of a criminal bankruptcy order, and what Parliament has in effect done, as we understand it, is to create a new kind of act of bankruptcy. So, when this section has to be construed, it would not be right, in our view, to construe it strictly as if it were a criminal statute with the various traditional methods and restrictions on construction of such a statute. We are construing here what is essentially a bridging section, designed primarily to simplify procedure.

With that in mind one comes to consider the phrase, "the offences which the court takes into consideration." It has been pointed out, quite rightly, that this phrase is first to be found, as far as researches go, in the Criminal Justice Act, 1972, and it was that Act which introduced for the first time criminal bankruptcy orders, and also introduced the concept of compensation orders, and at the same time significantly extended the powers of the court in relation to restitution orders under section 28 of the Theft Act. In all those three contexts the Criminal Justice Act, 1972, uses this same phrase which is to be found in sections 6 and 7, and in the compensation section also. The question is: Does that phrase mean offences taken into consideration in the technical procedural sense in which it is so often used, which can be shortly indicated by the initials TIC, or has it got a wider significance?

There are arguments both ways on this, but if this phrase is read literally as it stands in the statute, it means what it says, simply offences which the court has taken into consideration in determining the sentence. There is no doubt whatever that in this case the court below, in pronouncing a sentence of six years' imprisonment, which we yesterday reduced to four, unquestionably and indeed expressly took into account the fact that the total sum involved in the dishonesty was of the order of £26,000, far in excess of the total of the specific charges which had been proved. Is that right, or is that wrong? Well, the first observation to be made is that the whole idea of taking into consideration other offences is a matter of practice and not of statute. That is made perfectly clear by Archbold and by various decisions of this court in cases to which it is not necessary to refer. For various good practical reasons the courts have worked out a procedure to be followed in most of these cases; the procedure of making out a list of specific charges outstanding and submitting the list to the accused person, and asking him or her whether or not he or she wishes the other offences to be taken into consideration. From the point of view of the accused it has the advantage of clearing up his record and getting rid of a lot of outstanding offences which might otherwise bring him before the court again. It saves the court's time in hearing separate cases involving the other offences, and it is obviously a highly advantageous system. It has been necessary to introduce a fairly formal procedure in relation to it to avoid the consequent confusion which might arise if a fairly strict procedure has not been followed, but in the view of this court there is no compelling reason to read that procedure into the various sections of what was originally in the Act of 1972, and is now in the Powers of Criminal Courts Act, 1973, section 39.

That being so, what are the limitations on this phrase? The practical limitations are not very difficult to define. They are what the statute says they are, the offences taken into consideration in determining the sentence. Mr. Bagnall has pointed out that in certain cases such as, for example, deciding to pass an extended sentence, the court takes into account not previous offences, but previous convictions. The court here is only concerned with two possible circumstances, as we see it, and indeed as Mr. Mott has put it to us. We are concerned with the ordinary situation where a list of other offences is submitted to the accused or the defendant and he admits his guilt of all of those offences or some of them, and they are then cleared up by including them in the sentence passed. That is one situation. The other situation which arises in relation to fraud cases of all kinds, is that for convenience sake the prosecution elect to proceed on what are called sample offences. Police enquiries have revealed, very often, a whole series of offences, in some cases all committed against the same person, the same victim; in other cases of course, the offences will be committed against many different

236

people. In those cases, it is a matter of practical convenience for everybody, to select certain sample charges or counts and proceed only on them; it being understood by the prosecution and the defence that there are many other similar offences which could have been charged, but have not in fact been specifically charged. The trial proceeds on that basis, and sentence is in due course passed upon that basis.

If there is any doubt about it, there is, in the view of this court, ample opportunity for the defendant represented by counsel to make clear at an early stage whether or not the other offences not included in the indictment are in some way or other to be differentiated from those which have been included in the indictment. Here, as I said, there was no question but that all the other offences, which added up to the sum of £29,000 odd, were of almost precisely similar nature to the ones in the indictment.

The conclusion which this court has come to on the construction of section 39 is that the phrase "offences which the court takes into consideration" must be construed as meaning exactly what it says: the offences for which the sentence is passed. In this case that is the aggregate sum of £29,000 or £26,000, whichever it may be. That deals with the question of jurisdiction. The court below, therefore, was quite right in thinking that it had the jurisdiction to make a criminal bankruptcy order.

The only other problem which has arisen, and which has given us a considerable amount of thought, arises under section 39(3). This does not go to jurisdiction at all, but to the actual drawing up of the criminal bankruptcy order, and also to its evidential effect, and it is right that we should say something about it.

Subsection (3) prescribes that: "A criminal bankruptcy order shall specify—(a) the amount of the loss or damage appearing to the court to have resulted from the offence or, if more than one, each of the offences; (b) the person or persons appearing to the court to have suffered that loss or damage; (c) the amount of that loss or damage which it appears to the court that that person, or each of those persons, has suffered; and (d) the date which is to be the relevant date for the purpose of the exercise by the High Court of its powers under paragraph 10 of Schedule 2 to this Act in relation to dispositions made by the offender, being the date which appears to the court to be the earliest date on which the offence or, if more than one, the earliest of the offences, was committed."

Reference has now to be made to Schedule 2, which contains all the mechanism involved in this new concept. Turning to Schedule 2, paragraph 1 says: "Subject to the provisions of this Schedule, where a criminal bankruptcy order is made against any person he shall be treated as a debtor who has committed an act of bankruptcy on the date on which the order is made." That is the provision which was referred to earlier as being an additional act of bankruptcy, a new type of act of bankruptcy created by this statute.

Then, under paragraph 2 of the Schedule: "A person specified in a criminal bankruptcy order as having suffered loss or damage of any amount shall be treated, for the purpose of any ensuing proceedings pursuant to (a) . . . or (b) . . . as a creditor for a debt of that amount provable in the bankruptcy." That brings him into line with the ordinary creditor.

Then we go on to Part II of the Schedule. Under Part II, the next important paragraph is paragraph 6. Paragraph 6 reads: "For the purposes of section 5(2) and (3) of the Act of 1914 (matters to be proved before receiving order is made) the act of bankruptcy which a person is treated by this Schedule as having committed and any criminal bankruptcy debt shall be treated as conclusively proved by the production of a copy of the criminal bankruptcy order in question." So that for the limited purposes of leading to the making of the receiving order, the terms of the order as specified in subsection (3) of section 39, are to be taken as conclusively proving the matters set out in the order, but it is only for the purpose of leading to a receiving order that the contents of the criminal bankruptcy order are to be taken as proof, because when one looks at paragraph 9 of Schedule 2, which deals in substance with proof of debt or debts in the bankruptcy, it is then perfectly plain that the criminal bankruptcy order is no more than *prima facie* evidence of the existence of the debts specified in the criminal bankruptcy order. Under that paragraph 9 it is open to either the creditor or the criminal debtor to dispute the amount of the alleged debt, either by saying the criminal bankruptcy order understates the amount of the debt, or alternatively overstates it. So it is no more than *prima facie* evidence.

Mr. Bagnall rightly drew our attention to sub-paragraph (3) of that paragraph, which reads: "Nothing in sub-paragraph (1) above shall be construed as entitling any person to contend that the offence or offences specified in a criminal bankruptcy order were not committed by the person against whom the order was made." The effect of that sub-paragraph seems to be that, in so far as it is a question of whether the offences were committed by the person in question, the criminal bankruptcy order is conclusive; it is not, of course, equivalent to a conviction, it is simply conclusive evidence that he or she committed the offences referred to.

Paragraph 10 also contains an important provision in relation to dispositions of property, because under that paragraph, the relevant date for the purposes of setting aside dispositions of property goes back to the date which has to be specified in the criminal bankruptcy order, and that brings in subsection 3(*d*). Under that paragraph, the court making the criminal bankruptcy order is required to specify the date which appears to it to be the earliest date on which the first offence was committed. So it dates the period in respect of subsequent dispositions right back to the date of the first offence. It follows that it is very important for the criminal court making a criminal bankruptcy order to be explicit in specifying the date of the first offence in question.

The difficulty in applying subsection (3) arises principally in relation to the first of the requirements of the order, that the order shall specify the amount of the loss or damage appearing to the court to have resulted from the offence, or, if more than one "the offences". It is not immediately obvious why it was considered to be necessary to require the court to allocate the loss or damage to each individual offence, but the fact is that the order is mandatory in form and must be complied with. (*b*), (*c*) and (*d*) are all perfectly comprehensible, (*b*) identifying the persons who are in effect adjudged to be creditors; and (*c*) indicating the total amount which each of those creditors has lost. But (*a*) goes beyond that: (*a*) requires the court, in the bankruptcy order, to allocate the loss to each offence, if more than one. There is no doubt that this may cause considerable difficulty when it comes to drawing criminal bankruptcy orders.

In the present case the difficulty has been got round by the Central Criminal Court office. When I say "got round" I do not mean to criticise them, but they have resolved this problem, and they have dealt with it by specifying in Schedule A, the specific offences which appeared as counts in the indictment on which the Appellant was convicted, and in Schedule B they have set out a detailed list showing dates of offences and amount of damage or loss suffered in a schedule running to two and a half sheets. That is based, of course, on the enquiries and investigations that were made by the police, and in fact it represents a list of all the invoices which were affected by the same criminal deception as those on which the accused was convicted. What happened at the trial was that the prosecution in opening stated the total amount of damage or loss suffered in this case by the Appellant's employers, and produced all the relevant invoices and made them exhibits, and produced either a schedule in the same form as Schedule B or something very similar, and the trial proceeded on the footing that all these offences were of the same character and nature as the offences actually charged in the indictment, and the whole matter proceeded in the usual way in this type of case. In other words this is a case of system, and what the prosecution are doing is saying that the Appellant had been engaged in a systematic fraud over a period of some considerable time, involving a very large sum of money, and they proved that by selecting their six or so specific counts.

In the view of this court the method of dealing with the drawing of this order is a satisfactory one. The Powers of Criminal Courts Act makes it plain that in practice where a court is contemplating making a criminal bankruptcy order, it will be very important for the Judge making the order to ensure that in due time the order can be drawn up in accordance with the provisions of section 39, and that will or may involve having available some such schedule as was produced in this case. We need say no more about it.

238

It also follows from what we have said that it is of great importance to fix accurately the date of the first offence for the purposes of the criminal bankruptcy order. That being the position this court has come to the conclusion that the learned Judge below was entitled to make the order for the reasons we have given, and that the form of the order drawn up in the office at the Central Criminal Court itself was also right and in accordance with the provisions of the Act. Therefore we need say no more than, the criminal bankruptcy order stands.

We would like to say once more how grateful we are to counsel for all the assistance we have been given. We have not referred specifically to the three cases we were referred to, simply because we do not think they really take the matter any further. The only case which perhaps we should have mentioned in passing, is the case of *Hutchison* in (1972) 56 C.A.R. at page 307. We only refer to that case, because in the course of the judgment of this court given by Lord Justice Phillimore express reference is made to what he called "sample counts", simply to draw attention to the fact that that form of prosecution is a well recognised one in appropriate cases. For those reasons the criminal bankruptcy order must stand.

MR. BAGNALL: I appreciate that I have very much veered towards the neutral in addressing your Lordships, but as I did remind you there is this method of presenting the matter in Archbold which seems to rely heavily on the classic form of presenting the counts. I am wondering whether, therefore, it would be proper that I should apply for leave to take this matter to the House of Lords, because it is a matter of general public importance, as well as specifically relating to my client, and it would appear that there is an argument available for consideration by their Lordships' House, in this matter.

I put it in that neutral form, because I have, in attempting to assist your Lordships here, tended more towards the neutral rather than specifically following a course, and saying you must do so and so. But it seems to me to be a matter which could properly be considered by their Lordships.

LORD JUSTICE ORMROD: Thank you. The court will of course recognise and be prepared to certify this as a case which raises a matter of public importance, but we will refuse leave to appeal.

The Court subsequently certified the following point of law of general public importance:
"What is the meaning on a true construction of Section 39(2) of the Powers of Criminal Courts Act 1973 of the words 'offence or offences which the Court takes into consideration in determining his sentence' so as to found the jurisdiction of the Crown Court to make a criminal bankruptcy order?"[1]

---

[1] The Appeal Committee of the House of Lords granted leave to appeal; the hearing of the appeal is due to take place in April 1978.

APPENDIX U (Chapter 1)

LIST OF WITNESSES

Mr. J. B. Clemetson	Senior Official Receiver
Professor Sir Rupert Cross	Vinerian Professor of English Law in the University of Oxford
Mr. G. Emerson	Assistant Secretary, Probation and After-Care Department, Home Office
Mr. A. G. Flavell	Assistant Solicitor, Office of the Director of Public Prosecutions
Professor A. S. Goldstein	Dean of the Yale Law School
Mr. N. C. Honey	Governor of H.M. Prison, Wormwood Scrubs
Mr. J. M. Kress	Director, Criminal Justice Research Centre, Albany, New York
Sir Louis Petch	Chairman of the Parole Board
Mr. D. A. Thomas	Lecturer, Cambridge Institute of Criminology

TABLE OF STATUTES

---

[1]Otherwise known as the Piracy Act 1717.
[2]Otherwise known as the Transportation Act 1779.
[3]Otherwise known as the Garotters Act 1863.

243

TABLE OF CASES

INDEX

✻ Insert also
Criminal Law (mitigation) Bill 1911, 31

Burglary,
aggravated,
life sentence for, 104, 217
maximum penalty for, 81, 148
Alverstone Memorandum penalty for, 193
Churchill scale of offences, in, 198
combined sentences for, 125
consecutive sentences for, 211n
criminal bankruptcy, as additional
penalty for, 231
maximum penalty for, 79, 81, 148
sentences for, distribution of, 79, 159
Butler, Richard Austen, Lord, Home
Secretary (1957–62)
Committee on Mentally Abnormal
Offenders (1975), chairman of,
indeterminate reviewable sentence, 102
mandatory penalty for murder, 111
protective sentencing, 92
renewable sentence, 102n
restriction orders, 89
Home Secretary, 99n
Cairns, Sir David,
Justice report on *Legal Penalties* (1959),
chairman of, 74
Canada,
Law Reform Commission reports,
*Guidelines—A Report on Dispositions
and Sentences in the Criminal Process*
(1976), 166
Imprisonment and Release (1975), 8, 165
life imprisonment in, 166
maximum penalties, reduction of, 165
new maxima suggested, 166, 167
penalty structure, 165
Capital punishment, *see* Death penalty
Carnarvon, Henry Herbert, 4th Earl of
(1831–90),
Lords Select Committee on prisons (1863),
chairman of, 60, 61–2
prison discipline, debate on (1863), 60
Channell, Mr. Justice (1838–1928),
Alverstone Memorandum, signatory to,
196
flogging, in favour of, 196
maximum penalty for indecent assault, 40
Chapman, Mr. Justice,
minimum recommendation for murder,
100n
Children,
cruelty to or neglect of,
Churchill scale of offences, in, 198
maximum penalty for, 10, 43, 84–5,
85n, 86, 151
indecent assault on, *see* Indecent assault
Churchill, Sir Winston (1874–1965), Home
Secretary (1910–11),
new maxima, plea for, 1, 30
petty crime, 199
preventive detention, views on, 47, 49, 50
probation, 199

scale of offences suggested, 30–1, 198–9
suspensory sentences, 199
Cockburn, Sir Alexander (1802–80), Lord
Chief Justice (1859–80),
prison regime, severity of, 25, 57n
remission and licence, 25
short sentences, advocates 25
Coleridge, Bernard John Seymour, 2nd Lord
(1851–1927), 40n
Coleridge, Sir John, 1st Lord (1820–94),
Lord Chief Justice (1880–94),
sentence lengths, reduction in, 27, 28, 188
Collins, Victor John, Lord Stonham,
see Stonham
Combined sentences (*see also* Fines,
Compensation orders, Costs and
Criminal bankruptcy), 13, 124–7,
229–30
Commissioners on the Criminal Law: First
(1834–45), Second (1845–49), 4, 20, 59
consolidation Acts of 1861, impact on,
22, 23–4
maximum penalties,
deterrent effect of, 39
inconsistency of, 21–2
scale of penalties, 22, 77
Community service orders,
forerunner of, 31n
imprisonment, in combination with, 124,
229
Compensation orders (*see also* Criminal
bankruptcy),
courts' powers, 126, 229
custodial sentence, in combination with,
124, 126–7, 229
suspended sentence, in combination with,
118, 146
Concurrent sentences, 211
Consecutive sentences,
burglary, for, 211n
maximum penalty, exceeding the, 85–6,
96n
new maximum penalty, exceeding the, 12,
95–7, 145
principles governing, 12, 96, 211–13
robbery, for, 211
theft, for, 211n
Consolidation Acts of 1861, *see* Maximum
penalties and Parliament
Conspiracy to commit crime,
maximum penalty for, 83, 86n
Conspiracy to defraud,
criminal bankruptcy, as additional penalty
for, 231, 232, 233
maximum penalty for, 81, 148
Cork, Kenneth,
Insolvency Law Review Committee,
chairman of, 134
Corrective training, 48, 48n, 50n, 51, 65
Corruption,
maximum penalties for, 10, 33, 41, 43 ,84,

248

250

Fines,
    courts' use of, 125, 228
    custodial sentence, in combination with,
        125, 229
    lucrative offences, 126
    maximum, 5, 5n
    review of system of, 126, 146
    suspended sentence, in combination with,
        118, 122, 125, 126, 146
Firearms offences,
    consecutive sentences for, 211, 212
    maximum penalty for, 32, 33, 104, 147,
        151, 215
First offenders,
    partially suspended sentence for, 13,
        122-3
Flogging, 19, 24, 29, 194n, 196
Floud, Mrs. Jean,
    Committee on The Dangerous Offender,
        chairman of, 4, 89-90
Forfeiture (*see also* Deprivation of property),
    combination with other penalties,
        124-5, 229
Forgery,
    Alverstone Memorandum penalty for,
        193, 197
    Churchill scale of offences, in, 198
    combined sentences, for, 125
    criminal bankruptcy, as additional
        penalty for, 232, 233
    maximum penalty for, 81, 149, 214, 215
France,
    minimum and maximum penalties, 163
    sentencing bands, 163
    suspended sentences in, 116, 118
Fraud, 124, 125
    Churchill scale of offences, in, 198
Fraudulent trading,
    criminal bankruptcy, as additional
        penalty for, 232
    maximum penalty for, 10, 43, 84, 85, 86,
        154
Gardiner, Gerald, Lord, Lord Chancellor
    (1964-70),
    penalty for murder, Lords' vote on, 110
Garotting, 24, 24n, 25, 26, 29, 60-1, 61n
Gladstone, Herbert, Viscount (1854-1930),
    Home Secretary (1905-10),
    Departmental Committee on Prisons
        (1895), 63-5
    chairman of, 7, 27, 46
    deterrence and rehabilitation, twin aims
        of, 7-8, 63-4, 66
    preventive detention, recommendations
        on, 46
    recidivism, statistics on, 45-6
    rehabilitation and deterrence, twin aims
        of, 7-8, 63-4, 66
    Home Secretary, 46, 47

Goddard, Rayner, Lord (1877-1971),
    Lord Chief Justice (1946-58),
    corrective training, description of,
        48n
Greaves, Charles Sprengel (1801-81),
    consolidation Acts of 1861, draftsman of,
        24, 24n
Grey, Sir George (1799-1882), Home
    Secretary (1846-52, 1855-58 and
        1861-66),
    legislation on garotting, on, 24n
Guidelines, *see* Sentencing guidelines
Habitual criminals, *see* Recidivists
Handling, *see* Dishonest handling
Harcourt, Sir William (1827-1904), Home
    Secretary (1880-85),
    reduction in sentences, supports, 26,
        26n, 27, 27n, 176-86
Harm,
    as sentencing consideration, 89, 91
    serious, defined, 11, 89-90
Herbert, Henry, 4th Earl of Carnarvon,
    see Carnarvon
Hobhouse, Stephen (1881-1961) (with
    A. Fenner Brockway),
    report on prisons (1922), 65
Holland,
    maximum penalties in, 163-4
    prison sentences in, 8, 163, 164
    reducing imprisonment, policy of, 163,
        167
    suspended sentences in, 118
Home Office Research Unit,
    Life-sentence prisoners, research on, 100n
    maximum penalties, historical research
        on, 5
    Reports,
        Compensation Orders in Magistrates'
            Courts (1978), 127n
        The Effectiveness of Sentencing (1976),
            91n
        Parole in England and Wales (1977),
            87, 209
        Persistent Criminals (1963), 49, 50
Home Secretary,
    new maxima, need to review, 82, 144
    prerogative power of mercy, 28, 29, 30,
        39n, 98n
    prison rules, power to make, 64
    shorter sentences, 87
Hopwood, Charles (1829-1904),
    appellate court for sentences, advocate
        of, 27n, 29n
    biographical, 27n
    sentences, reduction of, 27, 27n, 187-8,
        189-90
    Times correspondence on crime and
        shorter sentences, 27-8, 187-9
Houses of correction, 44, 56, 58
Howard, John (1726?-90), 56, 57, 58, 59, 87

251

security in, 56, 67–8
Separate System in, 56, 57n, 58, 59, 61, 62, 68
Silent System in, 58, 59
Staff College for, 65
Probation, 66, 116, 117, 120–1, 125, 142, 199, 228, 230
Protection of public,
    serious harm, definition of, 11, 89–90
Provocation,
    potential redundancy as defence to murder, 14, 109
    research into, 14
Rape,
    Alverstone Memorandum penalty for, 194–5
    Churchill scale of offences, in, 198
    indeterminate sentencing for serious, 104
    life sentence for, 99, 217, 219, 222–4
    maximum penalty for, 81, 104, 147, 151, 215
    new maximum penalty for, 81, 83, 94–5, 147, 151
Receiving, see Dishonest handling
Recidivists, 44–54
    age and, 46, 47, 47n, 48, 49, 50
    disposal of, 46–7, 70, 87, 89
    extended sentences for, 11, 51–4
    legally defined, 46–7, 49, 51
    length of sentence, 46, 49, 93n
    leniency towards, 192
    petty, 50–51, 89
    preventive detention for, see Preventive detention
    register of, 45
Recommendation of minimum period, see Murder
Reconviction, 87–8, 185, 209–10
Rehabilitation, see Aims of penal measures
Remission, 53, 53n, 66, 95, 119n
    development of, 25n, 64, 64n, 65
    Lord Chief Justice Cockburn on, 25
Research (see also Home Office Research Unit), 15, 66
    criminal bankruptcy, 14
    life imprisonment, 14
    suspended sentences, 14
    system of new maxima, 14, 143, 145
Residential limitation order, 124, 125
Restitution orders, 229
Retribution, see Aims of penal measures
Robbery,
    Alverstone Memorandum penalty for, 194
    Churchill scale of offences, in, 198
    combined sentences for, 125
    consecutive sentences for, 211
    criminal bankruptcy, as additional penalty for, 231, 233
    life sentence for, 99, 217, 219

maximum penalty for, 81, 104, 148, 215
sentence lengths for, 37
Romilly, Sir Samuel (1757–1818),
    death penalty, campaign to abolish, 19
    penal legislation, on the state of, 17
Russell, Lord John, 1st Earl (1792–1878),
    Home Secretary (1835–39), 33
Salmon, Cyril Barnet, Lord,
    Royal Commission on Standards of Conduct in Public Life (1976),
    chairman of, 86n
Scarman, Leslie, Lord,
    on length of sentences, 78, 87
Scotland,
    criminal bankruptcy, absence of, 131n
    High Court of Justiciary, 78, 94, 161, 162
    length of sentences, 94, 162
    maximum penalties, absence of, 77–8, 161
    murder, penalty for, 114
    Scottish Council on Crime, 102
    sentencing powers of courts, 6, 161
    sentencing process, 162
    Sheriff courts, 161
    summary courts, 161
    suspended sentences, absence of, 118n
Sentences,
    appeal against, see Appeals against sentence
    consecutive and concurrent, 95–7, 211–13
    criminal bankruptcy, in addition to, 231–3
    deferred, 118n, 135, 230
    determinate, 93–4
    exemplary, 5, 76n, 91
    extended, 11, 51–4, 92n, 93n, 95, 145, 207–8
    imposable by various courts, 200–1
    indeterminate, 93, 98–101
    individualised, 37
    lengths of,
        1913–76, 206
        reduction in, 7, 26–8, 86–7, 173–90
    protective, 93–5
    renewable, 102, 102n
    suspended,
        partially, 118–123
        wholly, 116–18, 226–7
    tariff, 37
Sentencing,
    function of court, 36–8
    maximum penalties related to, 38–43, 200–1
    principles of, 37, 201, 204–5, 222
Sentencing guidelines, 8, 166–7, 168–72
Sexual offences, 33, 124, 125
    low reconviction rates, 90
    new maximum penalties for, 81, 147, 148, 149, 151, 152, 153
Shaw, Professor A.G.L.,
    Convicts and the Colonies (1966), 19n
Soskice, Sir Frank, Lord Stow Hill, Home Secretary (1964–65), 114

Printed in England for Her Majesty's Stationery Office by Oyez Press Limited, London.